THE RISE AND FALL
OF THE SHAH

THE RISE
*

AND FALL OF
*

THE SHAH
*

Amin Saikal

*

PRINCETON UNIVERSITY PRESS
PRINCETON, NEW JERSEY

FOR MY PARENTS

* CONTENTS *

* LIST OF ILLUSTRATIONS *

(following p. 70)

* LIST OF MAPS *

Preface

This book examines the rule of Mohammad Reza Shah Pahlavi of Iran (1953-1979) in the context of his regime's "dependence" on the United States in the 1950s for its survival, and of his attempts in the 1970s to transform Iran into a major pro-Western regional power with aspirations to eventual world power status. In this, it critically reviews both the domestic and foreign policy objectives and behavior of the Shah. It contends that despite all his achievements, the Shah's goals and policies were full of inherent contradictions and weaknesses. They were not responsive to the needs of Iran, and failed to achieve even their own objectives. In fact, they unleashed the very trends and developments that led the Iranian people in 1978 to launch the mass movements against the Shah's rule, forcing him from the throne on the grounds that he was the "enemy" of Iran and "puppet" of the United States.

Although it is too early to provide a comprehensive scholarly analysis of the Shah's fall, it needs to be stressed that I began research for this book in 1975. At the time, the Shah appeared, by all accounts, to be fully in command of Iranian polities. His absolute rule seemed so entrenched that not many, even among the Shah's opponents, dared to speculate about his possible overthrow, at least in the near future. The Shah's rule was, however, clearly plagued by certain fundamental contradictions and weaknesses. This encouraged me to pursue my research, and led me to the view that the Shah's rule was doomed unless he succeed urgently in modifying his goals and policies so that they would be more in line with the needs and means of Iran.

In late 1976, on a field trip to Iran, I talked to both the Shah's officials and his opponents, and studied the conditions of the Iranian people closely. By the end of the trip, I was firmly convinced that the Shah did not even seem to have enough time to bring about the urgently needed policy changes. At the time, this was a very unpopular view to advocate. In the West, especially the United States, where governments as well as press and media projected the Shah as a popular modernizing ruler, an over-whelming majority of even academics and policy makers had failed to perceive the gulf that was growing between the Shah and his people. They wrongly continued to identify the Shah with Iran, and thus analyze Iranian politics from a misleading angle. This became clearer to me as I traveled to England and the United States. Nonetheless, despite all odds, I completed the text of this book in late 1978. When the mass opposition movements finally forced the Shah from his throne, I needed no more than a few additional pages to confirm the thrust of my thesis and judgments.

Undoubtedly, the subject matter of this book could have been probed in a variety of ways and from different perspectives, de-pending on one's disciplinary and ideological interests. I found it both realistic and rewarding to study it from an integrative inter-disciplinary point of view. As a result, I have sought to provide an in-depth, macro-level analysis of the Shah's rule with respect to the linkage that existed between his domestic and foreign policy postures, as well as between these and the relevant evolving changes in regional and international politics. This approach is by no means unique. But it is rare among scholarly evaluations of Iranian politics.

In this book, I do not claim to have covered all the relevant issues concerning the Shah's rule. It must be stressed that research on Iranian politics under the Shah was, in many ways, a fearful task. The Shah conducted "closed politics," enforced strictly and brutally by his secret police, SAVAK. This made it extremely difficult to gain access to reliable sources of information and gather authentic data through normal research channels. Risking a great deal, I needed to obtain and authenticate part of my data through clandestine personal contacts in Iran and extensive checking and cross-checking in England and the United States. Most of the contact sources, including those Iranian officials who held high positions in the Shah's administration, but were not happy with his policies in private, wished to remain anonymous for reasons of either personal safety or official secrecy.

For this reason, the book contains many assertions that are attributed to unidentified sources. Despite all the difficulties and limitations that such type of research involves it has been my objective to include and evaluate as many relevant issues in the context of this book's argument as possible. This, however, does not involve a number of particulars of the Shah's rule that have already been detailed by other analysts of Iranian politics in one form or another.

In completing this research I owe much to many institutions and individuals. I wish to thank the Colombo Plan authorities, the Australian government and the Australian National University (ANU) for their financial support and sponsorship of a field trip that took me to Iran, Britain, and the United States in 1976. Among individuals I am very much indebted to J. L. Richardson, J.A.A. Stockwin, and Geoffrey Jukes for their valuable advice, encouragement, and guidance, and their help with many administrative problems at all stages of my research. I would also like to express my gratitude to Gordon White, who provided me with very helpful supervision in the early stages of my research, and Geoff Chandler of the Australian Development Assistance Bureau. Among numerous friends, I would like to thank especially Amanda Thornton for her tremendous intellectual and moral support throughout the research period, Mara Moustafine for her encouragement and advice, and Kristin Craig, who provided me with much inspiration when I needed it. I should also like to thank Paul Keal and John Atkin for reading parts of the draft of the book.

In Tehran, I wish to thank many individuals for their informative discussions. They included former Prime Minister Amir 'Abbas Hoveida, former Education Minister Manuchehr Ganji, and former Information and Tourism Minister Daryush Hymoyoon, as well as several senior officials and intellectuals, most of all, Harmoz Hekmat, Farhad Mehran, Majid Tehranian, Mansur Farsad, Mahmoud Faroughi, Amir Taheri, Cyrus Elahi, Reza Sheikh-ul-Islami, Ali Nik-Kha, Amir Ansawri, and Hassan Arfa, not to mention several members of the opposition who refrained from giving me their real names for reasons of personal safety. Moreover, I would like to thank Richard Bash of the American Embassy and Christine White of the Australian Embassy for facilitating my research in Iran.

In Britain, I am grateful to Peter Avery and Malcolm MacIntosh, both of whom enriched me with their knowledge of Iranian politics and furthered my enthusiasm about the project. I also wish to thank Lewis Turner for his conversation and Janet Calver of Australia House for facilitating my stay in London.

In the United States, I owe much to Marvin Zonis, who spent hours with me in helping me to shape what is now the topic of this book. I also wish to thank several other officials and scholars for their encouragement and help, including the British Ambassador, Sir Peter Ramsbotham, Alvin Cottrell, Bruce Van Voorst, Robert Haupt, William Griffith, Lincoln Bloomfield, Geoffrey Kemp, Richard Cottam, Rohullah Ramazani, Leonard Binder, Colonel Bill Thomas, Lloyd Henderson, George Green, Sepehr Zabih, George Lenczowski, Richard Frye, Bruce Kuniholm, William Hanaway, Jr., Jerome Clinton, Roy Mottahedeh, Sydney Cohen, Nathaniel Case, Timothy Case, and Alan Makowski. My thanks also go to David Stam, Rosella Murray and Lenore Cowan of the New York Public Library. Of course, this book could not have been produced without the direction and enthusiasm of Herbert S. Bailey, Jr., Margaret Case's fine and speedy editing, and the special and perhaps record-breaking efforts of other members of Princeton University Press. Moreover, two people who actively facilitated my stay in the United States during my field trip were Margaret Gray and Jonathan Thwaites of the Australian Embassy. I am also grateful to the Washington Post and Hoover Institute for letting me use their respective libraries. All interpretations (except where otherwise indicated) and any errors of fact are entirely my responsibility.

THE RISE AND FALL
OF THE SHAH

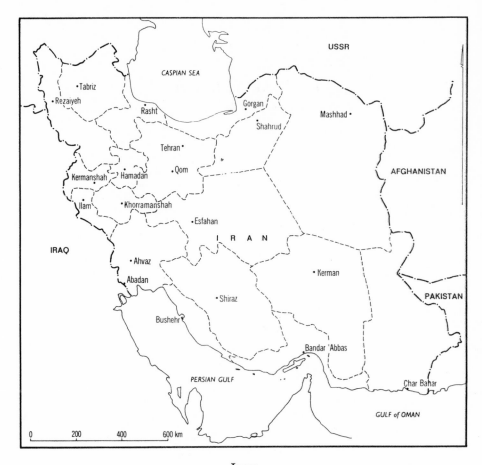

IRAN

Introduction

UNTIL THE BEGINNING of 1978, Mohammad Reza Shah Pahlavi of Iran was generally regarded as one of the world's most powerful and richest rulers. He ruled his strategically and economically important Islamic kingdom with absolute authority, and spent its enormous oil income as he saw fit. His publicly avowed goal was to transform Iran into a progressive, pro-Western self-sustaining industrial and military power before its exportable oil ran out, as the Shah estimated it would, by the end of the century. In order to achieve his goal, he pursued a forceful policy of domestic political repression, and, particularly from the early 1970s on, he worked hard to maximize Iran's economic and military capabilities on the basis of its growing oil wealth. In this, he was extensively supported by his major Western allies, led by the United States, which found him a very reliable ally, willing and able to look after Western interests in the Iranian region. The Shah was personally convinced of the strength and popularity of his government. He believed that he was rightly leading his 33 million subjects (of several ethnic, linguistic, and tribal origins) to achieve one of the highest standards of living in the world, with maximum peace and security, within the shortest time possible; and he believed that over 99 percent of Iranians, who had placed his commanding portrait wherever they lived and worked, were behind him in this task.

During 1978, however, the Shah was suddenly beset by nationwide riots, demonstrations, and strikes against his rule, which progressively undermined his authority at considerable human and material cost. By the beginning of 1979, amid increasing bloodshed, paralysis of the state machinery and of the economy, and lack of solid support from his armed forces, the Shah's power declined precipitously. He could no longer command substantial support from either his people or his leading ally, the United States, which found it inexpedient to back him further. After twenty-five years of absolute rule, the Shah had no choice but to leave Iran on January 17 for a "temporary" stay abroad. This paved the way for his chief religious-political opponent, Ayatollah Ruhollah Khomeini, the strongest leader of the Iranians' anti-Shah "revolution," to return to Iran after fourteen years of exile at the hands of the Shah, and proclaim the country an Islamic Republic.

Khomeini has undertaken to end not only the 2,500-year-old Persian monarchy and therefore the Shah's dynastic claim over it, but also most of the Shah's policies, particularly those connected with the pro-Western transformation of Iran into a primarily regional power. These events have been dramatic and world-shattering in many ways. They caught by surprise even most of those said to be best informed, including the CIA, for very few could foresee such a rapid collapse of the Shah's apparently well-entrenched and powerful administrative, security, and military apparatus. This has caused mounting debate and discussion around the world; the basic question confronting everyone is, why and how did these developments come about?

Clearly this question could be approached from several points of view. One approach would be simply to apply particular conceptual frameworks that have been worked out by Western scholars on the basis of case studies, and that reflect Western experience. Another is to refrain from applying these frameworks as such, but nevertheless to seek help from them when, for analytical purposes, they seem appropriate.

The first of these approaches is likely to be more misleading than helpful in exploring and evaluating the complexity of Iranian politics. As Bernard Lewis succinctly writes,

> It is no doubt tempting to try to explain Middle Eastern phenomena in terms of European, or North and South American experience. . . . But on the whole such comparisons—perhaps analogies would be a better word—obscure more than they explain. No doubt Middle Eastern societies and politics are subjected to the same human vicissitudes, and therefore to the same rules of interpretation, as those of the West, and [have] adopted Western outward forms in the organisation and expression of [their] political and social life, [but] it is fatally easy for the Western observer to take these alien outward forms as the element of comparison, and to disregard or misrepresent the deeper realities which they do imperfectly express. The Islamic society of

the Middle East, with its own complex web of experience and tradition, cannot adequately be labelled and classified with a few names and terms borrowed from the Western past.[1]

To acquire a better understanding of the deeper realities, this book examines the case of Iran largely on its own terms. It avoids the application of any specific model of analysis based on other countries' experiences and peculiarities. It goes beyond the Western journalistic evaluations that flooded the world press and other media, praising the "success" of the Shah (and occasionally criticizing him) in the few years prior to 1978, as well as stories about mass movements of opposition that preceded his fall. The book explores the root causes of the Shah's downfall by looking at the basic political and socio-economic features of Iranian society in the context of its contemporary history; the way the Shah assumed effective power, with the United States' help, in 1953; and the Shah's subsequent goals and policies, with their consequences for Iran in relation to his perception of the country's domestic, foreign, and particularly regional needs and interests. It particularly examines the dependence of the Shah's regime on the United States, and its consequent vulnerability to that country in the 1950s at the cost of Iran's relations with many of its regional neighbors, most notably the Soviet Union; the Shah's attempts in the 1960s to diversify his sources of dependence, normalize his relations with the USSR, and move toward realizing Iran's potential as an oil power, largely through a policy of accommodation with the West; and the Shah's goal in the 1970s of turning Iran into a strong regional economic and military power with global influence.

In this book, the use of the term "dependence" must not be confused with that of "dependency" as used in the "dependencia tradition," based largely on the experiences of Latin American countries.[2] Nor should the term "regional power" be understood in the same sense as that employed by various scholars of international relations in case studies and in classifying of world political units as "small," "medium," and "super" powers.[3] "Dependence" will be used mainly in describing the pattern and substance of the Shah's early political, economic, and military reliance on the United States, and his consequent alliance with the capitalist world against the background of strong feelings of domestic and regional insecurity. It will also be used in analyzing the consequences of this for Iran's socio-economic development and foreign policy position. This will be fully developed in Chapter II, where certain conceptual tools provided by the "dependencia tradition" will be used. The term "regional power" will be used to define the role that the Shah wanted Iran to perform within the limits of what he thought to be Iran's "region," given his perception of the country's national and regional security and interests. This will be discussed in the Introduction to Part Two and in Chapter V. The crucial link between the Shah's initial dependence (as well as the short- and long-term consequences of this for Iran) and his ultimate desire to transform Iran into a mighty pro-Western regional power will be discussed in the concluding chapter.

The first part of this book, Chapters I-IV, will explain and analyze trends and developments leading to the Shah's rise to power and the formulation of his goal to turn Iran into a regional power as a prelude to becoming a world power. Chapter I will provide a historical sketch of the development of Iranian politics from the mid-eighteenth to the mid-twentieth centuries, in the context of a growing major power rivalry over Iran, and the Iranian responses to this rivalry.

Chapter II will examine the nature and mechanisms of the Shah's dependence on the United States, his continuous search for a Western, mainly American, source of security, and the consequences of this for Iranian politics. Chapter III will discuss the Shah's efforts to implement, in accordance with American wishes, a number of selected socio-economic reforms in the 1960s within the framework of what he called "the White Revolution." This will be analyzed mainly in terms of the Shah's desire to expand his domestic power base and mobilize mass support in reaction against his vulnerability to American pressures. In doing so he hoped to achieve more flexibility in the conduct of his foreign relations, particularly with the USSR, from a position of growing domestic strength. Chapter IV will trace the development of the Shah's oil policy through various phases, leading in the early 1970s to his success in maximizing Iran's control over its oil resources and in realizing the country's potential as an oil power. This will be assessed in relation to the emergence of the Organization of Petroleum Exporting Countries (OPEC) as an effective bargaining cartel. It will be seen that the Shah was able to use OPEC, in the context of evolving changes in regional and international politics, to strengthen his position against both the international oil companies and the world at large, as a prelude to turning Iran into a regional and ultimately a world power.

The second part of the book will deal mainly with the Shah's policy of transforming Iran into an effective economic and military regional power. Chapter V will outline the Shah's vision of Iran as a regional power, the regional factors that influenced him in shaping his vision, and the policies that he adopted in order to bring it to reality. Chapter VI will analyze the policy programs and actions that he undertook in order to build up Iran's economic and military capabilities. Chapter VII will seek to identify the pattern of the Shah's regional behavior while he was engaged in maximizing Iran's resources capability and defining the country's regional role. Chapter VIII will examine critically the repercussions of both his domestic and regional policy behavior in terms of their consequences for the Iranian people, the Shah's rule, and regional politics.

PART ONE

THE SHAH AND IRAN: BETWEEN DEPENDENCE AND OIL POWER

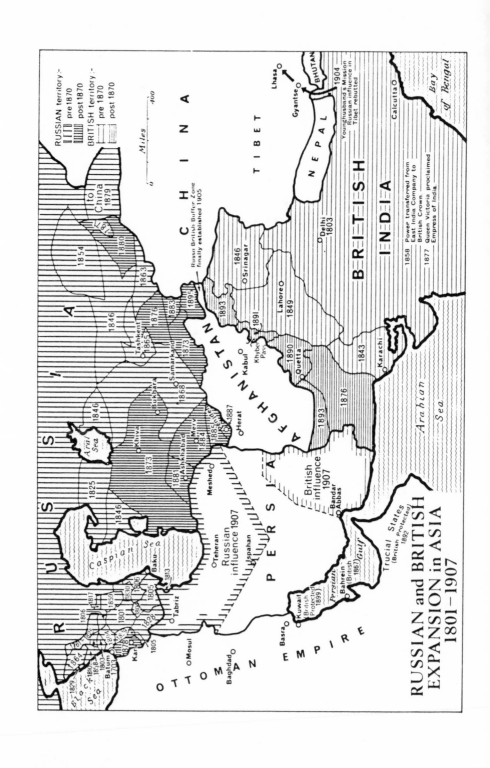

RUSSIAN and BRITISH
EXPANSION in ASIA
1801–1907

CHAPTER I

Iran and Traditional
World Powers Rivalry

THE POLITICAL HISTORY of Iran since the early nineteenth century reflects the country's importance in a zone of major power rivalry. Iran's strategic importance, enhanced during this century by its increasing significance as a major source of oil, has frequently stimulated the rival powers to seek domination of the country in order to strengthen their security and their political and economic interests in the context of changing world politics. Great Britain and czarist Russia began the modern rivalry over Iran which was already under way by the turn of the nineteenth century, when Britain had succeeded in entrenching its colonial rule in the Indian subcontinent. Anglo-Russian rivalry continued through different phases until its transformation into a conflict between the Soviet Union and the United States following World War II. This continuous interaction between the powers, at times resulting in the division of Iran into spheres of influence and occupation, has been instrumental in shaping Iranian politics.

EARLY RIVALRY

Anglo-Russian rivalry over Iran began in the second half of the eighteenth century, as a direct result of British colonial expansion into the Indian subcontinent. The strategic location of Iran in a zone between Europe and Asia placed the country within the geographical perimeters of Russian security and aspirations, as well as on the margin of British colonial expansion and on its imperial lines of communication. While Britain sought to enlarge and secure its colonial rule in Asia, Russia opposed such foreign control close to its borders; Iran's strategic position thus rendered it vital in the eyes of both powers for the security of their respective imperial domains. They regarded Iran, along with Afghanistan, Turkestan, and Transcaspia, as a buffer zone that separated and protected them from engaging one another directly. But the two powers entered into a prolonged and exhausting struggle aimed at rebuffing each other's encroachment into the country, either in terms of territorial acquisition or of political and economic penetration.

During the second half of the nineteenth and early twentieth centuries, this struggle manifested itself largely in a quest for respective spheres of influence within the country. The Russians tried to gain influence over the north, while the British endeavored to control the south. They both sought to divide Iran into zones of influence separated by a central buffer area under the administration of the Tehran government, which was to be vulnerable and responsive to their pressures and needs. Each zone was to be dependent on its respective patron power for protection and the conduct of its political and economic affairs.[1] By the late nineteenth century, Lord Curzon, the British viceroy of India and an outstanding defender of British imperial power, considered Iran to be essential for the defense of India, which he called "the inalienable badge of [British] Sovereignty in the Eastern Hemisphere." He believed that Iran, together with Afghanistan, Turkestan, and Transcaspia, constituted "the pieces on a chessboard upon which is being played out a game for the domination of the world. . . . The future of Great Britain . . . will be decided not in Europe . . . but in the continent whence . . . [the British] emigrant stock first came, and to which as conquerors their descendants have returned."[2] At the time, of course, Curzon did not realize that Iran, apart from its strategic importance, was also destined to offer Britain the economic incentive of oil, which was to impel Britain to work even harder for its strategic and economic influence, not just in southern Iran, but in Iranian politics as a whole.

Anglo-Russian rivalry continued for most of the first half of the twentieth century, even though the Soviet regime replaced that of czars in 1917. The discovery of major oil wells and the country's consequent emergence as an important oil producer introduced a new dimension to Anglo-Russian rivalry. It is necessary to look at these developments briefly before outlining the major implications of this rivalry for Iranian politics.

The discovery of oil in commercial quantities at the beginning of the twentieth century added to Iran's strategic importance and pointed to a promising future. The major deposits happened to be in southern Iran, where the British influence was at its strongest. Although in 1872 the Russians had forced Tehran to annul a concession that it had given to a British subject, Baron Julius de Reuter, for "exploitation of all minerals throughout Persia,"[3] the Iranian monarch, Mozaffar al-Din Shah, granted the first oil concession to an English entrepreneur, William Knox D'Arcy, in 1901. Under the concession, D'Arcy gained the exclusive rights to explore, produce, and refine oil in an area of about 480,000 square miles, covering all of Persia except the five northern provinces, for sixty years. In return he undertook to set up one or more companies within the following two years, to pay the Iranian government 16 percent of his annual profits, as well as £20,000 in cash and £20,000 worth of stock in the enterprise.[4] He formed the First Exploitation Company in partnership with the British Burmah Oil Company in 1905; but it was not until 1908 that oil was struck in commercial quantities in the foothills of the Zagros Mountains, about 150 miles from the Persian Gulf coast.

Having realized the future importance of oil as an energy source, the British government immediately intervened. Its representatives bought up D'Arcy's shares, and in 1909 formed the Anglo-Persian (later Anglo-Iranian) Oil Company with an initial capital of £2 million, to take over all the rights and privileges of the First Exploitation Company. In 1912 it linked the major oil well of Masjid-i Suleiman by a pipeline to Abadan, an island in the mouth of Shatt al-Arab in the Persian Gulf, where it was building the world's largest refinery. In 1913, the British Admiralty, after instructing the Royal Navy to change from coal to oil-firing engines, purchased on behalf of the British government a controlling share in the Anglo-Persian Oil Company by payment of £2.2 million of the new £4 million capitalization.[5] The British were soon able to develop the Iranian oil industry into a leading export sector. The net production of Iranian crude rose dramatically from 82,097 tons in 1912/1913 to 1,407,531 in 1919/1920, and 6,549,244 in 1932 (just before the replacement of the D'Arcy Concession by the 1933 Agreement), of which 37,000, 936,000, and 6,006,298 tons, respectively, were exported by the Anglo-Persian Oil Company.[6] Under the D'Arcy Concession's arrangement, the company, in conjunction with the British government, made huge profits compared with what the Iranian government earned in royalties, taxes, and profit sharing.[7]

The rapid evolution of British ownership and expansion of the oil industry tilted the balance of power between Iran, Russia, and Britain in favor of the latter. It provided Britain with a solid base to further its presence and influence in southern Iran, and expand its share in guiding and controlling Iranian economic and—for that matter—social and political affairs. Moreover, Iranian oil proved very beneficial to Britain in its domestic industrial development. It helped fuel its Persian Gulf and Indian Ocean fleet—the largest fleet in the region, and the badge of British supremacy—for both military and diplomatic purposes, and thus increased its offensive capacity; it also aided Britain financially in maintaining its far-flung empire. This speedy growth of British economic entrenchment in Iran developed at a time when the czarist regime was in decline. Internally, the Russian government was facing growing opposition; the abortive revolution of 1905 had shattered the basis of czarist autocracy. Externally, the government had been defeated and humiliated by Japan in the Manchurian War of 1904-1905, and it no longer impressed its neighbors, including the Iranians, as a powerful force to be trusted and relied upon.

Against this weakening position of the czars and growing British influence in Iran, Britain pressed for formalization of the long-standing but informal Anglo-Russian spheres of influence. The two powers reached an agreement in the Convention of St. Petersburg in August 1907, whereby, among other things, they agreed to a division of Iran into three zones: a Russian zone of influence in the north, a British one in the south, and a narrow central buffer zone under the control, at least nominally, of the Tehran government. They still pledged, however, to respect the territorial integrity and independence of Iran. The Russian line started from Qasr-i Shirin, crossed and included "Isfahan, Yezd and Kakh, ending at that point on the Persian frontier where the Russian and Afghan frontiers intersected." The British line commenced from the Afghan frontier, extending "via Gazik, Birjand, Kerman" and ending "at Bandar Abbas."[8] The Russians thereby recognized existing and future

British claims over the oil fields, with resulting political and economic influence not only in Iran but also in the Persian Gulf region as a whole; this meant a renunciation of their own aspirations to reach either India or the Persian Gulf. Tehran was not a party to this agreement, nor was its consent sought.

There is a major question of whether Tehran could have done anything about it. There is no doubt that the Anglo-Russian rivalry over Iran had caused a marked weakening of Iranian politics. In building their respective zones of influence, which often operated independently of the Tehran government, the two imperial powers not only forced Tehran to lose most of its initiative in the conduct of Iran's domestic and foreign policies, but also sought to pressure, buy off, and weaken successive Iranian leaders so as to make them obedient to and dependent on the two powers for their survival. For this, they used policies of divide and rule, whereby they established liaisons with different tribal authorities in their respective zones of influence, and exploited their ethnic, religious, and political differences, not only against each other but also against Tehran. These actions were often legally sanctioned by the various treaties that had been imposed on Iranian leaders, including the Treaty of Turkmanchai (1828) between Iran and Russia, and the Treaty of 1857 between Iran and Britain, which among other political and economic favors gave the foreign powers capitulation rights.[9] All this contributed to the social and political disintegration and economic impoverishment of Iranian society.

It is also true, however, that the frailty of political and socioeconomic structures in Iranian society helped the imperial powers weaken the country. Throughout the nineteenth and early twentieth centuries, Iran, a feudalistic society composed of different tribes, and bound together largely by a common religion, was ruled by the weak but autocratic, absolute, and bankrupt Qajar dynasty. The authority of the Qajar kings rested largely upon their divine claims and centralization of political power in the traditional institution of monarchy, to the supreme position of which the Iranian people had become accustomed for over two thousand years. While the word of the king was "the supreme law, against which there was no appeal," the Qajar dynasty suffered from steady decay, inefficient and corrupt administration, and the lack of a strong, loyal army. Its system allowed little room for the reforms that would have been necessary to strengthen Iran's position against British and Russian activities. In the face of foreign powers' interference, the system did not have the necessary potential to hold itself together. Iranian nationhood was already fragile, contending, as it did, with the country's difficult terrain, widely dispersed population, absence of an efficient communication network, and, above all, volatile society. The society rested upon a complex and delicate web of interactions between the different tribes, which opposed one another on a wide range of social and political matters.

At the start of the twentieth century, a movement, spearheaded largely by Western-inspired intellectuals, merchants, and clergy, began to articulate demands for constitutional reforms in an attempt to subject the power of the monarchy to the rule of law and somewhat liberalize the Iranian socio-political system. The movement, whose members subsequently became known as Constitutionalists, was short-lived and limited in its achievements. Its members succeeded in drafting the Iranian Constitution of 1906, which prescribed a monarchical parliamentary government and broader mass participation in the national political process; in establishing a lower house of parliament (the Majlis); and in putting some other provisions of this constitution into effect during 1909 to 1921.[10] But since the movement's first objective was to weaken the Qajar despotism as a precondition for reforming Iranian politics, after which it would seek to repel foreign intervention, the movement had to face stiff opposition from the monarchy and its supporters. Although the Constitutionalists found it imperative to seek British help in their struggle, which placed them at odds with Russia, the monarchy sought favors from both British and czarists against the Constitutionalists, in return for accepting the Anglo-Russian Agreement of 1907. This, and the Constitutionalists' own disharmony of principles and interests, led to the failure of their movement. They did not develop a national politics based on majority support and understanding, and they failed to reform the domestic system to the point that the Iranians could raise a national challenge to, rather than being largely manipulated by, the foreign powers.

Meanwhile, Anglo-Russian rivalry and attempts to strengthen their respective spheres of influence within Iran continued unabated, with Britain increasingly the main beneficiary. While the czarist and Qajar regimes were beset by serious internal problems, the outbreak of World War I provided Britain with further opportunity to enhance its position. Ironically, the war brought the two traditional rivals, Britain and Russia, into a wartime alliance against a common enemy, Germany. Tehran declared Iran's neutrality, but this was not respected by the warring factions. The northwest of Iran became a battleground for Turks and Russians. In the southwest, where the two major tribes of Bakhtiari and Qashqai had become disloyal to the central government, resentful of the British, and, consequently, receptive to German activities, the British landed forces to safeguard their recently acquired oil fields and installations, their Residency in Bushir, and imperial security against German threats. Moreover, the British exploited the situation by raising their own Iranian security force, called the South Persian Rifles, to assist in protecting and possibly expanding their zone of influence, especially in Khuzistan province, the location of most of the British-run oil industry.[11]

This rapid strengthening of the British political, economic, and military entrenchment in Iran contrasted with the continuously weakening position of Russia. At a time when the war had been taking heavy toll on Russians, the Bolsheviks overthrew czarism in the October Revolution of 1917, and in 1922 declared the Union of the Soviet Socialist Republics. Given its immediate needs of domestic consolidation, the new regime swiftly made peace with the Turks and the Germans. In January 1918, it announced its desire for friendly relations with its southern neighbors, and assured Iran of friendship and support for its independence and territorial integrity. It declared all czarist claims on Iran based on the Anglo-Russian Agreement of 1907 and other accords to be null and void. Thus, in effect, it encouraged the Iranian government to resist the British with Soviet support, and called on the British to reduce their activities in Iran. Tehran responded favorably to this Soviet assurance, and welcomed it as a lever against expanding British influence. But Britain considered the Bolshevik regime and its ideological bid for worldwide revolution a serious threat to the existence of the British empire and to the political and economic values that it upheld. When the British decided on armed intervention against the Bolsheviks, they resolved to stop at all costs the spread of communism to Iran, and to use it as a front-line base in its anti-Bolshevik campaign. The British maintained their

wartime lines of communication through Iran from Mesopo-
tamia to the Caspian, and extended active assistance to anti-
Soviet forces, including White Russians, who had established
bases in the czarist zone of influence in northern Iran. British
troops occupied the Iranian port of Enzeli (now Pahlavi) on the
Caspian, from which the Turks had made thrusts into the
Russian Baku oil fields, and a British naval detachment arrived
to patrol the Caspian. Thus, northwest Persia became in effect
a British zone of occupation. In addition, a British Indian force
controlled the area east of a line from Bandar Abbas on the
Persian Gulf to Meshed. In September 1918, Lord Curzon instructed the new British minister in Tehran, Sir Percy Cox, to
secure the agreement of the Iranian government to a new Anglo-
Iranian treaty, replacing the Anglo-Russian Treaty of 1907 that
had recently been denounced by the Soviet government.

Under conditions of uncertainty over the future of the Bolshevik regime, British occupation of a large part of Iran, domestic weakness of the Iranian government, and its growing
financial dependence on Britain, as well as Iran's internal disarray, Sir Percy succeeded in making the Iranian leadership sign
a new treaty in 1919, pending the approval of the Iranian Majlis.
This treaty provided for the British to take over complete
control of the Iranian army and finances.[12] Had it been implemented, it would in effect have reduced Iran, like many Persian
Gulf sheikhdoms, to a British protectorate. Had this happened,
there would have been serious repercussions for the Soviet Union
and regional balance of power. Meanwhile, attempts to overthrow the Bolsheviks having failed, early in 1920 the British
cabinet ordered all active British intervention on behalf of the
counterrevolutionary forces in Russia to cease, and subsequently British forces withdrew from Transcaucasia, Transcaspia, and northern Iran. Although this took much of the
pressure off Moscow, the Soviet government naturally opposed
the impending treaty proposal and sought its immediate
abolition.

In a surprise move, Soviet troops occupied the Iranian port of
Enzeli on the Caspian in April 1920, just a few weeks after the
British had left. Shortly thereafter, the Iranian Soviet Socialist
Republic of Gilan in northern Iran was set up, and the Soviet
Union sponsored the establishment of a pro-Moscow Iranian
communist group, which later led to the development of the

Iranian Communist party, called Tudeh (masses).[13] The long-run Soviet objective in these actions seems to have been to keep the British out of northern Iran and concurrently counterbalance the British build-up in Iran as a whole. In the short run, however, the Soviet Union aimed at exerting pressure on both Tehran and London to revoke their recent treaty, which needed the approval of the Iranian Majlis. Otherwise, Moscow appeared to have had no other aim in its actions that could justify a British assertion, upheld by pro-British Iranian circles, that the Soviets wanted to extend their Marxist revolution into Iran. In fact, Moscow was very careful to refrain from any action that could increase Iran's dependence on Britain at the time. This was evident in the common view held by Lenin and Rothstein, the Soviet Commissar of Foreign Affairs, that "any attempt on . . . [the Soviet] part . . . to start revolution in any part of Persia would immediately throw it into the arms of the British, who would be received as the Saviors of the Fatherland."[14]

This view had a considerable influence on Soviet policies in the coming years; and perhaps this is why the Soviet occupation and its support for the Gilan Republic were short-lived. As soon as the British, who had concurrently come under mounting pressure from a wave of anti-British nationalist feeling in the region, particularly in India and Turkey, completed their withdrawal from northern Iran and reduced their forces in the south of the country, the Soviets withdrew from Iranian territory, abandoned their support for the Gilan Republic, and signed a treaty of friendship with the Iranian government on February 26, 1921.[15] In this treaty, the USSR recognized Gilan as part of Iran under Iranian sovereignty, and expressed its support for Iranian independence and territorial integrity. But in return it secured the right to intervene in Iran whenever the country was being used by a third party to threaten the security of the Soviet Union and its allies. Thus, by implication, Moscow mounted its pressure on Tehran not to ratify the new Anglo-Iranian Treaty. This move, however, coincided with the dramatic rise to power in Iran of Reza Shah, on February 26, 1921.

THE RULE OF REZA SHAH

When Reza Shah rose to power, Iran was deep in social and political chaos, and the economy was floundering; the successive

Constitutionalist governments had failed to achieve domestic stability and democratic reform; many Iranians, particularly in the
towns, had become disillusioned and frustrated with chronic
instability in government, lack of reform or amelioration in their
standard of living, and continuous foreign interventions; the two
powers, Britain and the USSR, were coming close once again to
reaching some parity in their relationship in Iran, and their
pressing respective domestic problems had compelled them to
avoid further escalation of their rivalry; and nationalist-reformist
movements had become important in most parts of South Asia
and the Islamic world, where Ataturk in Turkey and King Ama-
nullah in Afghanistan rose high in their struggle for internal
reforms and against foreign domination.

Reza Shah, the commander of the Russian-trained Cossack Bri-
gade, the only disciplined force in Iran, seized power in a show of
force. He became *sardar sepah* or commander-in-chief of all the
armed forces, and entrusted his political collaborator, Sayyed Ziya
al-Din, a pro-British intellectual, with the prime ministership.
Subsequently, however, in a skillful display of statesmanship, he
replaced Sayyed Ziya in 1923, and succeeded to the throne of
Persia in 1925 by a vote of the Majlis and a constitutional amendment, thus becoming the Shah of Iran. He established the
Pahlavi dynasty and single-handed absolute rule—a rule that appealed to Iranians both socially and traditionally—but retained
the Constitution of 1906 and its symbol of expression, the Majlis,
as a source of legitimacy for his actions. Although he had come
from the north and was a Russian-trained Cossack officer, he was
trusted by the British, and many even saw him as a British agent.
Judged by his ideas and deeds, however, he was a nationalist,
deeply inspired by pro-Western reformist ideas. He ruled Iran
until 1941, and produced a strong dictatorial reformist regime
that strengthened the internal politics of Iran against Anglo-
Soviet rivalry, but did not save him politically once his grip on
power was shattered by the Allied occupation of Iran in 1941. His
actions show that one of Reza Shah's main goals was to reduce
Iran's dependence on Britain and the USSR, and hence insulate
it from their rivalry. For this, he considered it necessary to
achieve two major objectives: the consolidation of internal politics under the authority of the central government and, therefore,
the initiation of certain essential socio-economic reforms in order
to create internal stability and unity; and the establishment of a

regional friendship and close relationship with a third power to secure a counterbalance against Anglo-Soviet intervention and rivalry. In one of his very first acts, he asked the Majlis to reject the Anglo-Iranian Treaty of 1919 and ratify the Iranian-Soviet Treaty of 1921. This was carried out with little opposition in the Majlis, much to the dismay of the British, who were now deeply preoccupied with nationalist uprisings in the Indian subcontinent and many parts of the Islamic world. In domestic politics, after reorganizing and improving the armed forces, he moved swiftly and forcefully to consolidate the power of the central government vis-à-vis tribal and group powers, and banned all political parties and factions that had flourished during the so-called "quasi democratic" period, some of them having been sponsored by Britain and Russia in their own interests. His forces crushed the secessionists, including the local rebels, Kuchek Khan in Gilan and Sheikh Khaz'al in Khuzistan, who had been sponsored and manipulated by Russia and Britain, respectively. He succeeded in establishing the authority of the central government over almost all of Iran.

In the economic sphere, he gave priority to certain developmental projects that laid the base for the future Iranian economic infrastructure. His government built highways and the Trans-Iranian railway from the Persian Gulf to the Caspian, and established an airline and industrial complexes, largely on the basis of the limited Iranian oil and internal revenues.[16] In the social sphere, his government devoted attention to improving health and education, and laid the foundations of the University of Tehran. In a drive to secularize the state and reduce the power of the clergy in Iranian politics, he reduced religious holidays and introduced a new legal code modeled on the Napoleonic Code in what was a predominantly Islamic society. His social reforms included allowing women to discard veils and asking men to drop turbans. It was largely these reforms, in the context of his dictatorial rule in a traditional and strictly Islamic society, that caused the violent mass uprisings of 1935. The Majlis was burned, as a result of which the government cracked down violently on all opposition and closed the Parliament. The political party that suffered most was the pro-Moscow Tudeh, operating underground, whose leaders were prosecuted and imprisoned.

In implementing his reforms, Reza Shah attempted to balance British and Soviet involvement by seeking expertise and technical assistance from many other sources, including France, Germany, the United States, Austria, and China. In the long run, his reforms did not come to much, as he failed to undertake a coherent and comprehensive program to restructure the feudal, traditional, economically backward, and socially fragmented Iranian society. In the short run, however, they did result in the temporary social and economic stability that Reza Shah needed in order to reduce pressure on Iran from outside powers.

In foreign policy, Reza Shah moved to balance Iran's relationships with Britain and the Soviet Union. The Soviet leadership was deeply preoccupied with Stalin's policies of mass mobilization, collectivization, and "socialism in one country," while Britain was entangled with growing nationalist revolts in its South Asian and Middle Eastern colonies, as well as with the consequences of the Depression. Reza Shah acted to reduce Iran's dependence on Britain and to increase the country's oil revenues, which he needed to finance his reforms and military build-up. For this, he needed to restrain the increasing British economic and even political control in southern Iran. His regime was aware that any achievement in this direction would lessen the grounds for Soviet hostility toward Iran. At the time, Iran's income from its oil was the only sure source of substantial revenue, and was essential to the country's economy. But, largely due to the Depression, the Anglo-Persian Company paid markedly reduced royalties to the Iranian government in 1931-1932. This drop in royalties was enough to bring to the surface the long-standing dissatisfaction of influential circles in the Iranian government with the amount gained under the D'Arcy Concession of 1901, and with the way the company had monopolized the entire Iranian oil industry as an export-oriented sector benefiting mostly the oil company and the British government.[17] Reza Shah therefore canceled the original concession in November 1932, and demanded a renegotiated agreement. The British, in a display of gunboat diplomacy, which was to be repeated about twenty years later, refused to give in, and precipitated a crisis in Anglo-Iranian relations.

After a strong protest note to the Tehran government and a display of naval strength in the Persian Gulf, the British government took the matter to the Council of the League of Nations. Tehran considered the dispute a matter between itself and the concessionaires, not a concern of either the British government or the League of Nations. The Soviet attitude to the crisis was essentially one of "wait and see," but it commended Reza Shah's action as a "nationalist-reformist fight." As the crisis became prolonged, the British government grew anxious because any loss of British interests in Iran would not only seriously affect the British economy and its imperial power, but would also reduce Iran's dependence on Britain in favor of the Soviet Union. While the debate on the issue was before the League of Nations, the British, on April 29, 1933, signed a new concession with Iran that was to be valid for sixty years, and could not be canceled unilaterally again. Under the new concession, the company agreed to pay Iran "annually 20 per cent of dividends on ordinary shares in excess of £671,250 and royalties on oil fixed at 4 s. a ton sold and exported"; these figures were later increased. The area of the new concession was limited to 100,000 square miles, and provisions were made for participation by Iranians in managing the company and running the oil industry.[18] The British thus succeeded in retaining their monopoly of the Iranian oil industry from production to shipment.[19] Moreover, in the course of time, they were reluctant to implement the new agreement in its entirety. Many Iranian grievances thus remained, and eventually prompted Mossadeq's government to nationalize the Iranian oil industry in early 1951.

The showdown with the British, however, provided Reza Shah with some leverage to widen Iran's foreign policy options and improve relations with the Soviet Union and with other neighboring countries, as well as to seek closer ties with a third power to deflect the Anglo-Soviet rivalry. He devoted himself to strengthening Iran's relations with Turkey, Iraq, and Afghanistan, with the aim of forming a "small-power bloc" that could resist pressures from the imperial powers. This eventually resulted in the conclusion of the Sa'adabad Pact of nonaggression and consultation between Iran, Turkey, Iraq, and Afghanistan.[20] In his search for closer ties with a third power, Reza Shah preferred the United States, because it was a geographically distant and largely a noncolonial power, presumably less ready than others to intervene in Iranian affairs.

Given, however, the United States' policy of low-key involvement in world affairs at the time, particularly in a region that it had traditionally recognized as a British sphere of influence, Washington was unprepared to commit itself to close ties with

Tehran. After direct approaches had failed, Tehran attempted to develop relations by involving American oil companies in the Iranian oil industry. It arranged a visit by a representative of the Standard Oil Company in late December 1939, in search of a major oil concession. The mission, however, proved ineffective for two main reasons: first, the State Department completely disassociated the U.S. government from the mission and its purpose; and second, Moscow demanded that, if the American company were granted an oil concession, the Soviet Union should be given an equal concession, which Tehran was not prepared to grant.[21] Tehran therefore went so far as to provoke Washington into closer ties by threatening to strengthen its relations with Moscow. After concluding a Treaty of Commerce and Navigation with the USSR in March 1940, which promised closer ties between the two countries and made considerable economic concessions to the Soviet Trade Ministry and trade organizations, Tehran approached Washington with the details of the treaty in order to induce it to conclude a similar treaty with Iran. It also sought to purchase military hardware from the United States. But Washington remained reluctant to make any serious commercial, financial, or military commitment to Iran, and Reza Shah could secure nothing more than limited diplomatic and trade ties. The situation changed dramatically only after Reza Shah's death in 1944, when Washington began to commit itself to the security of Iran, and hence gradually to replace Britain as the major Soviet rival in the region.

The other power with which Reza Shah had sought to forge close ties was Germany. The rise of Germany as a nationalist and anti-British power had impressed the Iranian leadership, as it had many other nationalist governments and movements in Asia and the Middle East. Reza Shah had considerable success in furthering friendship with Germany. In his attempt to weaken the British position, Hitler rendered generous economic and technical assistance to Iran, as he did to Turkey and Afghanistan. By the end of the 1930s, more than six hundred German experts had been employed in various industrial, commercial, and educational projects in Iran. Trade developed rapidly, and by 1938-1939 Germany accounted for 41 percent of the total foreign trade of Iran.[22] Consequently, as Churchill put it, "German prestige stood high" among Iranians.[23] Britain was alarmed, but Moscow saw no danger in Iranian-German friendship because of its own treaty of friendship with Germany. In fact, to the Soviet leadership this was a fruitful anti-British development. At the outbreak of World War II, however, the two traditional rivals, Britain and USSR, were once again forced to enter a wartime alliance against a common enemy, Germany.

Iran in World War II

Under heavy pressure from the advancing German forces, Moscow requested London to open a second front against Germany in Europe. Churchill did not consider this to be politically or militarily expedient; instead, he promised all possible help to the Soviet Union in carrying on the war in its own front. He was determined to keep the Soviet front viable. London chose Iran, with its railway connection from the Persian Gulf to the Caspian, as the most suitable and quickest corridor through which war supplies could be transferred to the Soviet Union. For this, Churchill asked Stalin to join him in making a request to Reza Shah. But Reza Shah declared Iran's neutrality in the war; wishing to preserve his friendship with Germany, he rejected the Anglo-Soviet request. Without further ado, London proposed to Moscow a joint invasion of Iran.[24] Stalin agreed because he badly needed war supplies. The Anglo-Soviet forces, with American support, occupied Iran in almost the same pattern as had been prescribed by the two powers' agreement of 1907, with one major difference—their respective zones of influence were now transformed into zones of occupation. The Soviets occupied the north, the British took over the south, while the capital, Tehran, and the sovereignty of the whole country (though acknowledged to the Tehran government) were placed provisionally under the joint protection of the two powers.

The rewards for both powers were several. The Soviets secured a viable supply route and freed themselves from anxiety that the Germans might make a thrust from Iran against the Soviet oilfields at Baku. The British placed their interests, particularly their oilfields and oil installations, under their own direct protection. They made themselves immune against the possible use of Iran by Germans to implement Hitler's "Oriental Plan" in an attempt to weaken the British empire. They helped to keep the Soviet front active by facilitating, with the aid of the small American task force in the Persian Gulf, the transit of war supplies to the Soviet Union. Meanwhile, Churchill ordered British forces to ensure "that the Russian influence [in Iran was] kept within reasonable bounds" and to use "the leverage of a possible Russian occupation" of Tehran against the Iranian government in order to obtain all facilities Britain required; and finally to make "the Persians keep each other quiet while we get on with the war."[25]

Iran was humiliated, and lost its real sovereignty. The conduct of its domestic and foreign affairs was directly subjected to the dictates of the occupying forces. Under pressure, Reza Shah abdicated in favor of his son and went into exile in South Africa, where he died in 1944. Mohammad Reza Shah was 20 years old, inexperienced, and wielded little real power, but he suited the Allied forces in their desire to legitimize their actions in Iran.

The end of Reza Shah's absolute rule and the beginning of Allied occupation opened a new phase in the development of Iranian politics. Tehran lost control over a large part of Iran; the autocratic and centralized system that Reza Shah had built was loosened, and Iran sank into growing social disorder, political disarray, and economic hardship. Numerous social and political groups, including tribes, reappeared in the Iranian political scene with demands for domestic reforms and tribal autonomy. Some followed either the British or Soviet line. Some sought the evolutionary institution of some sort of "democratic" mass participatory system with the retention of monarchy; others demanded revolutionary "socialist" structural changes, with the establishment of a republic.[26] A nationalist current developed rapidly, supported by those Iranians who were anxious because of the chaotic domestic situation as well as the humiliation and instability that Iran had suffered at the hands of foreign powers. While foreign powers were using their favored social and political groups and tribes against each other, the Majlis emerged as a credible national forum for diverse political expressions, agitations, and demands. The conservative, traditional institution of monarchy, however, still controlled the demoralized Iranian armed forces and symbolized Iran's sovereignty, while the "old guard" that upheld this institution still dominated a government notorious for its corrupt and inefficient bureaucracy.[27]

In the meantime, with their traditional zones of influence transformed into zones of occupation, Britain and the Soviet Union intensified their rivalry in Iran. Each wishing to keep the other's influence at bay, and wishing to secure a government in Tehran friendly and dependent upon itself, the two powers once again engaged in a stable but intense struggle to entrench their respective positions. Churchill had already ordered the British forces to insure that Soviet influence be kept "within reasonable bounds" and to make "the Persians keep each other quiet"; the Soviets now found the opportunity to solve their Iranian problem once and for all: they began what may be called "Sovietization" of their zone of occupation.

Shortly after their occupation began, the Russians closed their zone to free entry; those Iranians and foreigners who wished to visit the zone were required to obtain special passes from the Soviet embassy in Tehran. The Soviets embarked upon a number of long-range policies designed to effect basic socio-economic and political changes in the northern Iranian provinces under their control, especially Azerbaijan and Kurdistan. This eventually led to the establishment of a pro-Soviet Tudeh government in Azerbaijan, independent of the Tehran government. Some of the major measures instituted by the Russians included issuing new regulations that would favor the peasantry over land owners in the sharing of crops, although this fell short of a land reform; confiscation or compulsory purchase of large amounts of grain from private individuals and government stores; and taking over some estates and establishing model farms to be operated with the help of the Red Army. These measures, together with a ban on the export of staple foodstuffs, enabled the Soviet zone to claim a better economic growth than the British zone, and thus attract increasing support for the Soviets from Iranian intellectuals, anti-British factions, and the lower working classes.

More significantly, the Soviets promptly and forcefully revived and strengthened Iran's Communist party. In his campaign against all organized opposition, Reza Shah had banned the Communist party in 1937. Under the general amnesty of 1941, however, fifty-two leading members of the party were released from prison. With Soviet help, and under the leadership of the strongly pro-Moscow Ja'far Pishavari, they soon reorganized the party and renamed it Tudeh (the masses), with its base in the Soviet zone. The renaming was largely an attempt to disguise its ideological leanings and avoid alienating those Iranians who believed in reform but not in communism. The party was a major critic of the Tehran government, and opposed the institution of monarchy and the British "colonial-imperialist" presence and interference in Iran. It advocated socialist reforms and autonomy for the province of Azerbaijan, with which Soviet Azerbaijan shared a common geographical, ethnic, and religious background. Similarly, it encouraged the Iranian Kurd community to stand up for its autonomy against the Tehran government. Eventually, the Tudeh succeeded in establishing an autonomous regime in Azerbaijan, where in 1944-1945 the Tehran government was barred from appointing a provincial governor. General Arfa, at the time Iranian joint chief of staff, has alleged that the Soviets' ultimate aim was to establish a pro-Moscow government in Tehran.[28] But it is at least equally arguable that the threat of doing so was being used chiefly as a bargaining lever by the Soviets against British activities in the rest of Iran.

The British were certainly alarmed by these Soviet activities in the north, which they interpreted as imminently dangerous to their security. With their closest ally, the United States, they charged the Soviet Union with violating the provisions of the Tripartite Treaty of January 29, 1942, under which the allied powers had undertaken "to safeguard the economic existence of the Iranian people against the deprivation and difficulties arising as a result of the present war," as well as "to respect the sovereignty and territorial integrity of Iran" and withdraw their forces from Iran "not later than six months" after the end of hostilities in all war theaters. This had subsequently been reiterated by the Anglo-American-Soviet Declaration of December 1, 1943.[29]

Meanwhile, the British had begun to reinforce their past policy of "divide and rule" in Iran. This time, it meant the reinforcement of the politics of "conservatism" and "tribalism" against the forces that sought "radical" changes either against the British position or in favor of the Soviets. In this way, the British sought to check both the activities of the anti-British forces and the Soviet influence in Iran. They exploited conservative beliefs against radical ones, Islamic beliefs against conservative convictions, and nationalist feelings against religious ones. In general, they vigorously supported conservative elements (largely the tribes, religious zealots, and the institution of monarchy), although, at times, they played these forces against one another.[30]

To oppose the strengthening of the Tudeh party, the British also eagerly assisted the formation and activities of a pro-Western but anti-communist political party called Erade-ye Melli (National Will). They used the threat of a Soviet occupation of Tehran as leverage in enlisting the support of the Tehran government for this party. To lead the party they brought back from exile the former Iranian prime minister, Sayyed Ziya al-Din, whom Reza Shah had replaced and sent into exile partly because of his strong pro-Western sentiments.[31] The party strongly opposed the Tudeh, accusing it repeatedly of "treason, subversive activities, anti-religious propaganda, violence, sabotage, hooliganism and hypocrisy."[32]

These measures and countermeasures in response to accusations and counteraccusations reactivated the traditional rivalry that had been inherent in British-Soviet relations even before their occupation of Iran. This local "cold war" was waged at a time when the United States was Britain's closest ally, and was committed not only to the Atlantic Charter, but also to the Tehran Conference, and had tacitly approved the Tripartite Treaty. While the British position as a leading world power was in decline, the position of the United States as a superpower was on the rise, and it could not remain aloof from Iranian developments any longer.

Up to 1940, Iran had a very small place in the arena of American foreign policy. The United States had neither significant military and economic interests in Iran, nor were there many Iranian voters, compared to those of other ethnic groups, such as the Poles, in the United States. Reza Shah had failed to secure any major American political and economic commitment toward Iran. After the occupation of Anglo-Russian forces, however, the situation began to change. During 1942 and 1943, the British called a number of American troops from the U.S. Persian Gulf Command, composed of about 30,000 men, into Iran to speed up the supply of American lend-lease aid and other war materials to the USSR. The Americans and British were to take care of the railway from the Persian Gulf to Tehran, and the Russians from Tehran to Bandar Shah on the Caspian. An Anglo-American agreement specified that British troops would provide security, and the Americans would handle technical operations. Although this American involvement was in line with Tehran's search for better ties with the United States, the Soviet Union considered it as the advent of yet another "imperialist" force at work in Iran. From the Soviet point of view, the presence of American troops in Iran without any agreement with the Iranian and Soviet authorities was illegal. Nonetheless, because of its wartime alliance with the United States, because it needed aid, and because U.S. policy was not initially very clear, the Soviet Union refrained from debating the issue publicly at the time.

In the meantime, Washington was becoming increasingly conscious of the growing strategic importance of Iran to the West, and its economic importance with respect to oil. A number of American policy makers understood that if Iran fell to Soviet communism, all Western economic and political interests in the Persian Gulf region would become vulnerable to Soviet penetration. In the early 1940s, a report had been submitted to President Roosevelt by American commission of experts, which stated that the center of gravity of the world's petroleum output was shifting to the Persian Gulf. Such considerations prompted the State Department, in late 1941, to appeal to American missionary schools in Iran to keep up their good work by "countering bad [communist] influences at work there." Wallace Murray, chief of the Near Eastern Division, urged the Presbyterian Board of Foreign Missions to see that its school at Tabriz restrain "Soviet separatist and ideological activities in that area, of which much has already been heard." He also advocated the resumption of trade negotiations with Iran "for reasons of political expediency and in order to safeguard American trade interests in Iran during the post-War period," and make sure that American oil companies interested in Iran could be welcomed in the region.[33] As a result, when the British requested lend-lease funds to build several pipe lines across Iran, Washington asked for assurances that these pipe lines would be made available to American companies after the war.[34] Meanwhile, the American special emissary, Patrick Hurley, upon his return from a Middle East tour, advised President Roosevelt that the United States needed to put in much greater effort and exert much more leadership if Iran were to remain independent in the postwar era. He advised Washington to help Iran in building a "democratic government," based upon a "system of free enterprise."[35]

In the context of these reports and suggestions, Washington committed itself to the development of close political, economic, and military ties with Iran, so that America's position would remain strong in the country. It bolstered its military mission in Iran, which was there to expedite lend-lease shipments to the

Soviet Union, by dispatching additional military experts and advisors to the Iranian government.[36] It sought to have a substantial role in the Iranian economy and access to the country's oil resources. Responding to a request of the Iranian government in 1943, it assisted an American financial mission to Iran, headed by Arthur C. Millspaugh, to reorganize the Iranian financial system. Millspaugh subsequently wrote, "our control of revenues and expenditure not only served as a stabilizing influence, but also was indispensable to the full effectiveness of Americans in other fields."[37] In February 1944, moreover, Washington raised its legation in Tehran to embassy status, and came out publicly in full support of the Iranian and British governments against Soviet moves to entrench that country's position in Iran. Before the war ended, therefore, Washington's New Deal diplomacy had been extended to Iran in opposition to the Soviets and in promotion of its own interests. This rapid change in American policy, from limited to extensive involvement in Iran, brought sharp public criticism from the Soviet Union, which increased during the so-called oil crisis of 1944.

The oil crisis was largely precipitated when, during the first half of 1944, two American oil companies, Standard Vacuum and Sinclair, sought to negotiate oil concessions with the Iranian government without informing either the British or the Soviets. In the background of rapidly growing American involvement in Iran, this added to the discomfort of the Soviet Union, which had already been troubled by the increasing influence of the Anglo-Persian Oil Company, the biggest in Iran. In a countermove, Moscow also demanded an oil concession that would cover all the five northern provinces of Iran, stretching from Azerbaijan to Khorasan, under Soviet occupation. The Soviet objectives in this demand were to rebuff the Americans and any further British demands for oil concessions, and thereby to undercut the influence of these two powers in Iran. The Russians also wished to combat the Western monopoly of Persian Gulf/Middle Eastern oil, and its possible future use by the Western powers against the Soviet Union in the arena of international politics.

On the grounds that Iran would become a victim of a round of foreign competition because of its oil at a time when the Tehran government was weak and rival forces had occupied Iran, Iranian Prime Minister Sa'ed refused any oil concession to any of the powers. He ordered all the talks about oil concessions to be postponed until the end of the war. The Majlis promptly passed a bill to this effect, prohibiting any government official from either discussing or signing any oil concessionary agreement with any foreign company or person. The principal author of the bill was Dr. Mohammad Mossadeq.[38] Sa'ed's refusal was very displeasing to the Soviets, who suspected the Iranian government of having made its decision in collusion with the United States and Britain. On October 24, 1944, the Soviet vice commissar for foreign trade, Kavtaradze, denounced the Iranian decision and declared, "the disloyal and unfriendly position taken by Premier Sa'ed toward the Soviet Union excludes the possibility of further collaboration with him." The Soviet and Tudeh press criticized the Iranian government as "reactionary" and an agent of "Western imperialism." In responding to the Soviet criticisms, the American ambassador to Tehran, Leland B. Morris, revealed that Washington "recognized the sovereign right of Iran to refuse the granting of oil concessions and did not reproach the Iranian government on that account." This strengthened Soviet suspicion of Iran's collusion with the West. As a result, *Izvestia* provocatively questioned the legality of the presence of American troops in Iran. It questioned how their presence without a treaty with the Iranian government "tallies with Iran's sovereignty and independence."[39]

The final blow to Washington-Moscow relations over Iran came when the Soviet Union showed reluctance to honor its treaty commitments to withdraw its forces from Iran within six months after the termination of the war. The final date for troop withdrawal, as agreed at the three powers' foreign ministers' conference of September 1945, had been set for March 2, 1946. But as the war neared its end, the Soviet Union continued to strengthen its forces in northern Iran. Meanwhile, an autonomous communist regime under Tudeh party leadership was formed in the two Soviet occupied provinces of Azerbaijan and Kurdistan.[40] This angered the Iranian government and deeply concerned the administrations in Washington and London. In January 1946, the Iranian government, with U.S. and British support, formally charged the Soviet Union before the Security Council under the United Nations Charter with creating "a situation which might lead to international friction" by interference in Iranian internal affairs. In reply, the Soviet Union introduced formal charges against Britain over Greece and Indonesia, and argued that the dispute over Iran "was not a matter which that body [the Security Council] was competent to handle." This provoked the British foreign secretary to comment that "many . . . were discouraged at the disintegration of the great wartime coalition behind a front of diplomatic verbiage which kept up the appearance of good relations and of unity but avoided the central problem, the adjustment of relations between east and west."[41] Thus, the Anglo-Soviet dispute over Iran, which so far had been kept at regional level, finally assumed its place in the arena of global politics, with the United States taking a leading part in the dispute.

On January 26, 1946, however, Premier Sa'ed was replaced by Ahmad Qavam, who was known to favor a compromise with the Soviet Union, and he proposed to enter direct negotiation with Moscow. The Security Council agreed to let the two parties settle their differences bilaterally. British and American troops had withdrawn from Iran formally on January 1, but President Truman, who had just succeeded Roosevelt, cast serious doubt on Qavam's chances of success in direct talks. He later wrote: "it was, of course, unlikely that Iran would be able to resist Russian demands while Soviet troops were still occupying her territory. Under such conditions there could hardly be any equality at the bargaining table." In a coordinated move, Washington and London sent two separate protest notes to the Kremlin, demanding immediate Soviet withdrawal. The American note explained the U.S. obligations to the U.N. Charter and certain treaties concerning its commitment to Iran, warned Moscow that Washington "cannot remain indifferent," and stressed that "the Government of the Soviet Union will do its part by withdrawing immediately all Soviet forces from the territory of Iran, to promote the international conference which is necessary for peaceful progress among the peoples of all nations." For President Truman, as for the British foreign secretary, the dispute over Iran was no longer regional. "Russian activities in Iran," Truman wrote, "threatened the peace of the world." He stressed, moreover, that "if the Russians were to control Iran's oil, either directly or indirectly, the raw material balance of the world would undergo serious damage, and it would be a serious loss for the economy of the Western world."[42] Hence the United States must fight Soviet influence in Iran at all costs. On the Russian side, Stalin remained concerned about Soviet security, which had been threatened for years by British activities in Iran, and the vulnerability of the

Baku oilfields to attack from Iran. And the Soviet desired, as a world power, to have a share in the "exploitation of world deposits," particularly those in the Persian Gulf region.[43]

Against this build-up of tension between the Soviet Union and Western powers, there was a sudden but major breakthrough in the bilateral talks between Tehran and Moscow. On March 24, 1946, Moscow unexpectedly announced that all Soviet troops would be withdrawn from Iran at once, pending the conclusion of an agreement between Iran and the Soviet Union in April. The two sides agreed that the Red Army would evacuate within a month and a half after March 24, 1946; a joint-stock Irano-Soviet oil company was to be established and ratified by the Fifteenth Majlis within seven months after March 24; and Iran would carry out improvements in Azerbaijan in accordance with existing laws (under Tudeh leadership) and in benevolent spirit toward the people of Azerbaijan.[44] The reasons why the Soviet Union so easily agreed to withdraw its troops and abandon the autonomous Tudeh regime in Azerbaijan have not yet been documented. Washington claimed that Moscow was yielding to its pressures, whereas London credited Churchill's Fulton speech, which recommended to the Western democracies a policy of "sedate and sober strength" against the Soviet Union. These may have made some contribution. But it seems that the Soviet decision was mainly a result of Moscow's increasing preoccupation with its interests in Eastern and Southern Europe, and Qavam's political shrewdness in handling negotiations.[45]

The Irano-Soviet agreement provided both sides with an honorable way out of the dispute, and it was, indeed, a partial victory for Moscow. But before the year ended, the situation changed dramatically in favor of the Tehran government. The Azerbaijan issue had had a marked impact on the Iranian people's view of the Soviet Union. It had not only reinforced the traditional conservative beliefs that the Soviets were determined to transform Iran into one of their socialist satellites, but it also disenchanted many other Iranian groups that adhered strictly to their own traditions and independence. The Iranian monarchy, heading the conservative forces—including the bureaucracy—as well as the British and Americans capitalized on this extensively in order to strengthen the anti-Soviet tide and consequently their own position in Iran. In the meantime, the United States had stepped up its military and economic aid to the Tehran government. The American police and military advisory missions had become active in reorganizing and equipping Iranian security and military forces. Millspaugh and his team of financial advisors had been engaged in reorganizing the Iranian financial system, though they had run into difficulties with many Iranian personnel, and had been forced to leave Iran by 1946. Later, however, Max Thornburg, formerly petroleum advisor to the State Department, headed a group of American advisors in planning the Iranian economy and eventually in drafting Iran's First Seven Year Development Plan in 1949. The Iranian government welcomed the increasing role of the United States in Iran, as against both the USSR and Britain.[46]

By October 1946, the Iranian government was in a relatively strong position to undertake certain bold anti-Soviet actions. Under the Shah's command (possibly at Anglo-American urging), Tehran forces crushed the secessionist Tudeh regime in Azerbaijan and Kurdistan. Premier Qavam urged the newly elected Majlis to denounce the whole Irano-Soviet Agreement of April 1946. In October 1947, the Majlis, led by Mossadeq, did so by 102 to 2 votes, and Irano-Soviet relations returned to a situation of mistrust and unfriendliness. For the first time, the young Shah had exerted his constitutional position as the commander-in-chief of the armed forces by personally commanding the military operation against the secessionist provinces. This bolstered his leadership and the power of the monarchy in Iranian politics. Meanwhile, as a result, Iran became further dependent on the West, mainly the United States, for its protection against any possible Soviet reaction. It was, indeed, a hard pill for the Soviet leadership to swallow—to let its southern neighbor slip into the Western camp at a time when U.S. international behavior was being guided increasingly by Truman's doctrine for the containment of communism within the Soviet borders. Moscow therefore stepped up its underground support for the Iranian communists and antigovernment groups. The role of these groups in Iranian politics, particularly during Dr. Mohammad Mossadeq's nationalist and reformist government (1951-1953), later provided London and Washington with an excuse to engineer the overthrow of the Mossadeq government.

MOSSADEQ AND OIL NATIONALIZATION

During the war, the loosening of central authority under Allied occupation had allowed various social and political groups with

reformist platforms but diverse ideological orientations to emerge
and develop on the Iranian political scene. The Anglo-Soviet
intervention had resulted in a strengthening of the pro-Moscow
communist Tudeh and pro-British Erade-ye Melli into major political parties. These, among the tens of other factions, dominated the Majlis, which had become the seat of political power
and symbol of democracy in Iran. But the disunity and group
animosities among the factions had become responsible for political instability and social disturbances. As a result, the life span
of no government was more than a year in the 1940s, and successive governments had failed to initiate and implement serious
and necessary reforms. After the war and the Azerbaijan affair,
the Tudeh and Erade-ye Melli parties had been weakened, and
subsequently, because of an attempt on the Shah's life in February 1949, the Tudeh party was officially banned. Qavam's
Democratic party, which had attracted a balanced membership
from various political circles, assumed control of the fifteenth
Majlis, and Qavam became prime minister once again.[47] He was
respected as a remarkable political tactician in the way he had
handled Iran's dealings with the Soviet Union. But an inner party
crisis resulted in loss of support for him in the Majlis on December 10, 1947, and his party disintegrated. From then until 1951,
there were three different cabinets, none capable of commanding
a working majority in the Majlis for more than a short period.
Amid growing unrest and constant attempts by the conservative
forces, headed by the monarchy, to assert their control over the
Majlis, the prime ministers and the Majlis seemed incapable of
significant decisions.

During this period, however, the Majlis approved in 1949 the
program of Iran's First Seven Year Development Plan and au-
thorized the establishment of a Plan Organization to execute its
projects. The Shah also paid his first state visit to the United
States, and pressed for economic and military aid; Washington
announced the extension of its first Point IV (economic aid)
program to Iran in 1949, and agreed to supply the country with
arms under the Mutual Defense Aid program in 1950.

In the meantime, Dr. Mohammad Mossadeq was emerging
rapidly as a leading nationalist-reformist figure. He had been a
prominent political activist, with a controversial background,
since early in the century. He had consistently advocated the creation of a parliamentary democratic system with the power of

monarchy limited and regulated by law; the exertion of Iran's ownership and control over its resources, particularly oil; and the implementation of rapid, fundamental socio-economic reforms. It was primarily in support of these interrelated objectives that, after supporting the Constitutionalist movement in the 1910s, and subsequently being elected to the Majlis, Mossadeq led a small group of deputies in opposing Reza Shah's succession to the throne of Persia in 1925 on the grounds that his rule could only be dictatorial. He had been imprisoned in the 1930s for his opposition activities, but returned to political life in 1941 under the Allied occupation, and was elected to the Majlis from Tehran. He subsequently initiated the bill forbidding oil concessions to any power in 1944, and played a leading role in the Majlis' rejection of the Irano-Soviet Agreement of April 1946.

By the late 1940s, Mossadeq gained increasing support, both inside and outside the Majlis, from the newly formed National Front (Jebhe-ye Melli), which was a loose grouping of diverse elements: the Iran party, Toilers' party, neo-Nazi Sumka party, the ultranationalist Pan-Iran party, the religious fanatics of the Devotees of Islam, and followers of the rabble-rousing religious leader, Sayyed Abol Qasem Kashani. Mossadeq emerged as the leading spokesman of the Front. He advocated, first, the assertion of Iran's ownership and control of its oil industry. The underlying considerations were to maximize Iran's income from its most viable source of capital, minimize the reasons for both British direct activities and Anglo-Soviet rivalry in Iran; and, as a result, improve Iran's relations with the Soviet Union as leverage against the British influence in Iran. He wished to harness Iranian resources in order to initiate and implement structural political and socio-economic reforms. The popularity of Mossadeq's program was greatly assisted by the fact that the monopoly of the Iranian oil industry by British Petroleum (BP), which owned the Anglo-Iranian Oil Company (AIOC), had proved to be very costly for Iran. According to one analysis,

> the magnitude of direct influences of the oil industry during the 1910-50 period was, for all practical purposes, negligible, and that the industry remained economically divorced from the rest of the Iranian economy. The only major connecting link between oil and the domestic economy was provided by payments of royalties, taxes and dividends to the govern-

ment. These payments, too, were of limited benefit, largely because of their relative order of magnitude in the over-all budget. Only owing to the limited scope and magnitude of Iranian non-oil exports and the growing needs of Iran for both civilian and military imports, the supply of foreign exchange in oil royalties and sterling conversion into rials (for the economy's domestic expenditure) was of relatively notable help to the Iranian economy.[48]

In this light, one of the AIOC officials has called the company's half-century effort "crudest exploitation."[49]

By now a broad cross-section of the Iranian people had not only become conscious of their oil resources and their exploitation by the British against Iranian interests, but were also easily persuaded, following defeat, humiliation, and pressure by the Allied occupying forces, to rally for a cause that could restore their dignity. As a result, there was growing popular support for Mossadeq when he rejected an oil concession to the USSR in early 1947, and firmly demanded a better deal from AIOC. The Majlis appointed Mossadeq to head a committee to consider the issue. Although by 1949 BP had devised a "supplemental agreement" that would have about doubled royalty payments made by AIOC, the concurrent Aramco offer of a "fifty-fifty percent profit sharing deal" to the Saudi Arabian government prompted the Majlis' oil committee under Mossadeq to reject the agreement unanimously. The British refusal to enter a fifty-fifty arrangement with Iran angered the Iranians, and the oil committee recommended the full nationalization of the Iranian oil industry.[50] This infuriated the British, and Prime Minister 'Ali Razmara, a conservative general and the Shah's choice as prime minister since June 1950, appeared before the Majlis on March 3, 1951 in an attempt to persuade the deputies against full nationalization on the grounds that Iran could not override its international obligations and lacked the capacity to run the oil industry on its own. But Razmara was shot dead within four days of his appearance by a member of the Feda'iyan-e Islam (Devotees of Islam), which two days later threatened to kill the Shah and other leading members of government.[51] Amid growing public unrest, the Majlis accepted its oil committee's recommendation, and on March 15 passed a bill providing for the nationalization of AIOC; the bill was approved by the Senate on March 20.[52]

Meanwhile, when Premier 'Ala, Razmara's successor, failed to reach any agreement with the British, the Majlis voted Mossadeq to the prime ministership on April 30, 1951.

Despite the foreseeable consequences, Mossadeq declared AIOC nationalized on May 1, and in return promised compensation. He set up the National Iranian Oil Company (NIOC) to take over from AIOC. The nationalization meant Iranian ownership and control of the oil industry; it did not, however, provide that the former company should withdraw all of its British employees and expertise. Mossadeq believed that the nationalization would not result in economic losses, as many antinationalization elements were vigorously arguing. He considered this move the most viable measure to procure sufficient capital for improving socio-economic conditions in Iran. On June 21, 1951, he declared,

> Our long years of negotiations with foreign countries concerning the legitimacy of our claims to ownership of the industry, which no power in the world can deny us, have yielded no results this far. With the oil revenues we could meet our entire budget and combat poverty, disease, and backwardness among our people. Another important consideration is that by the elimination of the power of the British company, we would also eliminate corruption and intrigue, by means of which the internal affairs of our country have been influenced. Once this tutelage has ceased, Iran will have achieved its economic and political independence.
>
> The Iranian state prefers to take over the production of petroleum itself. The company should do nothing else but return its property to the rightful owners. The nationalization law provides that 25 percent of the net profits on oil be set aside to meet all the legitimate claims of the company for compensation. . . .
>
> It has been asserted abroad that Iran intends to expel the foreign oil experts from the country and then shut down oil installations. Not only is this allegation absurd; it is utter invention. The Iranian government has never considered such a step. Rather, it will make every effort to carry out nationalization as smoothly as possible, so as not to interfere with production. Thus deportation of the foreign specialists is out of the question.[53]

Mossadeq had already declared that it was possible that the nationalization might not result in great economic gains immediately; but it was the moral aspect of the measure that concerned him most. Outlining his views on the matter on November 6, 1950, Mossadeq had stated, "I believe more in the moral than economic aspect of nationalization of the oil industry. Assuming that we could not extract and sell as much oil as the company, we should be able under any circumstances to satisfy domestic consumption and secure the equivalent of the current revenues received from the company; the remaining oil should stay in the ground until the future generation could better benefit from it."[54]

Mossadeq's nationalization, however, happened at a bad time for Britain, which was still recovering from the war and the degradation of losing, as Lord Curzon would have put it, the badge of its imperial sovereignty in the Eastern hemisphere—India. It was facing mounting postwar economic difficulties at home, and was battling, both politically and psychologically, against accepting the fact that its position as the Western world's leading power was rapidly being taken over by the United States. Meanwhile, Iran had become "the jewel in the crown of BP,"[55] whose chairman, Sir William Fraser, was convinced that BP could and should hold on to the monopoly of Iranian oil. This was significant because BP had emerged as the cornerstone of British interest in Middle East oil, and, together with six other Western international oil companies, held the monopoly of world oil outside the Soviet bloc, from production to shipment, and exercised tremendous political power in the conduct of the Western world politics.[56] This meant that there was no possibility that Britain, at this stage, would have given in to Mossadeq.

The British Labour government at the time, and its immediate Conservative successor in October 1951, were equally convinced that to give in to Mossadeq would mean not only the loss of British prestige, but also the crippling of BP and the British economy, since it would also threaten investments and other interests in the Persian Gulf and the Middle East in the face of growing Arab nationalism. This negative position was encouraged by the AIOC officials and by Sir William Fraser, who argued that since Mossadeq lacked manpower, technical skill, a tanker fleet, and access to the world market, he would have to retreat from nationalization in the end, provided Britain exerted

enough pressure on him, even to the point of military intervention if necessary. Britain, as a result, rejected the nationalization
as illegal and unacceptable.[57] The consequences of this crisis for
Iran were more far-reaching than anyone could have predicted.
As the British stepped up their pressure, Mossadeq became more
militant, and his militancy was encouraged by an outspoken
American ambassador in Tehran, Henry Grady, a first-generation
Irish American, who openly expressed his hatred for British im-
perialism, and who misled the Iranians to believe that the United
States would help them resist British pressure.[58]

While the British government was taking its case to the United
Nations and International Court of Justice—unsuccessfully—it
put on a display of gunboat diplomacy reminiscent of its actions
in 1932. The HMS Mauritius cruised into the Persian Gulf and
British troops were reinforced in Iraq; but the British were divided over military intervention. The foreign secretary, minister
of defense, and BP's chairman all favored it, but Prime Minister
Attlee succeeded in convincing them that the use of force was
unwise and damaging to the position of Britain in the region.
Events, however, moved very swiftly. By the end of 1952, the
British had withdrawn their assets and advisors from Iran, and
had frozen Iran's conversion privileges of deposits in the Bank of
England. They had warned all other fleets that they would be
liable to prosecution if they shipped or marketed Iranian oil,
and BP obtained an agreement with its sister international oil
companies not to enter any agreement with Iran replacing the
AIOC. BP and Aramco immediately doubled their production in
Saudi Arabia, Kuwait, and Iraq, and thus compensated for the
loss of the Iranian oil so that no hardship was felt in Britain, and
the British public rallied behind the cause of AIOC. These all
amounted to an economic blockade of Iran and, as a result, the
entire Iranian oil industry came to a virtual standstill, with oil
production dropping from 241.4 million barrels in 1950 to 10.6
million in 1952.[59] This reduced Iran's oil income to almost nil,
increased Iran's economic plight, and caused a severe strain on
the implementation of Mossadeq's promised domestic reforms.

The Soviet Union viewed the dispute as the surfacing of a
long-standing contradiction in Iran's relationship with the West.
It hailed Mossadeq's nationalist stance, and urged the Tudeh's
support for him, but approached nationalization cautiously because it would have meant no concession to the Soviet Union,

either.[60] The United States, with its growing interests in Iran and the Iranian region, and its global campaign against communism, could not remain aloof from the crisis. Summing up the U.S. government's view, Secretary of State Dean Acheson subsequently wrote that the American "interest lay in the threat that this controversy held for everyone's interest in the Near East: it upset relations with the oil producing states and opened rare opportunities for communist propaganda; Britain might drive Iran to a Communist coup d'etat, or Iran might drive Britain out. . . . Either would be a major disaster."[61] But the British government and the AIOC bureaucracy rejected Washington's reading of the situation, which reflected a consideration of the situation solely in terms of Washington's interests in the region and involvement in the Cold War. Sir Anthony Eden, the British foreign secretary at the time, later wrote: "I did not accept the argument that the only alternative to Mussadeq was communist rule. I thought that if Mussadeq fell, his place might well be taken by a more reasonable Government with which it should be possible to conclude a satisfactory agreement. I knew that the country was possessed of an elasticity and resilience which appearances did not suggest."[62] To Eden the alternative to Mossadeq was a pro-Western conservative government, headed by the institution of monarchy in Iran. But Britain needed American support to achieve this. After American mediation had failed several times to bring about a settlement, Acheson concluded that the British were "destructive and determined on a rule or ruin policy in Iran."[63]

Finally, in October 1952, just three months before the Eisenhower administration was due to take over from President Truman, Acheson decided that the United States should try an independent initiative to end the crisis quickly, and try to save Iran from further political and economic disasters that could pave the way for the communists to take over.[64] For this he needed the help of the major American oil companies, which had the capacity to buy and market Iranian oil. But Acheson's efforts were seriously hampered by the battle that was in progress between the U.S. Justice Department and the American international oil companies under American antitrust laws, in which the Justice Department was charging the companies with forming an "international petroleum cartel," dividing the world markets between them, and sharing pipe lines and tankers throughout the world for major interests of their own. The State Department intervened in the case, arguing that since the companies were, for all practical purposes, major instruments of American foreign policy toward the oil-producing countries and against the spread of Soviet communism in those countries, the case against them might seriously impair American foreign policy aims and weaken political stability in the Middle East. It urged, therefore, that a new commission should study the interrelationship of antitrust, security, and foreign policy so that the important role of the companies in the execution of American policy abroad was not overlooked. Despite the attorney general's rejection of this on the grounds that the companies' cartel as "an authoritarian, dominating power over a great vital world industry" could be damaging rather than crucial to national security, the State Department's argument eventually won the approval of President Eisenhower, and the Justice Department dropped the case. Eisenhower ruled that the global battle against communism must take precedence over antitrust laws.[65] This was too late for Acheson, who had been succeeded by the new hardline anticommunist secretary of state, John Foster Dulles.

The antitrust laws, meanwhile, reinforced Mossadeq's position against AIOC. In early January 1953, before Eisenhower took office, Mossadeq cabled him in an attempt to secure American understanding and support for the Iranian people's "aspirations for the attainment of . . . life as [a] politically and economically independent nation." Eisenhower's reply to a proud and noncommunist Mossadeq was one of hope that the future American-Iranian "relationship would be completely free of any suspicion" during his administration.[66] Although international opinion favored Mossadeq, the situation began quickly to sour for him at home. The British blockade of Iranian oil and that country's intervening actions for Mossadeq's downfall resulted in serious economic hardship and polarization of Iranians into pro- and anti-Mossadeq forces. The anti-Mossadeq forces were centered around the monarchy, which had the support of a large section of the armed forces. The situation worsened when, amid increasing unrest inside and outside the Majlis, Mossadeq attempted to take over the constitutional position of the Shah as commander-in-chief of the armed forces, rule by emergency powers legitimized by a referendum, and bypass the responsibility of the Majlis. He thus isolated himself from some of his close colleagues, including Seyyed Abol Qazem Kashani, the speaker of the Majlis, and laid himself open to criticisms of dictatorial rule, inviting a direct confrontation between his government and the conservative forces.[67]

By now, the Eisenhower administration, under the growing pressures of American global strategy against communism, and of British propaganda (supported by the Iranian conservatives) to the effect that Mossadeq was being influenced by the Tudeh, had been convinced that a reliable alternative to Mossadeq's administration would be a government headed by the anti-communist but pro-Western monarchy. In a dramatic turnabout, Washington hardened its position against Mossadeq. When Mossadeq appealed directly to Eisenhower on May 28, 1953, for American economic assistance against Iran's "great economic and political difficulties" because of the "action taken by the former company [AIOC] and the British government," Eisenhower refused to "bail Mossadeq out." He wrote that in the wake of the "failure of Iran and of the United Kingdom to reach an agreement with regard to compensation . . . it would not be fair to American taxpayers for the United States Government to extend any considerable amount of economic aid to Iran" so long as Iran could have access to funds derived from its own resources.[68] This provided London and Iranian conservatives with much satisfaction, though the latter disapproved not of nationalization but of Mossadeq's method of bringing it about. In the struggle between Mossadeq and the conservatives that followed the American refusal of aid, the Shah at first lost, and left Iran for Rome in mid-August. But less than a week later he was back, with his throne restored, largely as a result of a successful operation by the CIA.[69] The latter, in conjunction with the American embassy in Tehran, rallied thousands of nonpartisan Iranians—by distributing thousands of dollars to them—to support the conservative forces, which were being led by the Shah's loyal colleague, General Fazlollah Zahedi. The people who played a major role in the operation were Allen Dulles, the head of the CIA, Loy Henderson, the American ambassador to Tehran, and General Schwarzkopf, formerly commander of the New Jersey State Police and now a member of the CIA attached as military specialist to the American embassy in Tehran.[70]

Mossadeq was arrested and subsequently sentenced to three years solitary confinement. This was humiliating for him, but it did not make him a martyr. The triumphant CIA-backed Shah resumed his reign and later condemned Mossadeq for bowing to the communists and committing "treason" against his country. He wrote that Mossadeq preached "a definite doctrine of . . . 'negative equilibrium,' which stressed the ending of Iran's suffering from the influence and domination of foreign powers" by granting "no concession to any foreign power and accepting no favour from any"; and that he extended a similar "negative approach . . . to domestic as well as foreign policy."[71] The Shah called his own regime's politics "positive nationalism." However, given the widespread anti-British sentiment in Iran, the Shah could not establish his regime without relying heavily on the Americans. He thus urgently sought extensive economic and military aid from the United States, and worked to build a "special" relationship and alliance with that country. This proved highly effective, as Washington was only too happy to follow up its initial support for the restoration of the Shah's throne, seek the transformation of Iran into an anticommunist state, and secure an American share in the Iranian oil industry. This resulted in three major developments: Iran's growing dependence on the United States and alliance with the West in the 1950s; Iran's assumption of outright opposition to communism; and the transformation of the traditional Anglo-Russian rivalry into American-Soviet rivalry; from then on the United States, not Britain, was the major protagonist in Iran and the world against the Soviet Union.

CHAPTER II

Iran's Dependence, 1953-1963

As WASHINGTON'S SUPPORT of the pro-Shah forces was largely responsible for the overthrow of Mossadeq's government, the Shah's regime became dependent on the United States for its immediate survival and continuity. This initial dependence implied a narrowing of the regime's policy options to a pro-Western, mainly pro-American, stance in both its domestic and foreign policy behavior. The regime committed itself to a formal alliance with the West, and tied not only Iran's foreign policy but also the country's socio-economic development to the interests of the capitalist world. These constituted the basis for the development of Iran's "dependence relationship"[1] with the United States, at the cost of the country's traditional policy of nonalignment. The relationship had two major aspects. First, Iran's status as a dependent state made it extremely vulnerable to pressures exerted by Washington. Second, the Shah was provided the necessary security and the economic and military leverage to achieve his prime objective: the consolidation of his rule, as swiftly as possible, in the face of what he perceived to be strong internal opposition and external regional threats.

After the violent overthrow of Mossadeq's government, the Shah immediately reassumed his traditional and constitutional position as Iran's monarch and commander-in-chief of the armed forces. Under his leadership, General Zahedi formed a military government and put Iran under indefinite marshal law. The Shah's principal aim was now to consolidate his regime and establish his absolute dynastic rule as quickly and forcefully as possible, so that never again could the Majlis limit the power of the crown and never again could a figure like Mossadeq challenge his position. Internal opposition to the Shah continued, largely from four sources: 1. the National Front supporters of Mossadeq, although the latter had been arrested and his influential foreign minister, Fatemi, had been shot; 2. the Tudeh party, whose supporters had grown, and whose activities had been tolerated to some extent under Mossadeq, even though the party had been officially banned in 1949; 3. the nonpartisan intellectuals, as well as pro-British elements, including former politicians; bureaucrats and professionals; and the organized clergy, who were now frightened at the prospect that the Shah would restore the dictatorial rule of monarchy with American support; and 4. the antimonarchist tribes, particularly the Qashqai in southern Iran.

This broadly based internal opposition was coupled with some regional disapproval of the Shah's regime emanating from two main sources, the Soviet Union and "radical" Arab nationalists. Moscow referred to the grabbing of power by the regime as an "offensive by the imperialists and the Iranian reaction."[2] It was, however, careful not to denounce the regime outright because of the realpolitik dictates of its foreign policy. The "radical" Arab nationalists, who had just manifested their strength in the antimonarchical and anticolonial Egyptian Revolution of 1952, denounced the Shah's regime as an "agent of Western imperialism," whose existence was contrary to the Arab nationalist and revolutionary struggle against Western colonialism and imperialism. This "radical" Arab opposition was subsequently sharpened by Tehran's decision to pursue a policy of cooperation with Israel and claim the island of Bahrain as part of Iran. The Shah's regime felt acute threats from these sources, and from the possibility of an alliance between them and the domestic opposition.[3]

The internal opposition and the perceived external threats in the face of the disturbed state of the Iranian economy and the weakness of the country's armed forces (which formed the original domestic power base of the Shah's regime) meant that the Shah was left with little choice but to persevere with his original reliance on the United States for his survival. As a matter of conscious policy, therefore, he pressed for further American help. Washington responded with a full commitment to ensure the continuation of the Shah's regime.[4] America's purpose was to strengthen its influence in Iran, which was both rich in oil and strategically important as a front-line defense against the Soviet Union.

The Eisenhower administration extended two important grants to Tehran in the second half of 1953: $23,500,000 under the U.S. technical assistance program, which had been resumed to Iran in 1950; and a $45,000,000 emergency grant-in-aid. This was to enable the Shah's regime to meet quickly Iran's immediate economic problems of an empty treasury, unemployment, and lack of foreign exchange, which had resulted largely from the economic crisis of Mossadeq's period, and to improve its security forces. In the meantime, Washington sought long-term American involvement in the Iranian oil industry, the economy, the armed forces, and social reform.[5] Increasing U.S. involvement in these areas and a continuous feeling of insecurity on the part of the Shah's regime lay behind the rapid development of the internal mechanisms of Iran's dependence on the United States.

THE OIL INDUSTRY

Given the desperate need of the Shah's regime for capital and the West's desire to keep the communist bloc from having any share in Iranian oil resources, both Tehran and Washington deemed it desirable and necessary to settle the Anglo-Iranian dispute as soon as possible. The United States rather than Britain now had the initiative in Iran, and in October 1953 John Foster Dulles commissioned Herbert Hoover Jr., a petroleum advisor and the son of the ex-president, to find a solution for the Anglo-Iranian dispute, but to make sure that this time the U.S. companies had a share in the Iranian oil industry. Hoover's endeavors, which lasted several months, finally resulted in the formation of an international consortium of all major Western oil companies to take over the operation of the Iranian oil industry from the Anglo-Iranian Oil Company. The consortium was originally composed of British Petroleum, with a 40 percent share; five American companies (Standard Oil of New Jersey, Standard Oil of California, Texaco, Mobil, and Gulf), each with 8 percent, or a total of 40 percent; Shell, with 14 percent; and Compagnie Française des Petroles (CFP), with 6 percent.[6]

Theoretically, the consortium was to act as a customer of the National Iranian Oil Company (NIOC)—a legacy of Mossadeq's nationalization. It was to operate in an area of 100,000 square miles; its contract was to be for fifteen years, but renewable for three more five-year periods; the Anglo-Iranian Oil Company was to receive handsome compensation in cash and assets from both NIOC and the eight consortium members. The area outside the consortium's operation, together with the refinery of Naft-e Shah, was to be conceded to NIOC, which was entitled to make use of both its proven and unproven oil reserves in whatever way it wanted. As for Mossadeq's nationalization, the consortium was to acknowledge the Iranian ownership of its oil resources. Moreover, Iran was to receive more in royalties than it had in the past, and was to share the consortium's profit on a fifty-fifty basis.

The major architects of this arrangement, Dulles and Hoover, hoped to keep everybody happy, and meanwhile seriously undercut the chances for a recurrence of actions like Mossadeq's against a single monopoly. The participation of the American companies in the consortium was, of course, contrary to American antitrust laws; but President Eisenhower had already overruled the laws for the sake of national security and the fight against communism. The arrangement was urgently accepted by all parties concerned, and an agreement to this effect was signed in November 1954. It proved rewarding for all: the United States, Britain, the Shah's regime, and Western international companies, but largely at the political and economic cost of Iran. It enabled Washington for the first time to secure a key position in Iran's leading economic sector, which was heavily to influence both the direction and intensity of Iran's future economic development and, for that matter, political changes. It also enabled Washington to strengthen the American position against the USSR and British interests in the region. From now on, any event in Iran that affected oil either directly or indirectly concerned the United States. Britain was not able to achieve any better arrangement. Sir William Fraser and Sir Anthony Eden had finally to accept the fact that Britain was a declining power, not only in relation to the Soviet Union but also in relation to the United States. The Shah, although adamant in his aim to bolster his position and national image, and to erase the humiliation of his dependence on the CIA, secured the resumption of oil outflow and hoped for the necessary capital inflow, which he needed badly. In announcing the agreement in the Majlis, he declared that it was the best he could secure, given his regime's weak domestic and regional position.[7]

The agreement, however, fell far short of achieving nationalization on Mossadeq's model. On paper the consortium acknowledged Iran's ownership of its oil industry and NIOC's right to operate and produce oil outside the consortium's area with whatever local or foreign interests it wished to. In practice, however the consortium assumed full control of the Iranian oil industry from production to pricing and marketing. It did so through its capital, expertise, managerial capacity, its tanker fleet, and, above all, its monopoly of markets. The NIOC could not effectively exercise its right to operate outside the consortium area. Since it had neither the necessary capital nor the know-how and access to markets, it had to undertake joint ventures with foreign companies, all of which happened to be American except one, the Société Irano-Italienne des Petroles (SIRIP).[8] The international oil companies were placed, in fact, in such a powerful position that they could run the Iranian oil industry as their interests dictated. They increased and decreased production and prices, and finally controlled supply and demand in markets, to whatever degree and in whatever way suited them best.

It has come to light that for this, the consortium even embarked upon a clandestine operation under a "participant agreement," which was signed by its eight member companies, and was kept secret from the public and the Iranian government until 1974. The agreement described not only the terms under which the member companies would buy oil, but also how they would restrict production to avoid a glut and decline in their profits, even though this was detrimental to Iran because any drop in production or sale of oil meant less revenue for Iran. The aim of the "participant agreement" was achieved largely by the formula of the "Aggregate Programed Quality" (APQ). Anthony Sampson explains: "The APQ calculated total amount of oil that was to be 'lifted' from Iran in the following year, and it was reckoned by listing the needs of each participant, divided by their percentage share in the consortium, in order of magnitude, and then taking the last figure after seventy percent of the holdings had been listed. A company wishing to take more than its quota would have to pay more for it." This system "effectively held down production in Iran to the levels required by the least demanding of the companies. If Exxon and Texaco, for instance, were to want less oil (as they always did) because of their commitments in Saudi Arabia and elsewhere, BP and Shell would have to restrict their production, too."[9]

The system not only enhanced the controlling power of the American companies within the consortium and, for that matter, over the Iranian oil industry, but also enabled the consortium to make the real decisions on Iran's economic growth. Moreover, the consortium, like its predecessor, the AIOC, pushed for the development of the Iranian oil industry as an exporting sector, which meant that there would be restricted linkages connecting it with the rest of the Iranian economy. In effect, under the Agreement of 1954 Tehran essentially relinquished Mossadeq's nationalization, for ownership without control of the oil industry meant very little. The international consortium replaced AIOC, and the United States replaced Britain in influencing Iranian politics and socio-economic development. As for stimulating the distressed economy, the regime's income from oil was initially insufficient both to pay for the Shah's counter-Mossadeq operations and to help the ailing economy at the same time. Iran's oil income grew steadily from $22.5 million in 1954 to $92.5 million in 1955, and $285 million in 1960.[10] On the average, the government allocated only 55 percent of this revenue annually to the Plan Organization for economic development.[11] This was not enough, given the disturbed state of the economy. American aid was, therefore, crucial in supplementing the oil revenue.

AMERICAN ECONOMIC AID

In spite of its reluctance in the past to respond to requests by successive Iranian governments for economic aid, after Mossadeq's fall Washington found it necessary to give millions of dollars of economic aid to the Shah's regime. President Eisenhower had foreseen the need for such aid in 1953 when he wrote, "of course, it will not be so easy for the Iranian economy to be restored, even if her refineries again began to operate. . . . However, this is a problem that we should be able to help."[12] Under its various programs and agencies, including AID and the Export-Import Bank, the United States provided the regime, from 1953 to 1957 alone, with a total of $366.8 million in economic-financial aid. From this, $250.6 million was in the form of grant-in-aid and $116.2 million was in loan. The inflow of such aid continued at an average of $45 million a year for the next three years. In 1961, at a time when the Iranian economy had

failed to make substantial progress, Washington increased its aid
to $107.2 million: $35 million in grants and $72.2 million in
loan.[13] By now Iran had become the recipient of one of the
largest quantities of American economic aid outside the NATO
alliance in the postwar period. This increased aid, supplement-
ing Iran's oil income, enabled the Shah's regime not only to meet
the needs of its empty treasury and administrative and welfare
expenditure, but also to ensure the implementation of the remaining projects of the First Seven Year Development Plan
(1949-1956), which had been stalled during the nationalization
crisis, and the entire program of the Second Development Plan
(1956-1962).

Along with the inflow of American aid, a large body of U.S.
official advisors and technical experts, employees of aid agencies
and technical and commercial organizations, and private investors came to Iran. They were to assist the Iranian government
in its economic planning and allocation of American aid, provide technical know-how, and establish joint ventures with both
the Iranian government and entrepreneurs, who were now once
again confident that Iran was firmly set in developing a free
enterprise system. By the beginning of the 1960s there were more
than nine hundred American economic and technical experts
active in various capacities in Iran. They helped in drafting and
implementing Iran's Second Development Plan, which stressed
the essential role of both public and private sectors in Iranian
economic development, and called for increasing foreign investment. To this end, the government had promulgated the Law
for the Attraction and Protection of Foreign Investment in 1955.
The underlying objectives of this law were to encourage foreign
participation in economic development, particularly in the industrial sector; safeguard the interests of foreign firms, mainly
against confiscation; and upgrade foreign investors to an equal
status with private domestic investors.[14]

The American investors played a major role in stimulating the
banking system and, most importantly, in creating the Industrial
and Mining Development Bank of Iran in 1959. The Bank
supplemented the existing Revolving Loan Fund as a principal
source of credit extension to the private sector. It drew capital
from a variety of domestic and foreign, private and official
sources. Its initial capital was $42.4 million; equity came to $5.3
million, divided in a ratio of six to four between domestic and

foreign investors, the latter mainly Americans. Following its establishment, the Bank was very important in promoting private industry and in providing financial, technical, and advisory assistance to private investors. During the second half of the 1950s, private investment more than tripled, and imports of capital goods increased six-fold.[15] A number of key economic projects went to American firms, as an extension of the fact that they were financed largely by U.S. aid and investment. Other foreign firms, which either helped the American firms (or were commissioned by them), or entered private contracts with Iran, were mainly West German, French, and British. By the early 1960s, U.S. direct private investment in Iran was estimated in excess of $200 million.[16] At the same time, the United States was Iran's leading trade partner, with the balance of trade well in favor of the former. In 1963, for example, Iran's imports from the United States amounted to $103.7 million and its exports to the U.S. reached $40.4 million.[17] This rapid entrenchment of the American position in Iranian economic planning and operations was reenforced by the concurrent U.S. involvement in building up the country's armed and security forces, which acted as yet another paramount mechanism governing Iran's dependence on the United States.

AMERICAN MILITARY AID

The armed forces had traditionally been instrumental in consolidating the power base of monarchy in Iran. In the past the Iranian kings had used it as the most obvious available means to manipulate and govern the behavior of their subjects. Reza Shah had followed this pattern forcefully. The military, traditionally and constitutionally, had been controlled and commanded directly by the monarchy. It had, therefore, been trained to obey only the monarch and to operate only under the command of that authority. Some of the Qajar kings had not maintained this single-handed authority, and as a result eventually lost their throne.[18] When Mohammad Reza succeeded his father, the one thing to which he paid most attention was the defeated but not entirely demoralized Iranian armed forces, which he took special care to reorganize and expand. For this purpose, he attracted the support of an American military advisory mission in 1942, which led to the development of the United States Military

Mission with the Imperial Iranian Army (ARMISH) in 1943. In the immediate postwar years (1946-1952), when Iran adopted a tough stance against communism, Washington provided Tehran with two parcels of aid to help in improving the efficiency and capability of its armed forces: $25 million credit to strengthen ARMISH; and a $16.6 million grant for arms purchases.[19]

The loyalty to the Shah of a major section of these armed forces eventually helped General Zahedi and the CIA to lead the royalist forces to victory against Mossadeq. Following the latter's fall, Iran was placed under military rule, which lasted until 1957. The armed forces under the direct command of the Shah formed his major domestic power base, and assumed a special role in helping him to consolidate his rule. The American ambassador, John C. Wiley, had already stressed in 1950 that "Iran needs an army capable primarily of maintaining order within the country, an army capable of putting down any insurrection— no matter where or by whom inspired or abetted."[20] In the next few years, Washington extended massive military aid in arms, training, and expertise to the Shah's regime. The total U.S. military grant-in-aid to the regime during 1953-1963, the period of the Mutual Security Act, amounted to $535.4 million. This was the largest military grant that Washington had offered to a non-NATO country. During the same period, the number of American personnel present in Iran exceeded 10,000.[21] American aid and personnel played a decisive role in helping the Shah's regime, between 1953 and 1960, to reorganize and expand its army from about 100,000 men to 190,000, and build up a modern air force and navy with 8,000 and 4,000 trained personnel, respectively.[22] Between 1950 and 1965, some 2,000 Iranians received military training in the United States.[23] In the meantime, at least three U.S. military groups entrenched their operations in Iran: ARMISH; MAAG, the Military Assistance Advisory Group; and GENMISH, the United States Military Mission with the Imperial Iranian Gendarmerie. ARMISH was officially assigned to advise and assist the Iranian minister of war, the supreme commander's staff, and the commanders and staffs of the army, navy, and air force in matters concerning plans, organization, administration, and training. MAAG was to execute the objectives and ensure the effective implementation of the Mutual Defence Assistance program in Iran. GENMISH was to advise and assist the interior minister in improving the organization and operations of the Imperial Iranian Gendarmerie.[24]

In 1957, moreover, the CIA helped Tehran in establishing the Iranian State Intelligence and Security Organization (Sazman-e Ettela'at Va Amniyat-e Keshvar, or SAVAK), which was subsequently assisted by Mossad, the Israeli intelligence service. The organization was affiliated to the office of the prime minister, and its chief was directly appointed by the Shah, and held the portfolio of assistant to the prime minister. From its establishment, SAVAK bore principal responsibility for all types of intelligence and counterespionage activities; for preventing subversion, sabotage, and all such activities harmful to the security and independence of the state; and for checking and prosecuting all Iranian groups and individuals opposing the Shah's regime. Its officials were members of the armed forces, and by virtue of its duties it shouldered many civilian responsibilities, so that it became by far the most efficient organization in Iran. It soon grew to become an omnipotent and brutal force in running the affairs of the state, under the Shah's direct control.[25]

IRANIAN-WESTERN ALLIANCE

The rapid development of extensive American involvement in the economy and internal security of Iran was coupled with the growth of a formal military alliance. Under the impulse of Cold War politics and American global opposition to communism, Washington had expressed its willingness, prior to the overthrow of Mossadeq, for an alliance with Iran as a member of a regional pact. In February 1953, President Eisenhower professed a definite need for a U.S.-sponsored "system of alliance" in the Iranian region against what he called the "enemies [communists] who are plotting our destruction." His secretary of state, John Foster Dulles, subsequently envisaged the concept of the "Northern Tier" alliance, comprising Turkey, Pakistan, and Iran. He believed that these countries were aware of their common enemy, communism, and that they could not only defend themselves with American support, but also could prevent the spread of communism to the "core Arabs," south of Euphrates down to Egypt, where the Arab revolution would be more receptive to communism.[26] The idea, of course, could not have impressed

Mossadeq at all. In spite of his desire to have a close friendship with the United States as a leverage against Anglo-Soviet pressures on Iran, Mossadeq had opposed any alliance that could have undermined his nationalist stance and jeopardized Iran's relations with the Soviet Union and nationalist Arab forces.

The Shah's regime was, however, very receptive to such an alliance, given its need for Western support against its domestic and regional insecurity. Dulles' idea of a "Northern Tier" alliance did not materialize, largely because of opposition by Britain, which wanted to include its regional client, Iraq, and Washington's refusal of this on the ground that other Arab states, particularly Egypt, would be offended.[27] In 1955, however, when the largely British-sponsored military and economic Baghdad Pact was announced between Britain, Iraq, Turkey, and Pakistan (with the United States also expected to join), the Shah's regime was determined to join it, too.[28]

Before securing formal membership in the pact, the Shah paid an official visit to Washington in early 1955 in order to enlist the full backing of the latter. The Eisenhower administration supported the Shah, and agreed with him on the need to build up the Iranian armed forces and equip them with modern arms, and to construct strategic roads and airports in Iran.[29]

After Washington had sent General Carlson to Tehran to assess the military and defense requirement of Iran, Premier 'Ala, who had just replaced General Zahedi, announced Iran's formal accession to the Baghdad Pact on October 11, 1955. The Shah subsequently wrote that he considered "the system of alliances and mutual aid between states with common interests as the most effective way to ensure the stability and security not only of Iran but also of the world."[30] Iran's entry into the pact was widely opposed by the Iranian public, including a number of the Majlis deputies.[31] Premier 'Ala even became the target of an unsuccessful assassination attempt while he was on his way to a Baghdad Pact meeting, but the Shah's regime persevered with its policy of alliance. In July 1958, when a "revolutionary" republican group overthrew the pro-British Hashemite monarchy in Iraq and withdrew that country from the Baghdad Pact (which led to the pact being redesignated the Central Treaty Organisation [CENTO]), Tehran simply transferred its membership from the former to the latter.[32] In the meantime, however, the failure of the alliance either to prevent or reverse the

Iraqi events or help regional members in their regional disputes disillusioned the Shah's regime with the effectiveness of the Baghdad Pact and its successor, CENTO, as a source of support and security. The regime therefore pressed for an exclusive defense alliance with the United States. A bilateral military treaty was concluded between the two countries in March 1959. Under Article 1 of the treaty, Washington committed itself to take, in case of aggression against Iran, "such appropriate actions including the use of armed forces as may be mutually agreed upon."[33]

This extensive American involvement in Iran brought with it a great increase in Western social and cultural influence, particularly among those educated urban Iranians who found the Shah's regime and its pro-Western stance desirable and beneficial. This influence consolidated the overall structure of Iran's dependence on and vulnerability to the United States. Iran's socio-economic development and foreign policy objectives became closely tied to the interests of the capitalist world.[34] This confirmed the country's formal opposition to communism, at both national and regional/international levels, at the cost of its relationship with the Soviet Union—which, had it been improved, could have been used to some extent by Tehran as an effective lever to counter its dependence on the United States. In its relationship with Tehran, Washington acted as a "Patron power" in upholding and securing the Shah's regime and influencing the direction and substance of its policies in line with Western regional and international interests. By the start of the 1960s, the Shah's regime was so vulnerable to Washington that the latter was capable of influencing, for example, the Shah's choice of who should be the prime minister of Iran. The Shah was not in a position to complain, for it was his leadership that served as the necessary "bridgehead" in the whole process of the rapid transformation of Iran from a cautiously nonaligned nation, opposed to any type of domination by outside powers, to a state dependent upon the United States. In order to justify and enforce this transformation, the Shah noted as early as December 1954 that "the potentialities of friendly and close relations between the people of Iran and the United States are immense. There is a deep and fundamental identity of national interests, which overshadows everything else. We both believe that the individual is the central figure in society, and that freedom is the supreme blessing. . . . Iran has a great deal in common, in convictions, with the Western world regarding freedom and democracy. The way of life of the Western world fits in with our scheme of Islamic values."[35]

In this context, he subsequently declared that "Westernization is our ordeal." He branded his regime's politics "positive nationalism," against what he called Mossadeq's politics of "negative equilibrium." He claimed that, as a doctrine, "positive nationalism" implied "a policy of maximum political and economic independence consistent with the interests of one's country. On the other hand it does not mean non-alignment or sitting on the fence. It means that we make any agreement which is in our interest, regardless of the wishes or policies of others." But since, for the Shah, Iran's interests were served best in alliance with the West, he declared that it was his regime's determination to combat "internal communism" or "the new totalitarian imperialism," inspired by Moscow, as a necessary condition for building a modern, strong, and prosperous Iran with "social justice."[36]

The prize that the Shah expected out of Iran's dependence on the United States and alliance with the West was to achieve his prime objective: the swift domestic consolidation of his rule. In this respect, his efforts were, indeed, rewarding to some extent. By the end of the 1950s, he had succeeded in establishing his rule almost throughout Iran, and in surviving both strong domestic opposition and his perceived regional threats.

IRAN'S DEPENDENCE AND DOMESTIC POLITICS

In order to achieve his prime objective, following the overthrow of Mossadeq, the Shah found it essential to manipulate the organizational and institutional setting in which his regime acted in an attempt to create relative political and economic stability. In this context, the regime's foreign policy became its domestic policy writ large; and the conduct of the former was conditioned largely by the needs of the latter. The Shah, along with strengthening his regime's links with the United States, sought to centralize politics, perhaps more vigorously than ever before in Iran's modern history, around the institution of monarchy. He engaged in a counter-Mossadeq operation, involving a very forceful rearrangement of Iran's national setting and goals.

He drew heavily on Washington's economic, military, and political support in carrying out this operation.

Economic Maneuvering

The essence of this method lay in the Shah's attempt to stimulate the economy while manipulating the process of economic development, as well as the interactions between economic groups and organizations on the one hand and the government on the other, for political ends—the stability and security of his regime. In this respect, American aid, plus the reactivation of the oil industry and the resumption of the government's income from this sector, played readily into the hands of the Shah.

During the oil nationalization crisis, the First Seven-Year Development (1949-1956) had largely been abandoned, and recessionary conditions had set in, causing serious economic hardship for a majority of the Iranian people, and disillusioning many of Mossadeq's followers. Seizing upon the opportunity, the Shah's government, assisted by Americans, urgently drew up the Second Seven-Year Development Plan (1956-1962), with an eye on increasing oil revenues and American aid. The Plan, which was ratified by the Majlis in early 1956, called initially for a total outlay of Rls. 70 billion ($933 million), almost a quarter of which was to be used to complete some of the unfinished projects of the First Plan. A year later the figure was raised by 20 percent to Rls. 84 billion ($1,120 million). Of this sum, 40.48, 29.88, 11.19, and 18.45 percent were to be spent, respectively, on transportation and communication, agriculture and irrigation, industry and services, and social affairs. The Plan called for both public and private investments, and stressed the role of private industries as vital for the industrialization of Iran. Most of the needed finance for the public sector of the Plan was to come from government's oil income and foreign loans repayable out of the future oil revenues. At first, about 80 percent of the oil revenues was envisaged for development purposes annually. But this target was never achieved; the government could not manage more than 55 percent per year throughout the Plan, because of inefficiency and high military, security, and administrative expenditures, as well as inflation;[37] it therefore had to rely increasingly on American aid and smaller amounts of aid from other Western sources, namely, West Germany, France, and Great Britain.

In economic terms, the Plan's achievements were very limited. It was not based on a philosophy of economic development that involved comprehensive socio-political changes, including re-distribution of wealth. Rather, it aimed for some economic expansion in certain areas, to be exploited by the Shah's regime for political gains. The Plan could have hardly been called a "plan" in the strict sense of the term. It allocated finances, but it had no explicit philosophy or physical targets. Meanwhile, in its implementation, it suffered from numerous difficulties: "the uncertainties surrounding the magnitude of available financial resources (particularly foreign loans), the comparative inexperience in large-scale planning, lack of coordination among various government agencies, and other operating hurdles were instrumental in causing some delays and frustrations. Thus, many programs did not hold closely to their original allocations; projects that were started early naturally established themselves as preferred claimants for funds."[38] These difficulties were exacerbated by inefficiency and corruption, which were features of the Iranian political and economic system at all levels.

The Second Plan was, however, somewhat politically rewarding for the Shah's regime. Within the framework of the Plan's policies and expenditures, the regime made some progress toward several important interrelated objectives. The intensity of economic activity and commercial transactions were increased, and the job market expanded. Certain limited but influential entrepreneurial groups, which were given incentives under the Plan regained confidence in the regime; these were groups that had been opposed by Mossadeq because of their power and malpractices, which resulted largely from their interactions with outside interests. Under the Plan, the regime was also able to appease those professional and bureaucratic groups and individuals who had at first supported Mossadeq but had then become disillusioned with him because of the growing political and economic instability. The uneducated rural masses, who were politically inactive but traditionally obedient to the monarchy, were given some attention. Direct communication between the government and the rural people was attempted; numerous projects were initiated, so that the rural people could be preoccupied in their own areas away from the major urban centers, where opposition to the regime was strong and active. Finally, the Plan Organization was reactivated in order to work out and implement new economic plans, as an indication of the regime's determination to play a central role in creating economic stability and prosperity, but without apparently undermining the role of the private sector.[39]

In the meantime, the leadership made sure that economic organizations, agencies, and groups, both public and private, operated independently of each other, but that they checked and balanced one another in a way that would be favorable to the leadership's political needs. The Shah, as far as possible, would never allow separate groups to join together and acquire the possibility of undermining his authority. For example, the Iranian planners and their American advisors found it imperative to entrust the revitalized Plan Organization with the execution of the Second Plan. It had been originally set up as a semi-independent body by an act of the Majlis in 1949, so that it could operate largely free of the prejudices and influences of the political structure. Meanwhile, however, the leadership directly encouraged self-seeking local entrepreneurial groups, which provided part of the private sector of the Plan, to compete with the Plan Organization in securing a bigger share in the implementation of the Plan. This caused serious competition between the private and public sectors, and allowed entrepreneurial groups to influence the operation of the Plan Organization in their own interests. The head of the Organization, Abol Hasan Ebtehaj, a competent economist, who had assumed office with a pledge to purge the Plan Organization of endemic nepotism, inefficiency, and corruption, opposed the entrepreneurs' interference in the operation of the Organization.[40] A conflict developed between the two sides, and Ebtehaj could not survive, given the support that entrepreneurs received from the government. He resigned in 1959, even though he was regarded as a very competent manager.[41]

This episode impeded the accomplishment of the Second Plan, but proved politically rewarding for the government. The Shah personally did not favor the statutory status of the Plan Organization and the power that it wielded. He therefore used the new situation to bring the organization under the control of the prime minister's office, which by now had become well subordinated to his personal power. This brought economic planning and development under the direct control of the Shah, as part of his overall drive for rapid centralization of power,

though the private sector was encouraged to increase its participation in a government-dominated "free-enterprise economy."
The Shah was the major protagonist of such "divide and rule"
manipulations.

The Shah's policy was also enforced by another vigorous
method: political repression. His main instruments were the
armed forces and security forces, which were extensively reorganized, trained, and built up by the United States.

Political Repression

One of the major features of the Shah's rule in the 1950s, upon
which most of the analysts of the Iranian politics agree, was its
intensive political repression. Following Mossadeq's overthrow,
the Shah's regime moved swiftly to suppress all opposition,
imposed strict censorship on the mass media, and banned all
forms of political organization, activities, and even literary expression that it found threatening to its security. It maintained
the Constitution of 1906 and permitted the Majlis to function,
but only as a source of legitimacy for the regime's actions. In
managing this, the security forces, which after 1956 were spearheaded by SAVAK, were used excessively and indiscreetly. This
could have not been done without extensive American assistance
in increasing the efficiency and capability of the forces. Capitaliz-
ing on their efficiency and loyalty, the Shah entrusted the armed
forces with two major tasks: to establish a monopoly over the
means of physical violence; and to take over the civil power in
many areas, though the Shah's encouragement was perhaps less
explicit in the second respect.[42]

The brutal intervention of the military in the political sphere
became a pervasive characteristic of the Shah's rule. The military
and SAVAK were used effectively in crushing and demoralizing
opposition of all political coloring, manipulating the behavior
of citizens, and controlling and redirecting public opinion for
the benefit of the regime's stability and security. In this, the
military and secret police executed, imprisoned, and exiled hundreds almost indiscriminately. With respect to the organized
opposition groups, they forced the disintegration of the National
Front and of Tudeh, and crushed uprising by some southern
tribes. One of the most serious cases was the army purge in late
1954. About six hundred officers, alleged to have been Tudeh
supporters, were purged and tried by a military tribunal that

resulted in massive executions and imprisonment. By the late 1950s, the capacity of Tudeh to operate as an organized opposition was severely weakened, and many of its leaders were living in exile in Leipzig.[43]

Although a new Majlis was opened on March 18, 1954, and gave a vote of confidence to General Zahedi's government, the regime quickly moved to reduce the role of the Majlis to what it had been under Reza Shah. The legislature's procedures were brought under the control of the executive power, and its members were elected on the basis of selections made by the regime. Its function was reduced to that of a rubber stamp, legitimizing what the political leadership required it to do.[44] The Shah approved the formation of a two-party system in 1957 on the basis of his assertion that a one-party system was "communistic" and "dictatorial," and could not be permitted in a Western-inspired Iran.[45] This was to serve two purposes: to signal to the West his intentions to "democratize" Iranian politics; and to placate the internal opposition and his regime's pro-Western supporters.

In practice, however, both parties were instigated and controlled by the monarchy. The Hezb-e Melliyun (Nationalist party) was commissioned to form the government under Prime Minister Manuchehr Eqbal, who succeeded 'Ala. The Hezb-e Mardom (People's party) was asked to serve as the opposition under the leadership of the Shah's most trusted colleague, Asadollah 'Alam. The record of the opposition performance shows very rare deviations from its support of government policies.[46] The regime allowed no political activities outside these two parties. It enforced strict press censorship, and warned the press against any criticism of the royal family, or the military, or the Americans, whose support was crucial for the Shah to continue his political repression. Literature of a "radical" nature was suppressed, and instead literature in support of the regime and of the United States was widely published and disseminated. For this purpose, the American Franklin Book Program was set up in Tehran, and was followed by the establishment of the Imperial Foundation for Translation and Publishing. They both played a major role in reeducating the public about the "evils of communism," on the value of friendship with the West, and in support of the Shah's regime and its endeavor to build a state-dominated capitalist system. This had a marked impact on the reorganization of the Iranian educational system, turning it toward training youth with these values, and promoting the Shah as the sole and unchallengeable leader of the nation. In order to silence dissident students, intellectuals, and political activists, a method of cooptation through intimidation, bribery, and selected concessions became the order of the day.[47]

By economic maneuvering and political repression, based largely on the strength that it acquired from its dependence on the United States, the Shah's regime had largely succeeded by the end of the 1950s in establishing absolute rule in Iran. The Shah's personal executive power had expanded to the extent that no branch of government could act independently of his instructions.[48] In this sense, he had considerable success in achieving his prime objective; but this did not mean that he had secured the consent of a majority, safeguarding the continuity of his regime. The underlying causes of instability had not been redressed, but were only temporarily submerged. He succeeeded in weakening internal opponents; but he could not prevent their occasional reemergence in both physical and literary forms whenever they found the opportunity. He slowed down public agitation inside the country, but could not stop underground activities at home and public criticism of his rule abroad, which at times reactivated his feelings of insecurity in the conduct of both domestic and foreign affairs.

A number of examples will suffice to establish this point. In 1958, a coup attempted by General Qarani "came within hours of succeeding. The number of cooperating officers was impressive."[49] There were enormous, often violent, mass demonstrations against the regime from 1960, which continued over the next three years, and demonstrated the displeasure of a sizable portion of the Iranian people with the regime's behavior and with the discouraging social and economic conditions. Those displeased with the state of affairs comprised not only the supporters of the National Front and the Tudeh, but also a large number of nonpartisan students, intellectuals, professionals, craftsmen, small businessmen, landowners, religious leaders, and tribesmen.[50] They culminated in the massive uprisings of 1963, a widespread confrontation between civilians and the armed forces, in which hundreds of civilians were shot and arrested. The uprisings were spearheaded by religious leaders who opposed the Shah's oppressive rule, land reform, and Westernization measures.* The Majlis elections were aborted in 1960, and during 1960-1963 the Majlis was closed down twice, a state of emergency was imposed, and Iran was ruled by royal decrees. Outside the country, the voice of the Iranian dissidents, largely students, particularly in the United States, grew constantly stronger.[51] Against this domestic situation, the regime could not claim any major improvement in Iran's regional position, though its dependence on the United States and alliance with the West helped it to deter its perceived regional threats.

IRAN'S DEPENDENCE AND REGIONAL POSITION

The rise of the American-backed Shah to power against Mossadeq was, as we have seen, liked neither by Moscow nor by the Arab nationalist forces, which criticized him as an agent of Western imperialism in the region. The Soviet dislike was not because the Russians particularly favored Mossadeq, with whom they had already become disillusioned. Mossadeq was an aristocrat and a big landowner, and was the author of the 1944 bill denying oil concessions to any foreign power, at a time when Moscow was seeking such a concession; he favored friendship with the United States to counterbalance Anglo-Soviet pressures, was distrustful of

---

* The religious opposition was mainly led by Ayatollah Ruhollah Khomeini, an influential Shia theological scholar from the holy city of Qum. Although Khomeini had been active in promoting Islamic teachings and practices against what he perceived as repugnant to the religion of Islam, including the "oppressive rule" of the Pahlavi dynasty, since the 1930s, he came to public attention more prominently in 1961 when his religious superior, Ayatollah Borojerdi, died. He began issuing public statements in opposition to the Shah's "oppressive" rule and some of the government reforms. He opposed the government's program of female emancipation (in line with Westernization) as contrary to Islam. He was arrested by SAVAK in 1962 without any charges. Upon his release, however, he led the "June uprisings" of 1963, which resulted in bloody clashes between the Shah's troops and civilian population at high human and material costs. He was, consequently, arrested again by SAVAK in October 1963, following his order to his followers to boycott the current parliamentary elections, and he subsequently denounced the government's decision, endorsed by the Majlis in October 1964, to grant diplomatic immunity to American military personnel in Iran. He was never tried, but was ultimately sent into exile, which took him first to Turkey, then to Iraq, and then to France. For details, see Zonis, *The Political Elite of Iran*, pp. 44-47; I. Murray, "Battle for Iran's Soul."

Moscow, and sought little help from it during the nationalization crisis. The Soviets could have forgiven him neither for these actions, nor for his renewal of the agreement concerning American aid to the Iranian armed forces in April 1952. Immediately after Mossadeq's fall, they had no misgivings in criticizing his government on the grounds that in its struggle with Britain it failed to "rely upon the democratic forces within the country [i.e., Tudeh], as well as on the countries of the democratic camp [i.e., the USSR], but attempted to maneuver between them and the imperialist powers. It took no radical actions to stop reactionary provocations and intrigues. All of this created favorable conditions for an offensive by the imperialists and the Iranian reaction."[52]

The main reason for the initial strong Soviet dislike of the Shah's regime was the United States' involvement in its support. Moscow viewed this as detrimental to its own security and interests.[53] Iran's rapid drift into the Western camp irritated the Soviet leadership further, and this irritation often manifested itself in violent propaganda campaigns. When Tehran announced Iran's membership in the Baghdad Pact, Moscow reacted sharply, and warned Tehran that its membership is "incompatible with the interests of strengthening peace and security in the area of the Near and Middle East and is incompatible with Iran's good neighbourly relations with the Soviet Union and the known treaty obligations of Iran."[54] The last phrase was to draw Tehran's attention to Article 3 of the Irano-Soviet Treaty of 1927, whereby "each of the contracting parties undertakes not to participate, either in fact or formally, in political alliances or agreements directed against the security on land or at sea of the other High Contracting Party, or against its integrity, its independence, or its sovereignty."[55] As a result, the Tehran-Moscow relationship was further strained, and the Soviets cancelled a tour of their musicians to Iran and rejected a purchase of 40,000 tons of Iranian rice.[56]

Similarly, Moscow vehemently denounced the Iranian-American bilateral military treaty of 1959. This treaty was concluded against the background of a number of developments that favored Moscow but heightened Tehran's feelings of regional insecurity. Moscow was rapidly developing a close friendship with Egypt and Syria, who had just entered a formal union that was meant to increase the strength of Nasserism against the conservative forces of the region, including the Shah's regime. Meanwhile, the Suez crisis of 1956 had resulted in the establishment of Egyptian sovereignty over the canal, through which Iranian oil was exported to the West, and now this was largely at the discretion of Cairo. Moreover, the outbreak of a civil war in Lebanon in 1958 had brought Egyptian intervention, supporting the pro-Nasserite forces against the pro-Western forces, which upheld the Eisenhower Doctrine in the country.[57] Most importantly, the pro-British Hashemite monarchy was overthrown by a revolutionary republican army group in Iraq in July 1958. This, as far as Tehran was concerned, meant the extension of Nasserism and the prospect of a pro-Soviet regime on Iran's doorstep, though the new Iraqi regime under Staff Brigadier Abdul Karim Qasim was far from being Nasserite. These developments, complemented by some restiveness in the Iranian armed forces (reflected in General Qarani's coup attempt) and the Shah's realization that CENTO was not intended by its Western sponsors to help the regional members in their domestic problems and regional disputes, prompted the Shah to conclude the military treaty with Washington.

Moscow perceived this treaty to be a source of legitimacy enabling Washington to establish military, particularly missile, bases in Iran against the Soviet Union. It immediately condemned the treaty, and noted that it was concluded against a Soviet offer of a nonaggression pact to Iran, although Tehran claimed that such an offer, in return, demanded Iran's withdrawal from the Baghdad Pact—a demand unacceptable to Iran.[58] On February 17, 1959, Khrushchev stressed that the treaty would convert Iran into an American military base. He declared that the Shah "fears his people. He is none too sure, apparently, of his throne and for this reason he keeps his private capital in Britain, and not in Iran."[59] A war of nerves and propaganda broke out, and "The National Voice of Iran," broadcasting from the southern region of the USSR, began a vigorous campaign against the Shah's regime.

The Soviet criticisms coincided with disapproval of the Shah's policies by the growing radical Arab forces. The latter largely centered around the personality of Egyptian President Gamal Abdul Nasser (president from 1954-1970), who advocated revolutionary Arab nationalism and pan-Arabism against colonial, imperialist, and Zionist forces, as well as the Arab conservative forces, led by Saudi Arabia, with which the Shah's regime had a great deal in common both domestically and regionally. To Cairo, the conservative and absolutist dynastic regime of the Shah was essentially anachronistic, antirevolutionary, and antiprogressive; it was being upheld by Washington to promote and care for America's "imperialist interests" in the region. The de facto recognition of Israel by Tehran and the quiet entente that was developing between the two countries (involving, among other things, Israeli help for SAVAK and Iranian oil supplies to Israel),[60] were significant in shaping Cairo's perception of the Shah's regime. Against the background of historical, ethnic, cultural, territorial, and even religious differences between Arabs and Persians, Cairo branded the Shah's regime as the enemy of Arabs in their nationalist revolutionary struggle against Western "colonialism and imperialism" as well as "Zionism." It officially denounced Iran's accession to the Baghdad Pact and its successor, CENTO, and its military treaty with the United States; it advocated the overthrow of the Shah's regime, and severed its diplomatic relations with Tehran in July 1960.[61] Each side engaged in an intense war of propaganda against the other. The radical Arab opposition, concurrent with that of the Soviet Union, caused continuous anxiety for the Shah's regime, which claimed to be surrounded by hostile forces that threatened its stability and security. The regime, most importantly, was in constant fear that such hostile forces might establish effective links with the domestic opposition.[62]

It is, in fact, important to note that the regime's perception of Soviet and Arab threats was largely in relation to its feelings of domestic insecurity. There is no evidence to suggest that the Soviet and radical Arab opposition at any stage threatened to invade Iran, for this was unlikely under the prevailing regional and international circumstances. On the contrary, Moscow was willing from the start of the Shah's rule to improve its relations with Tehran. The Russians did not wish to exert enough pressure on the Shah's regime to drive it deeper into the Western camp, and thus prompt the United States to increase its presence and activities in a zone vital to the interests and security of the Soviet Union. Moreover, at the height of the Cold War and bi-polarization of world politics, Moscow was in search of regional friends and allies; its interests were unlikely to have been well served by taking direct military action against the Shah's regime, as this could have made even the radical Arab forces distrustful of Soviet friendship and support. And while the international situation was tense during the Cold War and the Soviet Union was laboring to establish nuclear parity with the United States, Moscow was careful not to be trapped in a conflict with America in a zone south of its borders.

As early as August 1953, after the death of Stalin, the new Soviet leadership tried to play down past Irano-Soviet differences, and indicated its desire for some sort of accommodation with the Shah's regime. Malenkov said, "the experience of the thirty-five years has shown that the Soviet Union and Persia are interested in mutual friendship and collaboration."[63] In the meantime, the Soviets initiated talks with Iran on the settlement of a number of frontier problems and mutual financial claims.[64] Moreover, Moscow adopted a rather calm attitude toward Tehran's persecution, arrest, and execution of numerous Tudeh members and supporters. Although it condemned such actions by Tehran as joining the Baghdad Pact/CENTO and concluding a military treaty with the United States, Moscow seemed to be consistently in favor of improving its relations with Iran whenever the Shah's regime assured the Kremlin of its good-neighborly intentions. For example, after denouncing Iran's membership in the Baghdad Pact, the Soviet leadership invited the Shah to Moscow and welcomed him warmly in the summer of 1956. The Shah pledged that his regime "would never allow either the Pact or [Iranian] territory to be used in furtherance of aggressive designs upon the Soviet Union,"[65] and soon thereafter Moscow relaxed its anti-Tehran propaganda. There seemed to be a degree of understanding in the Irano-Soviet relationship for the next three years, until the signing of the Iranian-American military treaty. Even then, amid a war of propaganda, the Kremlin again welcomed the Shah to Moscow in mid-1962, when the Shah gave his personal promise that he would not allow the Americans to establish missile bases in Iran under the military treaty. Thereafter, Irano-Soviet relations began steadily to improve.

As for the perceived radical Arab threat, it lacked the necessary potential either seriously to undermine or to oust the Shah's regime. The radical Arab forces were undoubtedly expanding under Cairo's leadership in some parts of the Arab world. But this did not mean that the forces were politically united or militarily strong enough to endanger the position of the Shah's regime in a country as distant as Iran. Cairo was deeply preoccupied in its conflict with Israel, and campaigned against what it called Western domination, particularly in the wake of the Suez crisis; the radical forces were divided, and engaged primarily in domestic struggles and rivalries. They had failed either to follow Cairo consistently, or, except in Iraq, to gain a strong foothold against their conservative rivals in the Persian Gulf states, who were backed by the British protectorate forces. Even in Iraq, Qasim's "revolutionary" republican regime, which the Shah perceived as a serious threat, soon proved to be more a rival than an ally of Egypt in its bid for the leadership of the Arab world. Besides, Qasim's regime was short-lived; it was replaced by the less radical regime of General 'Abd al-Salam 'Arif in 1963. 'Arif did not follow Cairo's rhetorical line of a pan-Arabist revolution against regional conservative forces, but rather sought better relations with Iran.

The separate but concurrent opposition to the Shah from the USSR and the radical Arabs was thus mostly rhetorical, and scarcely amounted to a direct physical threat against his regime. The most realistic source of threat against the regime was domestic opposition. The regime feared, in particular, that this opposition might receive assistance from outside its borders. It was largely a sense of domestic insecurity that made the regime continuously search for ways to strengthen its links with the West as a source of security. Nonetheless, the Shah's regime found it convenient to paint the Soviet and Arab rhetorical opposition as a serious threat against the sovereignty and territorial integrity of Iran, so that it could sustain and strengthen Washington's commitment for its survival, for use primarily against the strong opposition that it was facing domestically.

1. (*At left*) Reza Shah, father of
Mohammad Reza Shah, on the
Peacock Throne, 1926.

2. (*Below*) Mohammad Reza Shah
with Kurdish tribal chiefs, 1950.

3. (*Above*) W. Averell Harriman confers with Prime Minister Mohammad Mossadeq, 1951. An interpreter sits between them. 4. (*Below*) The Shah talks with Secretary of State John Foster Dulles, 1956.

5. (*Above*) In the Marble Palace, Tehran, the Shah transfers ownership of crown land to a peasant, 1951. 6. (*Below*) The Shah and his top army generals at Niavaran Palace, 1978.

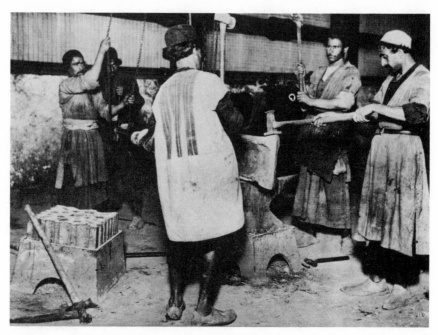

7. (*Above*) Persian workmen hammering a drill bit for the oil fields, 1933.
8. (*Below*) A modern highway being built with American aid, 1961.

9. The Shah during a pilgrimage to Mecca, 1971. To the left of the Shah stands
A. Zahedi, his former son-in-law and his last ambassador to Washington, D.C.

10. (*Above*) President Richard Nixon, the Shah, and Crown Prince Reza, Tehran, 1972.
11. (*Below*) The Shah wipes tear gas from his eyes as President Carter speaks during ceremonies on the South Lawn of the White House, 1977. Shahbanou Farah and Mrs. Carter stand behind. The tear gas is from a clash of pro- and anti-Shah protestors outside the White House fence.

12. (*Above*) Demonstrators burning the Bank of Tehran, November 5, 1978.
13. (*Below*) Painting a stencil of Ayatollah Khomeini during the Ashura demonstrations, Tehran, December 11, 1978.

14. *(At left)* The Shah and Shahbanou at Mehrabad air-port, January 16, 1979, leaving Iran for the last time. Prime Minister Bakhtiar follows them.
15. *(Below)* Supporters of the Ayatollah Khomeini massing at the U.S. embassy, Tehran, December 13, 1979.

CHAPTER III

The White Revolution

DESPITE ITS CLAIM to great achievements, by the end of the 1950s it was clear that the Shah's regime had consolidated its position in a way that was very costly for Iran and for the future of the regime itself. The regime had failed to bring about a marked improvement in the social or economic conditions of an overwhelming majority of Iranians. In spite of the country's oil riches, a majority of its people were still among the poorest in the world; they lacked basic civil liberties, and lived virtually under a reign of terror.[1] The masses were generally dissatisfied with the regime, and the Shah's domestic power base remained dangerously narrow. Neither the Shah nor Washington could have much confidence in the future of his monarchic rule. Washington, in fact, found it necessary to press the Shah for urgent socioeconomic reforms. Eventually, in 1963, the Shah unfolded a reform program, which had already been initiated by his American-backed prime minister, 'Ali Amini (1961-1962), within the framework of what the Shah called "The White Revolution" (Enqelab-e Sefid). The program entailed both domestic and foreign policy changes, with important implications for the Shah's domestic and regional position and for Iranian-American relationship.

The Shah's method of consolidating his rule during the 1950s left him with too narrow a power base to ensure the effective continuity of his rule. His support came mainly from the armed forces and security apparatus, and from the conservative groups of landlords, entrepreneurs, and bureaucrats who formed the most substantial part of Iran's small upper class and slowly growing middle class.[2] The Shah's other source of strength, as he claimed at the time, was his spiritual vision that he was being instructed by God to lead his predominantly Shia Muslim people.[3] This claim to divine right was bolstered by his belief that

there were indissoluble ties between the institution of the Shah
and the masses, defined and legitimized by long-established cultural, social, and religious traditions.⁴ But his spiritual vision was
of little empirical value, and his belief in traditional ties with the
people was to a considerable extent illusory. Iran was basically
a feudal society. A majority of the country's rural masses, who
made up to about 70 percent of Iran's estimated 20 million population in 1960, lived in about 67,000 isolated small and large
villages, at the mercy of their landlords.⁵ With a low political
consciousness and miserable standard of living, they had participated very little in politics. Their traditional sense of loyalty and
submission to positions of power and authority, of which the
Shah held the highest, was strongly affected by their conditions
of daily hardship and their relationship with their landlords.
These landlords, some of whom were also tribal chieftains, traditionally formed the most powerful base of support for the Iranian monarchy, and exercised great influence on Iranian politics.
They were able to prevent the central government from reaching
and affecting the bulk of the rural masses directly if their interests were in any way threatened. As a result, the monarchy maintained in practice little direct contact with the rural masses, and
enjoyed no popular political support in the rural areas.⁶

The Shah could not hope for significant mass support from
urban centers, either. It was in the cities that Iran's experiences
with democracy during the constitutional period (1907-1921) and
the period immediately after Reza Shah (1941-1953), as well as
Iran's growing contacts with the outside world, had most deeply
entrenched their influence. On the whole, the socio-political consciousness of the country's urban population (about 30 percent
of the total population) was relatively higher than the rural
people. The cities housed the politically active groups and most
of the opposition to the Shah's regime. A majority of the urban
dwellers were disenchanted with the regime and its dictatorial
and autocratic pattern of rule; they expressed their intense wish
for freedom of choice and political participation as well as for
better living conditions in a series of uprisings that engulfed Iran
from 1960 to 1963.

Despite extensive American aid and increasing oil revenue, by
the beginning of the 1960s the Iranian economy was not in a
sound position. The inequality of incomes was increasing, and
the urban population's standard of living, not to mention that

of the rural people, was making very slow progress. In the absence of any reliable data concerning ratio of income and distribution of wealth, we may only note that during 1959/1960, the top 20 percent of the urban population accounted for 51.79 percent of the total consumption expenditure, while the bottom 40 percent accounted for only 13.90 percent.[7] Meanwhile, the Iranian economy was sinking rapidly into a recession with a very high rate of inflation, worsening balance of trade, and a dramatic drop in the general level of productivity and economic activity.[8] Thus Iran continued to be one of the world's most slowly developing countries, with an illiteracy rate of over 85 percent.

In the meantime, the Shah presided over and nurtured an anachronistic power structure and corrupt administration that were very much responsible for the worsening socio-economic situation. During the consolidation of his regime, the Shah concentrated on subordinating the parliament, political parties and groups, social guilds, and economic organizations for the sake of entrenching his rule as forcefully as possible. As a result, although the Shah retained the Majlis and fostered two political parties under his control as token forces of legitimacy for his rule, he essentially acted within a traditional pattern of rule that promoted the personalization rather than the institutionalization of politics. In other words, the political institutions, rather than developing as bases for political stability and continuity, were relegated by the Shah to support favorite individuals within a system of personal relationships; and institutionalized political participation was played down in favor of controlled individual participation, which was allowed at the Shah's discretion. In this system of relationships, the Shah claimed the central position of authority and power by both traditional and divine right, and assigned his loyal and trusted men to key positions to carry out his dictates and policies. These men either checked on one another or were directed by their subordinates, who had been given independent authority by the Shah, and to whom they reported directly about their superiors.[9]

The key nonroyal participants in the system were those who had proved their loyalty to the Shah, and who often possessed political, economic, military, religious, and tribal influence, or a combination of these, as a result of which they commanded a large body of followers. The Shah and these key participants formed the autocratic ruling elite of Iran. But this elite was closely directed and overseen by an "inner elite" that was mainly composed of the Shah and his brother, two sisters, prime minister, chief of the secret police, joint chief of staff, and court minister. The role of the last was important in that he headed a ministry that formed a secret government parallel to the official one, guiding and checking the latter under the Shah's direct command.[10] The successful functioning of the system rested, in the main, upon three factors: the Shah's personal ability and shrewdness in remaining in a controlling position in the pattern of relationships with the chosen key participants; the satisfaction of the key participants with their subordinate roles within the power structure; and their willingness to give their continuous loyalty to the Shah.

This style of political operation enabled the Shah to promote an autocratic and monolithic political system, which he was able to control in the short run. But it had serious weaknesses that threatened the existence and continuity of the Shah's regime in the long run. It fostered a carefully controlled individual participation in politics, but failed to mobilize mass participation. Since the key participants did not hold equal power positions or benefit from similar privileges and status, there was often intense rivalry among them. At times this resulted in concentration of too much power in the hands of certain individuals, who in pursuing their rivalry even challenged the Shah's position. For example, among the Shah's men who rose to a very strong position of power in the 1950s and then challenged the Shah himself in the early 1960s was his chief of the secret police, General Teimur Bakhtiar; the Shah succeeded in overpowering him, and sent him into exile.[11]

Moreover, the politics of personal relationships promoted the growth of a top-heavy, centralized, and corrupt government administration. The participants in the power structure, by virtue of their powerful positions, manipulated the administration for their own ends and purposes, and constantly altered governmental decisions and procedures to suit their own individual interests. The roles of public servants were reduced to executing the dictates of the top few, and they had little or no part in decision making; they even hesitated to make the routine daily decisions. As a result, the entire governmental machinery was inefficient, and riddled with corruption, favoritism, and nepotism. It was out of touch with the public in general, and offered no effective avenues of communication with the opposition groups, in particular. The public, even in their necessary daily dealings with the bureaucracy (when paying electricity bills, for instance, and lodging applications for identity cards) had to resort to bribery and personal contacts in order to make government officials attend to their affairs.[12]

Moreover, the Shah was intensely disliked by many politically conscious Iranians for his close relationship with the United States and for what they perceived as Washington's role in aiding the Shah to pursue his oppressive policies. This strengthened the hands of both his domestic opposition and his opponents in the region, who labeled him a dictator and stooge of the United States, acting against the interests of the Iranian people.[13] By this stage Western, and particularly American, critics of the Shah's regime were also increasing in number.

Some Americans were alarmed that, despite extensive American aid and increasing oil revenue, Iran appeared to be on the brink of economic bankruptcy and social chaos.[14] As early as January 1957, a U.S. Congressional report had expressed its concern over the way U.S. aid was being administered and used for purposes other than economic development.[15] On December 15, 1959, in a speech before the Iranian Parliament, President Eisenhower hinted that it was not military strength alone, with which the Shah seemed to be obsessed, that ensured stability and a just peace. He added, "the spiritual and economic health of the free world must be likewise strengthened. . . . While we must, at whatever cost, make freedom secure from any aggression, we could still lose freedom should we fail to cooperate in the progress toward achieving the basic aspirations of humanity."[16] Nonetheless, it was too late in the Eisenhower administration for it to take action.

The Kennedy administration resolved in 1960 to press the Shah for socio-economic reforms and relaxation of political repression. It immediately set up a task force for this purpose. The American ambassador to Tehran, Armin Meyer, recently revealed: "That task force did nothing but work on Iran. The idea was that Iran's demise was about to take place . . . that it was about to go down the drain, and we just had to take some dramatic and drastic steps."[17] Using the leverage of the Shah's dependence on the United States, Washington applied pressure on the Shah for reforms in several ways. First, it put the matter directly to the Shah and received coldly his request for further military equipment against the Soviet and Arab threats that he perceived. Second, it courted General Bakhtiar twice during 1960-1961, at a time when the general had fallen out of favor with the Shah and held no official position in Tehran.[18] This underlined Washington's attempt to make clear to the Shah that there were still alternatives to him should he fail to speed up the process of reform necessary both for his own rule and for the continuation of Iran's alliance with the West. Third, when the Shah's regime was facing severe financial difficulties, it promised the regime $35 million with "special strings" attached, including that a "particular individual" be appointed as prime minister of Iran. This was to be 'Ali Amini, whom Washington had in mind to carry out the necessary process of reform. Amini, an independent-minded economist, had previously served as Iran's ambassador to Washington, and had special ties with the Kennedys.[19]

In view of his poor domestic position and narrow foreign policy options, the Shah had no choice but to name Amini as Iran's prime minister in May 1961, though he never favored him. This symbolized the height of American influence in Iranian politics, and the Shah's submission to American pressure clearly indicated that the Iranian-U.S. relationship had indeed developed very asymmetrically in favor of Washington. Amini began his term of office by declaring that his country faced "economic poverty." He pledged to free Iran of corruption and injustice, and to carry out reforms for deep social and economic changes. For this, he pleaded for further American aid.[20] Meanwhile, Phillips Talbot, the assistant secretary of state for Near Eastern and South Asian affairs, noted Amini's premiership as a turning point in the American attempt to save Iran from going "down the drain." He declared: "In Prime Minister Amini it seems to us there is now a prospect that we can foresee to see Iran move toward a government with a somewhat broader base than it has had and to move toward strengthening its public life. . . . It would appear very much in the American national interest to support these [Amini's] objectives and support the present government of Iran to the extent that it can carry out these objectives."[21]

The first reform that Amini's government undertook was a comprehensive land-reform program, which had been attempted twice since 1960 by his predecessors, but had been aborted by the

Majlis, which was dominated by the landlords. In May 1961 the Shah dissolved the Majlis, and it was now easier for Amini to start the land reform under a royal decree. As the implementation of the reform got under way, Amini soon acquired personal prestige for his independence, both at home and abroad, and his able agriculture minister, Hasan Arsanjani, captured popularity and emerged as the champion of the land reform.[22] When the Shah visited Washington in April 1962 he had grounds to assure Kennedy and Congress of his government's strides in initiating fundamental reforms and promoting "equity and social justice" in Iran. He stressed that the reforms required time, though "we have no time to waste." He asked for continuous Western "moral and material support" to help his country reach its goals. He once again drew on Soviet activities to explain the disturbing domestic situation. He accused the USSR of doing its utmost every day "to beguile and delude and divert us from the path we have adopted." It did this, he said, "in order to seize this gateway [Iran] to the Middle East, the Indian subcontinent and Africa, by means of falsehoods, threats and subversion." He pleaded that his efforts for reform deserved better understanding from the United States in continuing and increasing both its military and economic aid to his regime.[23]

Thus the Shah survived a major crisis in his relationship with Washington. In August 1962, Vice-President Johnson, during a state visit to Tehran, praised the Shah's leadership and Amini's reform efforts. He promised the continuation of American aid, and disclosed that he had been assured by the Shah that the latter would cut down his military expenditures in favor of socio-economic reforms.[24] Meanwhile, in order to increase the strength of the Shah's real domestic power base, Washington agreed to the Shah's request for $200 million of modern military equipment.[25]

Amini's government, however, soon ran into serious difficulties. His land reform was firmly opposed by landlords and certain religious groups, which held large owqaf (religious) estates. Public agitation over land reforms increased and culminated in the mass uprisings of 1963. After fourteen months in office, Amini's government resigned. Amini publicly blamed the United States for the failure of his government, claiming that Washington did not live up to its promise of further aid.[26] Washington firmly rejected this, announcing that during Amini's term, the United States had provided $67.3 million in economic grants and loans, and had committed itself to provide an additional $20 million for a development loan. "This level of assistance compares with an average of $59.4 million in United States economic aid to Iran during each of the preceding four years."[27]

There was, however, more to Amini's resignation than was immediately apparent. The Shah's experience gained from his own rise to power had led him, so far, to consolidate his rule at all costs. But he had learned that for the effective continuity of his rule he could not rely on a policy of repression, a narrow domestic power base, and American support forever. He had re-marked as early as 1959 that a "country cannot be ruled by the force of the bayonet and secret police . . . for all times. . . . Only a majority can rule a society."[28] He had also thought in 1960 that U.S. support could not be regarded as permanent.[29] Moreover, the American pressure and his consequent appointment of Amini as prime minister had alerted the Shah to two important facts: the degree to which he was dependent on the United States for the continuation of his rule; and, largely a result of this, his vulnerability to American pressures and, therefore, to regional criticisms. When Washington backed Amini to initiate the long-overdue process of reform, and when Amini and his minister, Arsanjani, were emerging as its major architects, it must have become clear to the Shah that he could lose his leading position in dealing with Washington, or that he could lose the initiative over the reform program, which was considered vital for the future of his leadership and rule. Either of these possibilities could easily have undermined his supreme position in Iranian politics, and could have reduced his position to what it was during the first twelve years of his reign (1941-1953).[30]

The Shah, therefore, felt it necessary to take over the reform initiatives himself. He wanted to launch reforms in accordance with the dictates of his own vision of political, social, and eco-nomic progress, under his direct leadership, without causing any major political change that could undermine his own and the monarchy's supreme position in Iranian politics and his alliance with the West. By mid-1962, he was in a position to accomplish this. Despite all the socio-economic disturbances that had be-sieged him, the Shah had by now consolidated his regime and centralized sufficient power under his control to initiate innovative policies. He had averted a possible crisis in his relationship with Washington, and had the latter's full support for reforms. Amini's initiation of land reform had tested the strength of the public reaction to a reform program, and the Shah must have been convinced that he could cope with such reaction effectively. Thus when Amini's government became embattled with opposition to its reforms and with the socio-economic crisis that it largely inherited, and when Amini blamed Washington for the failure of his government, the Shah was in a strong and safe position to welcome Amini's resignation and draw on his failure to boost his own credibility in both his relationship with Washington and his domestic standing. He promptly appointed his close and loyal colleague, Asadollah 'Alam, in place of Amini.

The Nature of the White Revolution

Within seven months, on January 26, 1963, the conservative Shah unveiled a "revolutionary" front, still at considerable risk to his personal position, and successfully put to the Iranian people, in a referendum, his own reform program within the framework of what he called "the White Revolution." It was a "revolution" designed to appeal to and benefit a majority of the Iranian people of different political leanings, ranging from conservatives ("White") to radicals ("Revolution"), under the leadership of the traditional institution of monarchy. The Shah later declared that "Iran's internal situation and . . . international position" made him feel "an empirical need for a revolution based on the most advanced principles of justice and human rights that would change the framework of . . . [Iranian] society and make it comparable to that of most developed countries in the world."[31]

There are many ways that one could examine the White Revolution. For example, J. Bill and M. Zonis have looked at it as "the politics of system preservation" and "the politics of maneuvering," respectively; R. Ramazani has regarded it as "the politics of independence"; and C. Prigmore has analyzed it in terms of the politics of social modernization.[32] It could equally well be analyzed in terms of what Gabriel Almond identifies as four major "revolutions" that leaders of the changing societies in Africa, Asia, and Latin America confront in their attempt to change their societies to meet the challenges of time: "national revolution," "authority revolution," "participation revolution," and "welfare revolution."[33] For the present purpose, however, I am most interested in evaluating the White Revolution as a means whereby the Shah attempted to achieve two objectives: to solidify and widen the popular bases of his rule; and to reduce his dependence on the United States. The White Revolution represented an attempt on the part of the Shah to carry out a systematic process of centrally controlled general mass mobilization and selected socio-economic reforms, largely in line with Westernization, in support of his leadership and rule, in order to achieve a higher degree of independence. If successful, he could increase his foreign policy options and alter Iran's relationship with the United States to one of greater symmetry. In order to substantiate this argument, it is necessary to outline the ideological nature and philosophy of the White Revolution, and then the Shah's major gains from it.

In expounding the philosophy and working program of the White Revolution, the Shah, though not very coherent and consistent, drew on several sources, ranging from the Iranian cultural heritage and Islamic principles to "democracy" and "Westernization." And yet he and the Iranian official sources exalted the program's originality. One government publication claimed that the "idea and the philosophy as well as the measures themselves are purely Iranian in concept, planning and execution." It was a "White" revolution because its accomplishment was to be "through no disorder and no bloodshed; not even class hatred."[34] In this context, the Revolution was to encompass a wide range of innovative changes affecting the whole spectrum of socio-economic life in Iran, which the Shah visualized in terms of what he called political, economic, and social "democracy" and "Westernization" for social justice, self-sufficiency, and "true" or "complete" political and economic independence. His use, however, of terms such as "democracy" and "Westernization" must be understood within what he called an Iranian context. He declared that by "political democracy" he meant the blend of "the Western principle of parliamentary [system] with the Persian monarchical tradition." This was to involve the institutionalization of politics, expansion of political participation, and dispersion of power through the formation of "political parties" that, under the sovereignty of monarchy, would form the "actual" and "alternative" governments. He made it clear that he preferred a two-party system over a one-party system, which he condemned as "communistic" and absolute "dictatorship."[35]

By "economic democracy" the Shah meant the equal distribution of resources, goods, and services according to the ability and needs of the individual, and the establishment of a mixed economic system to be composed of private and public sectors. By "social democracy" he meant enabling every Iranian citizen to develop himself fully and act freely in every direction within such bounds as the social welfare, national interest, and security of the Iranians, as a single and united society, permitted.[36]

In implementing such a "democracy," he concluded, "as a nation we must demand steady progress, but we must also realize that the achievement of political, economic and social democracy perforce takes time. It requires education and psychological development, the reconciliation of individual wishes with social responsibility, the rethinking of moral values and individual and social loyalties, and learning to work in cooperation more than ever before."[37] With regard to the relationship between such an understanding of "democracy" and "Westernization," he emphasized that he talked of "Westernization" only in "selective and judicious" terms, whereby Iran would liberalize its political system and Westernize its way of life only as far as this was compatible with and served to strengthen those Iranian traditions that are important for the preservation of Iran's identity as an old and sovereign nation with a glorious past and rich cultural heritage. The monarchy, to the Shah, was a pivotal tradition of Iranian society; and he sought sanctuary in the important traditions in order to legitimize the innovational changes that would blend the traditional institution of monarchy with the requirements of modern times. He wrote:

> Especially in a country with such venerable traditions as ours, rapid change naturally brings its strains and stress. These are the price we must pay for Westernization and modernization. But I do not propose that we abandon our great heritage. On the contrary, I have every confidence that we can enrich it. Religion and philosophy, art and literature, science and craftsmanship—all will prosper more as we develop our economy so that the common people of this ancient land can enjoy all the essentials of life. Instead of the few flourishing at the expense of the many, they will do so

with the many. Selective and judicious Westernization can help us towards the goal of democracy and shared prosperity; that is why I refer to it as our welcome ordeal.[38]

Against the background of these convictions, the Shah officially launched the White Revolution in January 1963. The Revolution's philosophy and reform program were declared to be instrumental in transforming Iran from an economically poor, socially feudal and divided, and politically bankrupt country into a prosperous, just, industrialized, self-sufficient, and truly independent sovereign nation.[39] This goal, however, was to be achieved largely within the existing framework of Iran's close friendship and alliance with the West. The Revolution's policy guidance stressed the need for strengthening the government-guided free-enterprise capitalist economic system, and for conducting Iran's foreign policy interests largely in convergence with those of the "Free World," as underlined by the Shah's vow that "Westernization is our welcome ordeal."[40]

Originally, the Shah started off his Revolution by introducing six major reforms: a comprehensive land reform, which Amini and Arsanjani had initiated; the nationalization of forests and pastures; public sale of state-owned factories as security for land reform; workers' profit-sharing in industry; amendment of the electoral law and franchise for women; and the formation of Literacy Corps. By the end of the 1960s, he joined to these the creation of Health Corps, Development and Extension Corps, and Houses of Equity; the nationalization of water; national reconstruction; and "administrative and educational revolution." During the first seven years of the 1970s, he added five other reforms: expansion of ownership of industrial and manufacturing units; price stabilization and a campaign against profiteering; free education; provision of free nutrition and care for all children from birth to the age of two years; and provision of health insurance to the general public.

In order to implement the initial reforms of the White Revolution, the Shah had already promulgated a Third Five Year Development Plan in September 1962. This Plan represented the first serious attempt at comprehensive and consistent national planning in Iran. It defined the government's underlying development strategy and objectives, and made projections of the available financial and other resources for the Plan period much more clearly than ever before. The Plan called for speedy development of agriculture, industry, and the social sector. While stressing the importance of both public and private investments, it initially proposed a total outlay of Rls. 190 billion, soon raised to Rls. 230 billion ($3,262 million at current prices). Over 66 percent of this expenditure was to be met from oil revenues, estimated at about $3,000 million during the Plan period, and the rest from domestic financing and foreign loans. Thus, for the first time, a substantial portion of oil income was to be channeled into national development. Of the total outlay, 25.6 percent was allocated for transportation and communication; 21.5 percent for agriculture; 15.8 percent for power and fuel; 12.3 percent for industry and mines; 7.9 percent for education; 6.0 percent for health; and 3.3 percent for regional development.[41] Transportation and communication were given top priority as a vital condition for rapid improvement in all other sectors. The defense sector, however, was not discussed in detail in the Plan, though it continued to consume about 10 percent of Iran's annual GNP during the Plan period.[42]

THE POLITICAL CONSEQUENCES OF THE WHITE REVOLUTION

The Third Plan provided the basic working framework for the White Revolution, and the Shah made some important short-term political gains from implementing a number of the Revolution's reforms during the 1960s: he was able to mobilize some sectors of the masses in support of his leadership and rule. He began the process by putting his reform program to the Iranian people in a referendum. This in itself was unprecedented; no Iranian monarch in the past had ever sought a formal mandate of the kind from his subjects, though the idea of a referendum itself was not new to the Iranian people, because Mossadeq had held one in his quest for emergency powers in early 1953. There is ample controversy over the government's administration of the referendum and its reports of the referendum's representativeness. This did not, however, invalidate the government's claim that from 5,593,826 voters (of a population of about 21 million), 5,589,710, or 99 percent, voted for the Shah's program.[43] The results of the referendum provided the Shah with an effective instrument of "popular democracy" to claim that his subjects not only overwhelmingly endorsed his revolution, but also confirmed their support for his regime.[44]

Drawing on this source of "popular legitimacy," the Shah moved speedily and forcefully to implement his reforms. He started with land reform, which had been initiated and executed to some extent by Amini under the Land Reform Law of January 1962.[45] After approving some supplementary articles to the Land Reform Law in January 1963, the Shah proceeded with the program to implement the land reform in three stages. Under the first stage, the government purchased a total of 16,000 villages (about 19.5 percent of the arable land) from landowners, and transferred them to some 743,406 farm families. It limited the landlords' individual holdings to one village. Moreover, it launched a campaign urging the newly land-rich peasants to join the government-guided cooperatives. The second stage of the reform began in 1965. Landowners were offered a choice of five methods of settlement: tenancy; sale to peasants; division of land in the same proportion as the crop-sharing agreement; formation of agricultural cooperatives; and sale of peasants' rights to landowners. In addition, the land reform was extended to cover the religious endowment lands, and individual landholding was reduced further to 370 acres. There were, however, many local differences in the execution of the second stage. The peasants were generally given tenure; "they did not all receive ownership of the land, and the conditions under which the land was transferred to them were less favorable than those under the first stage." Nonetheless, from 1965 to 1969, a total of 9,505 publicly endowed lands were leased to farmers; 211,822 small landowners leased their lands to farmers; 54,480 villages were affected by the land reform; and 5,629 rural cooperatives were established, making the total number of cooperatives 8,102, with a total membership of over 1,399,000. The third stage of the reform was launched in 1966. This stage, as was stated officially, aimed at the expansion of agricultural production in line with the need of Iran's industrial development; a rise in the per capita output and standards of living of peasantry; and the improvement of marketing and production techniques, and consequently the stabilization of food prices.[46]

Meanwhile, the government nationalized forests and pasture lands. As was officially stated, this was to put these resources in the service of all citizens; to prevent their misuse and waste in the hands of private owners; to expand and develop them efficiently according to the needs of the country; and, above all, to support the land reform and strengthen the position of farmers. For the pasture lands, the government legislated that "public ownership" be available to sheep and cattlemen, and canceled all the charges that had been collected in the past by private owners. It subsequently nationalized water resources, and established the Development and Extension Corps, trained cadres to help farmers and rural cooperatives. The nationalization of water, which came into effect in July 1968, supported both agricultural and industrial development. According to the government, it was to make water utilization more efficient, and increase water supply by whatever means possible so that there should be enough water available for the expanding agriculture, industry, and electric power.[47]

The land reform, whatever its socio-economic results for the Iranian people—an issue that will be examined later on—proved to be politically rewarding for the Shah in several ways. He succeeded in almost liquidating the large landholdings of all major landlords, undermining their traditional power base, and consequently weakening their ability to separate the central government (or the Shah himself) from a majority of the peasants.[48] He was thus able to increase his direct access to the 70 percent of the population in the countryside who had previously been isolated from the effects of his policy actions, and endear his leadership to the newly land-rich peasants. He simultaneously met one of the popular demands of his ideological and political opponents, who had been advocating land reform as a popular and democratic measure. Thus, by the end of the 1960s, the Shah could claim not only to have abolished the traditionally land-based feudalism in Iran, but also to have "revolutionized" the life of the peasantry.[49] In their turn, a large number of land-rich peasants, whose behavior was mainly conditioned by their traditional way of living and political thinking, submitted themselves to the power of the Shah in the hope of a better life, and exalted him for his benevolence. The land reform thus provided a peasant-based start to the White Revolution and opened up a potential source of rural support for the Shah's leadership and rule.

The Shah, however, wanted neither to alienate the landlords altogether, nor to have a prolonged confrontation with them—

which he could ill afford at the time. The land reform was thus balanced, to a considerable extent, by the public sale of state-owned factories to private shares.[50] This reform was intended to achieve two interrelated objectives: to enrich the government with an additional source of revenue, so that it could finance the land reform effectively; and to provide the former landlords with a necessary stimulus to reinvest in industry the money with which they had been compensated for their lands. In this latter objective, the government sought to buy off the former landlords, and yet increase the share of private investment under its own guidance in developing the industrial sector. Many former landlords, however, soon managed to become industrial lords, and in shifting their power base from land to industrial urban centers, they still found the Shah's regime very beneficial.[51]

Concurrently with land reform, the White Revolution's program stressed the rapid industrialization of Iran and improvement in the working and living conditions of the country's industrial labor force. A certain amount of infrastructure had been built during the Second Development Plan, but the government allocated a relatively larger share of its funds for industrial development under the Third Plan. It sought direct investment to establish heavy industries such as steel and petrochemicals; it promoted, together with private investment, light industries such as the manufacture of refrigerators, heaters, and assembly factories for motor vehicles, radios, and the like; and it sought to protect and strengthen traditional industries such as textiles, carpets, and food processing.[52] The increasing government investment, coupled with the growing private investment that was enhanced by the flow of funds from former landlords, caused increased economic activity and industrial growth, and improved job opportunities in urban centers. During the Third Plan period, the industrial sector registered an average annual growth rate of 12.7 percent—2.7 percent more than had been planned.[53] By the end of the Plan, the number of industrial plants had grown from about 8,520 in 1961 to over 112,500, including some 4,000 large ones; and the number of industrial workers had increased from about 121,800 to over 540,000.[54] (During the same period, Iran's population rose from about 21 million to over 26 million, about 35 percent of which was urban.) The traditional textile and food industries, however, absorbed most of this labor force.[55]

In the meantime, the government legislated a minimum wage and workers' social insurance policy, as well as a profit-sharing scheme for workers in industries. According to the latter scheme, in each factory up to 20 percent of the net profit was to be distributed among the workers or, alternatively, workers were to be entitled to extra compensation based on production norms, through higher productivity or less waste. The profit-sharing law came into force in June 1963. At first it covered a limited number of factories, but later it was amended to cover all workshops with more than ten workers. The regime hoped that the law, together with the labor and social security laws, would ensure workers reasonable wages, increased employment, and welfare incentives. By the end of 1968, as was reported officially, a total of 1,412 large industrial plants had implemented the profit-sharing scheme, affecting over 125,692 workers.[56] All this undoubtedly created some improvement in the working and living conditions of a good number of urban industrial workers, and raised the hope of a majority of them for a better future; it also provided some impetus for the growth of an urban working class, largely under the Shah's leadership. Yet another source of support for the Shah's rule, this time mainly urban, began to mature. It must be stressed that previously the urban centers had produced most of the opposition to the Shah's regime.

The agrarian and industrial measures were accompanied by the Shah's efforts to mobilize women and youth behind his regime. Women had been denied the right to vote under the electoral law that had been passed by Iran's first elected parliament under the Constitution of 1906. In 1963, however, the Shah amended the electoral law and gave women the franchise, so that they could "contribute their share to the administration of the country" and participate actively in the process of socio-economic change and political mobilization. A substantial majority of the Iranian women, of course, could not make effective use of the franchise, given their low level of literacy and political consciousness at the time.[57] Nevertheless, the small educated group of women could express their growing support for the Shah's leadership by participating in government administration, public and private enterprises, and social schemes designed to propagate and execute the White Revolution's reforms, and exalt the Shah for his enlightenment. The government also legislated a family protection law and established family courts in support of "equal right" for women in all fields.[58]

For the educated youth, the Shah instituted what he termed "Literacy Corps," "Health Corps," "Development and Extension Corps," and "Houses of Equity." Under the first three schemes, the government drafted thousands of unemployed university and high-school graduates as trained cadres to work in rural areas in lieu of a part of their compulsory three years' military service. The Literacy and Health Corps were to help improve rural literacy, and health and sanitation standards, respectively; the Development and Extension Corps were to guide and assist farmers and rural cooperatives in new production and operational techniques. In addition, the corps were collectively entrusted with the task of propagating and disseminating the White Revolution throughout Iran. From 1963 to 1971, according to an official estimate, a total of 98,599 men and women served in twenty-one teams of the Literacy Corps, and educated about 1,625,000 pupils.[59] By 1972, the corps were active in over 20,000 villages, some of which had previously been out of reach of the central government. Moreover, Iran's literacy rate rose from about 15 percent at the end of the 1950s to about 25 percent at the beginning of the 1970s, though the number of students enrolled in rural areas still lagged behind that in the cities by 50 percent.[60] The Health Corps was established in 1964. By 1972, as was reported officially, there were 400 medical groups, each of which covered about twenty to forty villages with a total population of 8,000 to 20,000. The Development and Extension Corps were founded in 1965. By 1972, the number of corps members serving in the scheme amounted to 4,692.[61] Added to these schemes were the "Houses of Equity" or village courts of justice. They were originally founded in 1963 to deal with misdemeanors and petty offenses, and thus lighten the burden of official courts above the village and prevent minor rural disputes from developing into major ones at the cost of peasants' time and work. By 1973, there were reported to be 300 Houses of Equity with 2,400 corps members/judges on service in Iran.[62]

These schemes, apart from achieving something similar to the Maoist idea of linking the mental and manual labor of youth, helped the Shah's regime in several ways. Through the corps, the government recruited the personnel it needed to propagate and execute the White Revolution, and to expand contacts between the rural and urban population, under its own control. Since the corps members were fulfilling part of their military service in civilian form, they provided the government with a source of legitimacy to emphasize the importance of the civilian role of the armed forces, and thus boost the image and justify the expansion of the Shah's military power base. In addition, the schemes created employment and opened government-controlled avenues of political participation for graduates, a majority of whom had previously been bitterly critical of the Shah's regime for lack of jobs and opportunity for participation, and had taken part in public agitation. Thus the schemes mobilized a good number of the educated Iranian youth (who possessed more potential for revolt than any other section of the population) behind the Shah's leadership.

The Shah declared "National Reconstruction" to be a necessary follow-up of these reforms, involving the reconstruction of both urban centers and rural areas. By the late 1960s, the government legislated urban renewal and urban reconstruction acts. The "National Reconstruction" reform, according to an official source, was to narrow the gap in the standards of living between the cities and villages; to eliminate discrimination among various areas through greater attention to less developed areas; to accelerate rural development and reconstruction, and to continue with urban renewal; and to introduce all modern amenities for transforming Iran into a prosperous and powerful country in its region.[63] The Shah, however, realized that these reforms could not be fulfilled efficiently without at the same time adopting fundamental measures to reform Iran's administrative and educational system according to the changing needs of the country. He therefore called for an "Administrative and Educational Revolution"—the last of his reforms for the 1960s.

The administrative aspect of this reform was to improve the efficiency and working standard of Iran's fast-growing public service. It stressed the need for public servants, in whatever capacity, to "work honestly, consciously, and by accepting the responsibilities of their duty. The spirit of procrastination and red-tape must disappear from . . . offices."[64] It promised the "decentralization" of the administrative system and the protection of the "public interest," as well as improvement in the social welfare and security of public servants. The reform therefore envisaged new public service regulations, including the Public Auditing Law that came into force in 1972. The educational aspect of the reform was stressed as essential for the continuing success of the administrative and all other introduced reforms. It emphasized the need of Iran for trained educational, agricultural, technical, and administrative personnel. This was to be met at whatever expense by training students inside and outside Iran, particularly in Western countries.

The Shah failed, however, to couple these socio-economic reforms with any major political reform toward realizing his promise of "political democracy." He left the political structure and machinery under his supervision almost intact, and continued to centralize politics under his absolute control to strengthen his traditionally central position in Iranian politics. In general, the Iranian people were still denied the basic political freedoms and civil liberties necessary to fulfil the Shah's promise to democratize and decentralize the Iranian system. The people were allowed neither to criticize government policies nor to seek redress for their grievances individually and collectively. The Shah continued to maintain the parliament, which was reopened in 1963 after a lapse of three years, and the two-party system, which he had instigated in 1957, and formally allowed the people to elect the Majlis every four years. As in the past, however, party membership and elections were strictly controlled by the government, and the opposition was suppressed to prevent the public expression of criticism. Some representatives of the peasants, workers, and women did find their way into parliament in the 1963 and 1967 elections at the cost of the landlords, but they signified new bases of support for the Shah, not opposition.[65] In fact, by 1964 even the principle of the two-party system dwindled. The Shah instigated a new ruling party called Iran-e Novin (The New Iran), which was at first led by his loyal colleague, 'Ali Mansur, Iran's prime minister from 1964 to 1965. After Mansur's assassination in early 1965, he was succeeded by his finance minister and a former intellectual critic of the Shah's regime, Amir 'Abbas Hoveida, who soon made Iran-e Novin virtually the sole political party contesting elections; the formal opposition party, Mardom, continued as nothing more than a name. Those opponents who could not be coopted into the Shah's system either through the formal process of parliament and the two parties or through the informal process of the White Revolution's program were to be effectively suppressed, as in the past, by SAVAK.[66]

Thus, despite his frequent promises, the Shah largely failed to democratize or increasingly institutionalize the Iranian political system.[67] Although it is true that he initially needed a degree of political centralization to put his reforms into practice, his failure to disperse political power for fear of losing his own central position in the long run undermined the Shah's ability to plan and execute his reforms according to the needs of Iran, as we shall see.

Nevertheless, by the end of the 1960s, the Shah had come a long way from the unpopular and insecure domestic position that before 1963 had caused him and Washington grave concern about the effective continuity of his regime. By initiating his reforms, no matter how undemocratic, autocratic, and unfruitful they were in the eyes of his opponents and in terms of their results for the Iranian people, the Shah had achieved several short-term objectives in improving his domestic credibility and security. He had generated a process of controlled mass mobilization and opened up new bases of support among peasants, industrial workers, women, and youth, and among those intellectuals, professionals, technocrats, and bureaucrats who had previously been unhappy with his regime for other than ideological reasons. He had stimulated a higher degree of economic activity, which, together with his mass mobilization, improved the prospects for immediate social and economic stability, and raised the people's hopes for a better future. Iran's middle class grew more quickly than before—a factor necessary for the Shah's regime in pursuing a guided capitalist mode of socio-economic development. He had thus stimulated some social and economic bases on which to transform an "autocratic" model of economic development, which he pursued in the 1950s, into a combination of this model with "bourgeois" and "populist" models of socio-economic development.[68] Meanwhile, he had gained a reputation for his "revolutionary" strides, based on a national ideology, to reform his society and improve the living conditions of his subjects. It was for the lack of such strides that he had been criticized in the past by his opponents and critics both inside and outside Iran. Moreover, he had adopted a "revolutionary" rhetoric that had previously been adopted only by his ideological opponents.

The generally improving domestic image of the Shah, indeed, enabled him to initiate and pursue certain changes in his regime's regional policy in order to attain what he declared to be the White Revolution's goal of a "national independent foreign policy." The resulting achievements, in turn, helped the Shah's regime not only to strengthen its regional security, but also to gain regional—particularly Soviet—economic and technical support for its reforms.

A National Independent Foreign Policy

By the beginning of the 1960s, it was clear to the Shah that his past policy of exclusive alliance with the West and those "friendly" regional countries that shared with his regime the convictions of firm opposition to communism and regional "subversion" had done his regime more damage than good. It had caused the displeasure of the Soviets and radical Arabs with his regime, the suspicion of Afghanistan and India, and his own increasing vulnerability to Western, mainly American, dictates. While Washington was pressing him for reforms, Cold War tensions were losing the intensity of the 1950s, and the Shah found it imperative to couple his domestic reforms with changes in regional policy. He began to emphasize the importance of the country's bilateral relationship with other countries, particularly the neighboring ones, on the basis of peaceful coexistence, cooperation, and interdependence. He considered it essential for Iran to conduct its foreign relations with more flexibility and independence, within the bounds of his regime's alliance with the West and opposition to communism. He therefore stressed the foreign policy goal of the White Revolution to be one of "national independence." He subsequently declared:

> Our policy is based on the maintenance and preservation of peace. We in Iran have adopted a policy which we call a policy of independent nationalism. Its essential principles are non-interference in the internal affairs of other countries and peaceful co-existence. We must go beyond this

stage and convert peaceful co-existence into international cooperation and understanding especially to countries with different political and social systems from ours, for without them the basic difficulties facing the world today, such as illiteracy, sickness and hunger, cannot be solved. We believe that the way to safeguard the real interests of our country is by co-existence and sincere cooperation with all countries . . . on the basis of mutual respect for national sovereignty. . . . At the same time . . . the establishment of . . . understanding and peace cannot be achieved without sincere respect for the principle of co-existence between different ideologies and systems of government, or without respect for the principle of non-interference of countries in the internal affairs of others.[69]

In pursuit of such a goal, the Shah found it both politically and economically expedient to normalize Iran's relations with the Soviet Union at government-to-government levels, without abandoning his strong opposition to communism. He gave his personal undertaking to the Soviet leadership in 1962 that he would not allow any foreign power to establish bases in Iran against the Soviet Union, and he set out to rectify one of the underlying causes of the Soviet dislike of his regime: Iran's membership in CENTO. CENTO was originally established as both a military and economic organization. But thus far its military aspect had been stressed more than its economic aspect, as a defense against the spread of "Soviet communism" and "regional communist subversion." Meanwhile, it had become clear to Iran and other regional members that CENTO was not of any great value as a military alliance at the regional level unless the Soviet Union invaded one of them—a contingency that none of them regarded as very likely in view of changing world politics. The Shah, therefore, began stressing the fact that CENTO was important not merely because of its military functions, but also because it could foster cooperation and understanding in nonmilitary fields.[70] Sharing a common concern in this respect, Iran, Pakistan, and Turkey eventually announced in July 1964 the formation of the Regional Cooperation for Development (RCD) as an offspring of CENTO. The objectives of RCD were declared not to be opposed to the CENTO alliance, but to be an improvement on and adjunct to it. It was to expand "the field of mutual cooperation into those areas where the CENTO alliance had not been effective."[71] In other words, it was to further cooperation in economic, technical, and cultural fields outside the existing framework of bilateral and multilateral collaboration. At the time of its formation, the original member countries hoped that RCD would soon be joined by Afghanistan and other states of the region, excluding the USSR. Although this did not occur, and although during the 1960s Iran gained much less from RCD economically and technologically than did Turkey and Pakistan, which commanded stronger manpower and economic/industrial capabilities than Iran,[72] the formation of the scheme was in line with the Shah's need to improve his regime's relationship with the Soviet Union. He sought to reassure Moscow of his readiness for better ties, involving expansion of economic and technical cooperation between the two sides.

Meanwhile, the Johnson administration classified Iran as a "developed" country in 1965, and planned to end American grant-in-aid to it by November 1967. The United States was to remain committed to its alliance with Iran and to meet most of the Shah's economic and military requests upon cash payment or long-term loan. Washington was, of course, confident that Iran's commitment to the West and its dependence on the United States had grown deep and strong enough to ensure the continuation of its special relationship with the West.[73] The American decision, nevertheless, strengthened the Shah's position in his efforts to normalize the Iranian-Soviet relationship, reduce his vulnerability to American pressures, and counter his opponents' criticism that he was a Western stooge.

THE CHANGING FOREIGN POLICY POSITION

These developments must have been pleasing to the Soviets.[74] Since it had become obvious that only a domestically strong and secure Shah could normalize his relations with the USSR and reduce his dependence on the United States, it was in Moscow's interest to help him as much and as soon as possible. In this, Moscow could seek to achieve several objectives: 1. to secure some access to Iranian resources, particularly oil, which had hitherto been monopolized by the West; 2. to manifest its desire for improved ties with the conservative Arab states and attract their confidence, since they had been resentful of the rapid development of close ties between Moscow and radical Arab states; and 3. to promote its general policy of "good neighborly relations," "peaceful coexistence," and "friendship" with as many developing Afro-Asian countries as possible. Although at the time the Soviet Union did not need Middle Eastern oil, it was economical for it (quite apart from its need to strengthen its international bargaining position) to meet the fuel needs of its southern areas from the fields lying near its southern borders.[75] For this purpose, it had already concluded a natural gas agreement with Afghanistan in October 1963—the first Soviet venture outside the communist world in search of energy supplies.[76] It had tried to conclude similar agreements with Iran, but had failed largely because the Shah could not trust the Soviets while he was still domestically weak, given active Soviet support for the outlawed Tudeh and other left-wing groups against his regime. With the changing position of the Shah and of international politics, however, both sides were now ready to improve their relationship. Moscow made fresh offers of economic and technical aid to Tehran, and the Shah was pleased to make use of such offers in support of his domestic reforms and changing foreign policy objectives.

During the Shah's state visit to Moscow from June 21 to July 3, 1965, the groundwork was laid for Irano-Soviet economic and technical cooperation. This resulted in the conclusion of two major economic and military agreements. The first was concluded in January 1966. Iran was to supply the Soviet Union with more than $600 million worth of natural gas, beginning in 1970; in return, the USSR undertook to build Iran's first large steel mill complex in Isfahan, construct a pipe line from northern Iran to the Caucasus, and establish a machine tool plant in Shiraz.[77] Under the second agreement, initiated in February 1967, the Soviets agreed to supply Tehran with some $110 million worth of armored troop carriers, trucks, and antiaircraft guns in return for natural gas from Iran.[78]

Although the agreements were not to affect Iran's alliance with the West, they marked a major breakthrough in Irano-Soviet relations and, consequently, provided the Shah with a bargaining leverage in conducting his relations with Washington. Moscow, on its side, secured a firm beginning toward expanding its share in the Persian Gulf's oil resources and exerting greater political influence in the region. This, however, resulted in a dilemma for Moscow in dealing with the mutually hostile revolutionary Arabs who were its allies, and the pro-Western conservative Shah. As for the Shah, he not only found a market outside the capitalist world for Iran's gas, but also another source of economic and technological aid in accelerating the White Revolution's program of heavy industrialization. The Soviets' construction of the Isfahan steel complex was to provide Iran with sufficient steel to meet its domestic needs and to export a considerable amount by the 1970s. The arms deal was not very significant in military terms. But it was important in political terms, insofar as it marked the first Iranian arms deal with a non-Western and, above all, a communist country.

Politically, the Shah gained several things from improved Iranian-Soviet relations. For the small price of letting the Soviets have limited access to Iran's petroleum wealth, the Shah gained Soviet support, and Moscow stopped both its propaganda and its backing of certain Iranian groups against the Shah's regime. Soviet support strengthened the Shah's regional and international position. It enabled him to improve his position against Cairo and the Nasserite forces in the region, as well as against Iraq. Moreover, the Iranian-Soviet rapprochement undercut the chances of any serious cooperation between the domestic opposition and hostile regional forces. Moreover, the improved Iranian-Soviet relationship strengthened the position of the Shah's regime in its relationship with the West, particularly Washington.[79] From now on a domestically confident Shah could use his country's friendly ties with the USSR as a leverage against Washington should the latter decide to exert pressure on him, as it had in the early sixties. Thus, by the end of the 1960s, the Shah was in a sufficiently strong position to conduct Iran's affairs with considerable flexibility and less vulnerability to outside dictates. He drew heavily on this to challenge the Western monopoly of the Iranian oil industry, realize Iran's potential as an oil power, and call for an "interdependent" relationship with the West in the 1970s.

CHAPTER IV

The Emergence of Iran
as an Oil Power

THE OIL POLICY OF "POSITIVE EQUILIBRIUM," 1953-1960

IN ITS CONCERN that Iran own its oil industry and control it in the interest of its national development and stability, the Shah's regime shared a common purpose with the Mossadeq government. But the two regimes differed widely in their methods of pursuing this aim. The Mossadeq government believed in a "revolutionary" method, and the Shah's regime favored an "evolutionary" method, stipulating that Iran's sovereignty over its oil industry should be achieved gradually through accommodation rather than confrontation with the West.

From the start of his reign in 1941, the Shah had experienced the hazards of British monopoly of the Iranian oil industry, which had minimized Iran's benefits from its own resources and made the country vulnerable to outside interference at the same time. He had seen that these effects limited and frustrated many Iranian governments in their attempts to implement reforms and stabilize the domestic situation, on the one hand, and to exercise greater independence in the conduct of Iran's foreign affairs, on the other. By the time Mossadeq declared the Iranian oil industry nationalized in May 1951, the Shah was aware that as long as Iran's oil was dominated by outsiders, Iranians could not assert their national sovereignty effectively.[1] He and his close supporters, who later helped him to wrest the reins of political power from Mossadeq, at no stage opposed a renegotiation of the 1933 oil agreement between Iran and the Anglo-Iranian Oil Company (AIOC). On the contrary, they agreed with the opposition that Iran's controlling share in the running of its oil industry should be increased. When confronted with popular demand, the Shah fully supported Mossadeq's nationalization as an exercise of Iran's national legitimate right, even at a time when his political differences with Mossadeq were mounting.

When, however, Mossadeq failed to achieve immediate nationalization and was unable to cope with the ensuing crisis, which led to the overthrow of his government, the Shah faced his most urgent task: to establish his own rule against strong domestic opposition and the perceived Soviet threat. This resulted in the rapid growth of Iran's dependence on the United States and a weakening of its regional position. The Shah's regime clearly saw that it was necessary to end the nationalization crisis as quickly as possible. Given its weak and dependent position, the regime could not persist with Mossadeq's original prescription for simultaneous Iranian ownership and control of its oil industry. The Shah and his close supporters therefore retracted their support for Mossadeq's original nationalization program, and discredited Mossadeq's method of achieving his objectives through his doctrine of "negative equilibrium." The Shah adopted instead a policy of what he called "positive equilibrium." He equated this with his doctrine of "positive nationalism," which was designed primarily to meet the requirements for the rapid establishment of his rule.

Under this policy, the Shah's regime largely abandoned the "control" aspect of nationalization and opted mainly for "ownership." It welcomed U.S. mediation in settling the oil dispute between Iran and Britain, and aimed to put the oil industry into operation as rapidly as possible, in order to help finance its campaign against the opposition and generate a higher level of economic activity. This is precisely what was achieved by its 1954 agreement with the Consortium of International Oil Companies, concluded under U.S. auspices.

In terms of fulfilling the Shah's short-term objectives, the agreement was significant. By the end of 1954, Iran and Britain had reestablished diplomatic relations, and Iran had agreed to a 40 percent share for BP in the newly formed consortium. Within three years of the agreement's conclusion, the Iranian oil industry under the consortium had achieved its prenationalization level of production. In 1957, Iran's crude output at 263 million barrels surpassed the record of 242 million barrels established in 1950. In the same year, its oil exports reached 232 million barrels, and its oil revenue amounted to $212 million.[2] The consortium companies accounted for virtually all of the production and export. They fixed the posted prices for the Iranian crude between $1.67 and $1.86 per barrel (the Iranian government tax and royalty were calculated on the basis of posted prices), which was below the prenationalization posted prices. The companies' "off-take" per barrel amounted to 87.6 cents. The consortium achieved all this at a total capital expenditure of $34 million, which covered its fixed and movable assets as well as exploration and drilling costs.[3]

The reactivation of the oil industry at this level effectively supplemented the extensive U.S. support for the regime. Together, the two factors helped the regime to achieve its immediate prime objective of domestic consolidation. The regime had traded control over its oil industry for what it needed to establish its rule. In fact, the regime's oil policy in the 1950s was one of modus vivendi with the West and the oil companies, which now collectively controlled the Iranian oil industry. The 1954 oil agreement simply embodied the code of legitimacy for such an oil policy. It governed the regime's relationship with the consortium companies for almost nineteen years. Only when the Shah abrogated the agreement in 1973, and enforced Iran's control over its oil industry from production to pricing, did he finally begin to realize Mossadeq's nationalization goal, and fulfill Iran's potential as an oil power.

When the Shah's regime concluded the 1954 agreement, it did not mean that it had given up forever the goal of complete nationalization. The Shah was fully aware of the shortcomings of the agreement, and later voiced his displeasure over it on several occasions. Given the prevailing circumstances, however, as he remarked in 1960, "it would have been difficult at that time to have concluded a better agreement." His prime minister, General Zahedi, also stressed that the agreement "left much to be desired."[4] The Shah believed that only "through *steadily* increasing control over the production and distribution of our oil, shall [we] be re-asserting our national sovereignty."[5] As became evident later on, the Shah incorporated the goal of complete nationalization into his regime's long-term objectives. This was to be achieved through what can be seen as an "evolutionary" method, which would develop gradually and peacefully in accommodation with the West and in the context of the Shah's strengthening domestic position and the changes in the regional and international situations in favor of Iran. Meanwhile, without challenging the consortium companies in any way, it appears that the Shah's regime concentrated on strengthening the National Iranian Oil Company (NIOC) as a government organization, and enabling it to make effective use of the area outside the consortium concession area according to the 1954 agreement.

To this effect, it passed the Oil Law in 1957, which made the NIOC responsible for the development of oil resources in all parts of Iran outside the consortium or "agreement area," including the continental shelf, and made provisions for it to enter into direct partnership with other companies or organizations than the consortium companies.[6] During 1957 and 1958, the NIOC signed two agreements, with an Italian and an American company, with 50 percent NIOC participation in each arrangement. They set up two companies called Société Iranio-Italienne des Petroles (SIRIP) and the Iran-Pan American Company (IPAC). In each case, NIOC's 50 percent share, plus the 50 percent government tax on the profits made by the foreign partners, gave Iran a total share of 75 percent. This became known as the 75-25 percent agreement in favor of Iran.[7] The first of its kind in the world, the agreement was an important achievement in itself. It provided a basis for the Shah's rhetorical comment that it marked the beginning of the end for the 50-50 formula, which characterized Iran's agreement with the consortium. He considered the agreement a result "of more than 17 years of agony and adversities" of his regime.[8] Moreover, he stressed that although he did not want to challenge or "kill any goose which lays golden eggs that benefit my country . . . we intend to regulate each goose's behavior in the public interest."[9] The implication was that the regime was not happy with the 1954 agreement, and was working toward complete nationalization, while trying to gain some domestic and regional support for the regime and its current oil policy stance.

In practical terms, however, the 75-25 percent agreement neither resulted in substantial economic benefit for Iran, nor did it affect Iran's relationship with the consortium companies. The NIOC controlled only about 10 percent of the resource area outside that of the consortium, and SIRIP and IPAC were very small ventures operating in a very limited area. Furthermore, the two ventures did not start production until 1961-1964, and their full production levels were negligible in comparison with that of the consortium companies.[10] The agreements, therefore, had more symbolic than practical value. They underlined the desire of the Shah's regime to strengthen the NIOC and its hold on the area under its control, as well as to achieve better deals for resources outside consortium control so as to strengthen its own position in possible future bargaining with the consortium companies. It was, however, clear that if Iran were to maximize the benefits it was to derive from its oil potential, it must control the policy and production of all its oil industry, and not just 10 percent of it. In this respect, the regime failed to make any notable progress in the 1950s, when the regime was weak and the international oil companies were formidable in their unity against Iran and the other regional producers. Moreover, the global political and economic circumstances were not favorable. These restraining factors began to change with the foundation of the Organization of Petroleum Exporting Countries (OPEC) in 1960. This marked the beginning of a new phase in oil politics.

THE OIL POLICY OF "MORE PRODUCTION, MORE REVENUE," 1960-1970

Until the end of the 1950s, the international oil companies held virtually a complete monopoly, not only of the Iranian oil industry, but of all the Persian Gulf oil resources. While the postwar boom in the West was increasing the demand for oil, the companies kept increasing their Persian Gulf production, and explored more fields in both old and new areas there and elsewhere. But they concentrated on increasing their Gulf production because of the cheapness of oil there: a barrel of oil was produced for as little as 10 cents.

Having been caught up with the availability of cheap oil and the growing available markets, which brought them enormous profit, the companies failed to assess the world demand accurately. When there was a minor downturn in the world oil market in 1959, the companies found themselves with a considerable surplus supply. There were several reasons for the downturn, including excessive production by the companies themselves, a downward fluctuation in the postwar reconstruction and industrialization boom in the West, the U.S. decision to adopt protectionist policies in order to help its domestic oil industry against the inflow of cheap oil from outside,[11] and the sudden rise of the Soviet Union as a major oil exporting country. The USSR offered its oil to many of the less developed consuming countries at prices between 10 and 25 percent less than the Persian Gulf oil prices fixed by the international companies, and often in return accepted payment in local currencies or in nonoil commodities.[12]

Although the downturn was minor, the companies panicked at the prospect of a world glut in the oil market. In order to protect their own interests, they immediately used their controlling power over pricing, and cut the posted prices twice, without consulting the producing governments, during the first six months of 1959. The posted price for Venezuelan crude was reduced by 5 to 25 cents and that of Persian Gulf crude by 22 to 32 cents per barrel.[13] In the case of Iran, the posted prices of crude dropped from $1.80-$1.99 in 1958 to $1.62-$1.81 in 1959.[14] Since the companies paid royalties and taxes to producing governments on the basis of posted prices, there was a substantial drop in the latter's revenues. The first Arab Petroleum Conference (April 16-22, 1960) rejected the companies' unilateral price reductions as illegal. Venezuela, a hard-liner in oil politics, and Saudi Arabia, a fundamentally pro-Western state that was being pressured by growing Arab nationalism, called on the producing states, on May 13, to formulate a "common petroleum policy" in order to defend themselves and prevent the companies from further unilateral price cuts.[15]

By now the Shah's regime felt secure enough to use this opportunity to pursue its long-term oil objectives, put aside its differences with the two other Gulf producers, Saudi Arabia and Iraq, and join them in promoting their common cause against the companies. Such a move on the part of Iran would neither put the Shah in direct confrontation with the companies, nor would it single out Iran as a rebel against the West. In fact, it was Saudi Arabia, another close Western ally, not Iran, that initiated the call for a common petroleum policy. In return for its cooperation with other producers, the Shah's regime was unlikely to lose anything, and was likely to gain a source of collective strength and protection from other producers. The Shah could promote this policy to strengthen his bargaining position not only against the consortium companies but also against his domestic and regional critics, who denounced him for allying with the West and Western companies at the cost of Iran's interests.

The Shah's government therefore joined the governments of four other major oil exporting states, Venezuela, Saudi Arabia, Kuwait, and Iraq, in a series of consultations in Baghdad in order to coordinate their oil policies. Although the major capitalist consuming countries and oil companies expected little from the meeting, the participants founded the Organization of Petroleum Exporting Countries (OPEC) on September 14, 1960. It was set up as a permanent intergovernmental organization, the first of its kind. Its membership remained open to any less-developed country with a sizable petroleum capacity. Given the political aims and leanings of its founding members, the principal aim of the organization from the start was a compromise between the two "radical" governments of Venezuela and Iraq, and the two pro-Western "conservative" governments of Saudi Arabia and Iran.

The Organization stressed two major aspects of its aim: first, the determination of OPEC to coordinate and unify "the petroleum policies of member countries" in an attempt to safeguard "their interests, individually and collectively" and ensure "the stabilization of prices in international oil markets with a view to eliminating harmful and unnecessary fluctuations." Second, it emphasized the importance of "an efficient, economic, and regular supply of petroleum to consuming nations; and a fair return on their capital to those investing in the petroleum industry."[16]

This policy objective of OPEC was modest, and made no attempt to produce any substantial change in the relationship between governments and companies. It was, therefore, in line with the Shah's long-term oil policy, which looked toward the gradual expansion of Iranian control over the country's oil industry through accommodation. As could have been expected, the immediate achievements of OPEC were very limited. The member countries' general weakness, lack of sufficient determination and unity, as well as the unfavorable international situation of the Cold War period, did not permit them to pressure the powerful and united companies even to acknowledge OPEC's existence, let alone respond seriously to its demands. One way to exert pressure on the companies was to restrict production.

But the leading **OPEC** producer, Saudi Arabia, was not interested in this, and Iran never approved of it, either. Another way
that Iran and Iraq proposed was to "program" production according to population—both countries having large populations.
But other member countries wanted programming according to
need.[17] Finally, in mid-1962, the fourth **OPEC** conference, in
which Iran played an active role, resolved to establish a uniform
rate for royalties in each country; it also recommended that
prices be brought up to their pre-August 1960 levels and royalty
payments should not be deductible from income tax paid to
producing governments.[18] By 1966, however, all that **OPEC**
could claim to have achieved was, as Rustow and Mugno rightly
argue, "to have prevented further cuts beyond the decline in
real prices implicit in a steady nominal price. On the other
hand, the companies by 1965 agreed with each of the several
countries not to claim the royalty as a credit against the 50 per
cent income tax."[19]

The immediate result for Iran was that the posted prices of its
crude stabilized between $1.58 and $1.73 until 1970, and the
government's per-barrel revenue increased from 75.7 cents in
1961 to 83.3 cents in 1966, short of the 1958 gain of 89.7 cents
per barrel.[20] This gain was substantial neither financially nor in
terms of domestic political gain for the Shah's regime. Iran's
revenue from oil was increasing steadily but slowly, largely
according to the interests of the companies that controlled the
posted prices and resisted any major rise in production. Iranian
production rose from 390 million barrels in 1960 to 780 million
barrels in 1966, of which 356.2 and 700 million barrels, respectively, were exported. This increased the government's oil revenue from $285 million to $608.1 million during the same period.
The consortium companies were responsible for about 90 percent
of the production, exports, and revenues paid to Iran.[21] The
NIOC and its joint ventures, to which six more were added in
1966, made up the remaining 10 percent. Despite NIOC's "expansionist" moves, such as investing in India's Madras refinery,
extending its exploration activities to the continental shelf on
the Persian Gulf, and enlarging and modernizing productive
facilities in the area under its control,[22] its progress since the
1954 agreement was proportional to that of the companies, and
nothing more.

Meanwhile the White Revolution was urgently in need of more oil revenue to finance the reforms. The Shah was able to allocate an average of about 70 percent of the nation's oil income to the Plan Organization for economic development after 1962, as against an average of over 50 percent in the 1950s. But the increase in oil revenue could not keep up with the growing demands created by the reforms and people's rising expectations, in the light of the Shah's unwillingness to cut down on his high security and administrative expenditures, and his inability to curb corruption in the bureaucracy. The problem became more acute in view of Iran's limited achievement through OPEC, and of Washington's decision to end its grant-in-aid to Iran by 1967.

The Shah's domestic and regional position had dramatically improved since the 1950s, however. The White Revolution was mobilizing new bases of domestic support for the Shah's rule, and Iran's relations with the Soviet Union had taken a turn to steady normalization and increasing friendship. Moreover, despite the oil companies' panic in the late 1950s, the world demand for Persian Gulf oil was growing rapidly.[23] From this improved position, the Shah's regime intensified its efforts to pursue an old tactic of "more production, more revenue" on its own, although it maintained its close links with OPEC. Since the regime could not force the companies to increase posted prices and, therefore, government revenue, it took advantage of its partial control over supply, and pressed the companies for greater increases in Iranian production and exports. In 1965, for the first time since his protest against the companies over their unilateral price cuts in 1959, the Shah complained bitterly to the oil companies, and threatened them by declaring that "Western oil companies' dealings with us have not been fair. We have often warned them that our production, in view of the country's socio-economic requirements, must be much higher than it is now. But on every occasion, they have found a way to avoid meeting their commitments. If the present trend persists we will have no option but to meet our requirements by dealing with other markets."[24]

The Shah's complaint was genuine, but he had little chance to carry out his threat of "dealing with other markets" without bringing about a major crisis in his relationship with the West. The consortium companies firmly controlled the Iranian oil industry on the basis of the 1954 agreement, which was still fully enforced. Above all, Iran had neither marketing capability nor any direct access to major noncommunist oil markets, which were dominated by the companies. The only possible alternative markets that the Shah could have turned to were the Soviet Union and East European countries. In fact, the NIOC concluded two separate bilateral agreements with the Soviet Union and Romania during 1965-1966, for the sale of Iranian natural gas and oil to the two countries, respectively.[25] One could look at these agreements as tactical moves by the Shah to strengthen his position against the companies. But this was as far as he could go. The Soviet and East European markets were not big enough to provide Iran with effective alternatives. Even if they were, the NIOC did not have the strength and sanctions to divert the consortium's share of oil to other markets. It could have done so only after abrogating the 1954 agreement; but the regime was by no means ready for this yet. The companies were fully aware of these weaknesses on the part of Iran, and, despite the Shah's increasing persistence, there was no major rise in Iranian production and exports before 1967.

During 1967 there was, however, a sharp rise in Iranian crude production and export, as well as in government revenue, under the same consortium operation—a greater rise than for any other OPEC member. The major factors were the Arab-Israeli war of June 1967, the consequent closure of the Suez Canal, and an Arab oil embargo against certain Western countries supporting Israel, which the Shah exploited very successfully in promoting his own interests. In order to weaken the Israeli position, the Arab oil ministers met during the war (June 3-9) at Baghdad and decreed an oil boycott, particularly against Britain and France, which were alleged to be aiding Israel against the warring Arab states, especially Egypt. The boycott was the first of its kind and, perhaps, the most radical action since Mossadeq's nationalization. Although the boycott was short-lived and proved ineffectual, it, together with closure of the Suez Canal, caused a temporary oil shortage.[26] The companies were not prepared for it, and began to be concerned, not so much about the shortage itself—as it was small—but how to prevent its repetition. Moreover, the boycott demonstrated that despite the companies' control over their oil industries, the producing states could influence supply if they had the political will to do so. Given the growing world demand for oil, any degree of control over supply could work out in the interest of producers.

Meanwhile, Tehran's relationship with Cairo was at its lowest ebb. While voicing his support for the Arabs' "just cause" and endorsing the Security Council's Resolution 242, the Shah disassociated Iran as a non-Arab state, though a Muslim country, from the Arab boycott, and expressed his concern over the use of oil as a political weapon.[27] When the companies sought to overcome the oil shortage, the Shah agreed to increases in their production in Iran. As a result, Iranian production went up sharply, by about 20 percent in 1967 alone. By 1969, Iranian production increased to 1,234 million barrels; its export to 1,158.5 million barrels; and its total oil revenue to $1,136 million. By the end of 1970, with a record annual production of 1,403.8 million barrels, Iran surpassed Saudi Arabia as OPEC's leading producer and exporter. Moreover, during 1967 Iran reached a complementary agreement with the consortium, whereby the latter returned 25 percent of the area under its contract to NIOC, and agreed to deliver to NIOC supplemental crude production for export to East European countries.[28]

The political consequences of the Middle East war also brought dramatic improvements in Iran's regional position. Egypt's defeat had two closely related implications for the Gulf region. Cairo became deeply preoccupied with recovering its military, economic, and territorial losses in the war; therefore it could no longer pursue its aim of regionwide "Arab revolution" as vigorously as before. And to pursue its recovery, Cairo became financially dependent on the conservative, oil-rich Arab states, led by Saudi Arabia. Despite their differences with Nasser, the Arab states offered Egypt substantial monetary aid to make up for the closure of the Suez Canal and help reequip the Egyptian army. Nasser thereupon greatly reduced his revolutionary aspirations against the conservative Persian Gulf regimes, and withdrew Egyptian forces from South Yemen (the present People's Democratic Republic of Yemen), where they had been engaged in support of pro-Nasserite republican forces against the Saudi-backed monarchists in the north. The conservative Arab forces emerged strong and triumphant in the Persian Gulf.[29]

Thus the Shah's regime became free from its long preoccupation with the threat of Nasserism. This, together with Iran's emergence as OPEC's leading producer, strengthened the regime's position in regional politics. On the one hand, it could now base its relations and dealings with the conservative Arab producers, not on the common ground of anti-Nasserism, but rather on its own emerging position as a strong force in the region. On the other hand, it could cultivate and promote relations with all the regional states from a position of strength, as its own interests dictated. The Shah's regime had gained a central position in oil politics.

At a time when the capitalist consuming countries and companies were deeply concerned about a repetition of the Arab boycott, the Shah assured them that Iran would continue to honor its commitments and meet their oil needs in the event of a shortage created by an Arab boycott. Meanwhile, Iran's increasing production proved the effectiveness of the country's position as a potential "boycott breaker."

Thus, Iran became very important to the West and its companies, on the one hand, and the Arab producers, on the other. The former needed it to moderate the Arab producers and compensate for an Arab boycott, and the latter needed its close cooperation if they wanted their use of oil for political purposes to be effective. Tehran assumed a crucially influential position, not only in the network of relationships between the West, the companies, and the Arab producers, but also in OPEC politics. It was clearly in the Shah's interest to see OPEC emerge as a more effective cartel, so that he could use its strength in collective bargaining to realize Iran's oil potential for its own benefit. Changes in the world political and economic situation, as well as in oil politics, helped OPEC to become a very effective cartel by the beginning of the seventies.

The Oil Policy of "Price Rise, Price and Production Control," 1970-1975

There is a general belief that the emergence of OPEC as a more effective cartel largely reflected the political awakening of the oil producing states, including Iran, which, at last, decided to exert their will collectively in order to maximize their benefits from their oil resources. This is not altogether correct. Long before the start of the seventies, many producers were aware of their oil potential, and knew that their oil would neither be exhausted nor replaced by an alternative in the near future. Mossadeq's nationalization in 1951 and the formation of OPEC in 1960 were manifestations of such an awareness. But what the producers had lacked all along were the appropriate national, regional, and international political and economic environments to allow them to manage their own national resources either individually or collectively. By the end of the 1960s, however, changes in national, regional, and global politics had worked in favor of the producers. The national governments had become stronger, with increased control over their respective political situations. A strong trend had emerged for cooperation, at least at OPEC level, between the Persian Gulf producers themselves, and between them and other OPEC producers.

What suddenly enhanced these tendencies was the realization by a number of producers that the changes in the world political and economic situation were finally swinging in their favor.[30] The weakening of Cold War politics of bipolarity in favor of a politics of detente provided for more lucidity in the conduct of international relations. This meant an opportunity for small states, particularly those with resources such as oil, to conduct their foreign relations more flexibly and manage their dealings with the outside world more forcefully, without risking strong unfavorable repercussions from the major powers. Also, there had been a steady upward trend in the world oil market, which gave the edge to demand over supply, and thus strengthened the position of the producers who controlled the supply to some extent. Despite the international companies' claim in 1959 that the world oil market was facing a glut, during the 1960s the world demand for oil almost tripled, and world oil imports increased from 9.03 million barrels per day in 1960 to 25.60 million barrels in 1970. Western Europe and the United States between them accounted for about 50 and 70 percent of these figures, respectively. Most of the rising demand was met from the resources of OPEC members, whose oil was produced at less than 50 percent of the production cost of United States oil. OPEC's total production rose from 7.89 million barrels per day in 1960 to 22.13 million barrels per day in 1970, and its exports increased from 7.50 to 21.05 million barrels per day. The Persian Gulf members of OPEC accounted for over 80 percent of the organization's production and exports. In the face of such growing demand for OPEC oil, and increasing Western dependence on it, the position of the producing nations as the owners of the sources of supply had been strengthened against the companies and the consumers. The short-lived Arab boycott in 1967 had demonstrated clearly to the producers that they could, if they wanted, influence the world market by exercising collectively their power over the sources of supply. Meanwhile, the position of the companies had been weakened by the fact that from the mid-1960s onward, when royalty payments were added to, rather than deducted from income tax payments to OPEC countries, the companies began to accumulate vast excess tax credits. "These details of tax-accounting procedure meant that the division of production profits, which in 1948 had been approximately 63:37 in the companies' favor, passed the 50:50 mark in 1955-56 and became approximately 70:30 in the governments' favor by 1970."[31]

These changes in the world political and economic situation, and the firm grasp of them by a number of OPEC countries with strong national leaders, led the member countries to coordinate their policies and activities to a greater degree than ever before. The result was the so-called "OPEC revolution" by the beginning of the seventies. OPEC's "Declaratory Statement of Petroleum Policy in Member Countries," adopted by the organization's sixteenth meeting in June 1968, embodied what amounts to the charter of this revolution. It clearly stated that it was time for the producing governments to exert themselves in order to increase their oil revenues according to the value of their oil in the international market, increase their control over their oil industries by expanding their participation and determining posted prices, and keep the companies under close surveillance to prevent being misled about their profits and general accounts. It emphasized that the governments should have the right to set reasonable standards of accounting and information, to formulate the conservation rules to be followed, to exercise full jurisdiction in their "competent national courts" in any dispute with the companies, and to invoke against the companies the rule of "the best of current practices" for such matters as incorporation, labor relations, royalties, taxes, and property rights.[32]

Iran played a major role in the formulation of the Declaratory Statement, from a position that empowered it to hold the balance between the two major factions that had developed within OPEC: the "moderates," led by Saudi Arabia, which, in many ways like Iran, wanted OPEC's objectives to be achieved through steady negotiation rather than confrontation with the companies; and "the radicals," led by Iraq, which pressed for swift collective action against the companies. Iran's continuous presence in OPEC was not only essential for the unity and collective bargaining strength of the organization, but also proved to be a balancing force in the subsequent dealings between OPEC and the companies. In maintaining this position, the Shah was at first content to call for negotiation with the companies. When the companies failed to acknowledge the existence of OPEC, let alone agree to negotiate its demands, he did not undertake immediately any direct radical action. Instead, amid uncertainty as to what alternative means were available, the Shah supported certain radical Arab producers, particularly Libya under the leadership of Muammar al-Qaddafi, in their radical actions against the companies. For example, between September 4 and October 9, 1970, Qaddafi ordered production cuts and the threat of shutdown against individual companies. He simultaneously raised the posted prices of Libyan oil by 30 cents per barrel, and increased the tax rate from 50 to 58 percent, retroactive to September 1.[33] The Shah's government not only refrained from undermining Qaddafi's efforts, but hailed his actions as "Libya's national right."[34] This was not done out of any admiration for Qaddafi's regime—the Shah and Qaddafi were ideological enemies then, as they remained in the following years.[35] His support was largely for reasons of political expediency.

Qaddafi's actions and achievements helped the Shah in three important ways. First, they saved the Shah from having to initiate pressure against the companies. While the companies were being pressured by Qaddafi, the Shah maintained Iran's strong and central position in oil politics without directly engaging with the companies and, as a result, avoided antagonizing the companies and the major consumers against Iran. Second, Libya's actions tested for the Shah the intensity of the companies' and Western reaction, and of the potential of radicalism for achieving Iran's goals. Third, they paved the way for the Shah to implement similar measures, justifying them by the precedent of what Libya or any other radical Arab member of OPEC had already achieved. The Shah noted that Qaddafi's radical measures succeeded, and the companies could not do anything but give in. Western reaction did not go beyond verbal condemnation of Qaddafi's behavior, and the Arabs, not Iranians, once again gained the reputation in the West of being unreasonable and xenophobic. In November, the Shah felt he had sufficient justification to act more forcefully in raising Iranian posted prices and the tax rate by as much as Qaddafi had done.[36]

This allowed Iran to participate in OPEC's twenty-first conference at Caracas, between December 9 to 12, from a position of strength and accomplishment at least equal with that of Libya. OPEC's Caracas Conference explicitly recalled its 1968 Declaratory Statement, and reiterated the member countries' determination to implement its provisions. It adopted its 120th Resolution of five principles, which called for: fixing 55 percent as the minimum net income tax rate that the companies would pay to the OPEC members; elimination of differences between the posted prices in effect, taking into consideration the geographical situation and the type of oil of the exporting country; adoption of a new policy for adjusting differences between the posted prices and the prices used as the basis for tax calculation; fixing a uniform total increase in the posted prices and the prices used as the basis for tax calculation; and complete abolition, effective from 1 January 1971, of the discounts granted to oil companies. The conference also instructed the Persian Gulf members of OPEC to start negotiating the implementation of this resolution with the companies.[37]

The Shah's government played a prominent role in composing the resolution, and fully supported implementation of the principles. Although Iran had already increased its crude posted prices and tax rate, the consortium companies had failed to accept them. Any longer delay in the implementation of this and other provisions of the 120th resolution might have had serious repercussions for the Shah's regime, which urgently needed extra revenue. By now the White Revolution reforms had generated new social groups with rising political and economic expectations. Since the Shah had failed to execute substantial political reforms along with his socio-economic reforms in the sixties, the country's political system could not cope with the growing demands made by the new groups. The most convenient way out of this was to increase the level of economic activities and business transactions so that the people in general, and new groups in particular, would be placated by financial gains from accelerating economic growth, and thus be diverted from their aspirations for expansion of political participation and political reforms.

Moreover, in the previous few years, the rapidly weakening position of sterling, which was followed by the American dollar in the early 1970s, and growing recessionary trends in the Western economy, had had an inflationary impact on the oil revenues of the producing states. The Shah complained that "during the past ten or twelve years the value of money paid to us for oil extracted in Iran had been reduced by about 28 percent."[38]

Following the Caracas Conference, the Shah found it timely to pursue a more direct and harder line against the companies. When he found the companies as intransigent as before, he tried to strengthen his and OPEC's position further by rallying the support of the less developed countries in general. For this, he identified the OPEC cause as common to that of the less developed countries as producers of other raw materials, and widened the scope of his criticism of the companies by attacking the West as a whole for promoting its interests and welfare at the cost of the "third world" countries. In a press conference, he complained that while the Western countries insisted on cheap oil and other raw materials from the less developed countries, they sold their own goods at increasingly high prices to these countries. He stressed, "perhaps it is time to have the prices of raw materials corresponding with the increased prices of industrial goods in the world. Is there a simpler quest? You [the West] buy from us at cheaper prices and sell us your goods at dearer prices; we become leaner every day, and you become fatter every day." And he warned, "Well, one day you are going to explode. There is no doubt about that." The Shah expressed his awareness that such "clear policies by Iran will make certain enemies"—perhaps the type of enemies that were invoked by Mossadeq's nationalization exactly twenty years previously.[39] But, unlike Mossadeq, the Shah was now ready and equipped to cope with such an eventuality.

By turning the issue from one between OPEC and the companies to one between the Western industrialized nations and the less developed countries, the Shah painted an image of himself as a forceful spokesman not only for OPEC, but for the third-world developing countries at large. This image became more identifiable in early 1971. In order to implement the 120th Resolution, Tehran seized upon an instruction of the Caracas Conference and hosted a meeting on January 12, 1971, between a three-member committee of oil ministers from Iran, Saudi Arabia, and Iraq, representing six Persian Gulf members of OPEC, on the one hand, and the Iranian oil consortium companies, which were later joined by twelve smaller companies, on the other. This was the first time that the companies had agreed to meet and open dialogue with OPEC as a collective organization. The meeting broke down the same day, largely because representatives of the companies disclaimed any authority to negotiate; they said that they were there simply to find out more about the 120th Resolution. But if nothing else, as the Iranian daily *Ettela'at* claimed "for the first time, the oil companies . . . accepted the existence of OPEC."[40] The Gulf committee called the refusal of the companies to negotiate "illogical and unjustified . . . [and] an attempt [on the part of the companies] to avoid facing justice and legitimate rights of the producing states." Moreover, it threatened the companies and called for an extraordinary conference by the ten OPEC members to be held in Tehran in order "to take appropriate decisions."[41]

The Shah blamed the companies for the breakdown of talks, and called their refusal to negotiate "unreasonable and provocative." When the talks resumed and broke down again, the companies informally consulted the U.S. State Department. Although they were told to settle their differences with OPEC through negotiation,[42] President Nixon dispatched his under-secretary of state to Tehran and Riyadh to assess the situation, and see if the United States could mediate in any way. The United States had mediated in 1954 in settling the dispute between Iran and Britain. That mediation had restored Western control of the Iranian oil industry and left the Shah's regime with a major problem in the subsequent years. When the companies now reportedly consulted the State Department, it must have alarmed the Shah. He immediately denounced the companies' approach, and warned the West against exerting any pressure in their support. He stressed that the companies' intransigent attitude and any Western support for it could cause not only a "crisis" but also an OPEC oil embargo against the West. He declared:

> it could become a crisis if the oil companies think that they could bluff us or they could put up such a pressure on us [word indistinct] that we are going to surrender. It would be a still more dangerous crisis if the big industrial countries in the world tried to back up the companies and defend their interests. That would be then a confrontation between what

we will call the economic imperialists or imperial powers, or the new aspects of the neo-colonialism which would create then a terrible crisis between these countries and either the oil-producing countries and the countries who are not yet fully developed. Then [anything] could happen. Not only the stoppage of the flow of oil but maybe a much more dangerous crisis. It would be a [word indistinct] of the have-nots against the haves and if this [started] one day it would be beyond at least my control.[43]

Meanwhile, the Shah made it absolutely clear that he would go beyond achieving the objectives of the Caracas Conference. He emphasized that Iran's ultimate objective was to achieve a status such that it could "act as seller and the companies or other organizations as purchaser."[44] Since the build-up of his regime's heavy dependence on the United States and alliance with the West, this was the first time that the Shah had warned the West against doing anything that could harm what he called "the national interests" of Iran. Furthermore, he made it clear that if necessary he would join in an OPEC oil embargo as an "economic weapon" against them. In view of his previous refusal to join an Arab boycott and his assurances to the West that Iran would continue to meet its oil needs without interruption, this indicated the extent to which the Shah was prepared to confront the companies and the Western consuming countries. Negotiations resumed once again on January 28, but broke down on February 2 despite the efforts of the Iranian oil minister, Jamshid Amuzegar. The major point of difference between the two sides was the companies' demand that OPEC assure them of an "uninterrupted flow of oil," and that it would not "restrict oil availability" to them in the face of threats.[45] OPEC, and especially its Arab members, was of course reluctant to give such an assurance. The Shah did nothing, at least publicly, either to undermine OPEC's reluctance or help the companies. If anything, his attitude hardened against the companies during the special OPEC conference held in Tehran from February 3 to 4, following the breakdown of negotiations.

At this conference, the Shah urged the Gulf producing governments to raise their tax rates and prices by conserted unilateral action, along the lines of legislation enacted by Venezuela in 1970. He proposed that the total receipts by the producer governments should be increased by about $1 to $1.25 per barrel. This was to be the actual amount of receipts, quite separate from the national posted price.[46] The Shah's proposals substantially influenced the terms of OPEC's Resolution 131. This resolution, in its most important parts, declared the decision of the conference that "every member country in the Persian Gulf region take appropriate measures on February 15 to implement the provisions of Resolution 120 of the twenty-first OPEC Conference and enact necessary legislation." Should any oil company fail to comply within seven days, the resolution added, all the member countries concerned "shall take appropriate measures including total embargo on the shipment of crude oil and petroleum products by such company."[47]

The resolution was endorsed unanimously by all member countries, both "radicals" and "moderates." In the light of the Shah's previous warnings, the threat of embargo was particularly significant in reflecting America's closest ally's determination to win the fight against the companies. It took many Western political and business quarters by surprise. The companies at last bowed to OPEC demands. Following a meeting between the Iranian oil minister, Amuzegar, and Lord Strathalmond, managing director of British Petroleum, in Paris, and three days' discussion between the two in Tehran, the companies concluded an agreement with the six Gulf members of OPEC on February 14. This provided for an immediate rise of 35 cents a barrel in posted prices at Gulf terminals to an average of $2.15; a standard 55 percent income tax; a new system of payment for gravity differentials; fixed increases for the following five years; and an undertaking by the governments concerned not to seek further improvements in the five-year period. The companies justified the agreement by stressing that it established "security of supply and stability in financial agreements for the . . . period, 1971-1975." It was, however, to yield the Gulf states concerned an estimated additional revenue of over $1,230 million in 1971, rising to about $3 billion in 1975. Of the figure for 1971, Iran's share amounted to about $800,200,000.[48] Iran's total oil revenue thus increased from $1,136 million in 1970 to $1,944 million in 1971, and kept up a similar pace of increase until November 1973, when it amounted to $4,100 million. In return, the companies were to adjust their prices upward by 2.5 percent from June 1, 1971, and thereafter every January 1 until 1975.[49]

The Tehran agreement was, indeed, historic in its implications. It marked a watershed not only in the relationship between OPEC member countries and the companies, but also in oil diplomacy and world politics as a whole. It set the stage for the oil-producing governments to increase their control over their respective oil industries, from production to pricing, according to their own interests in the next few years. From now on, the world, particularly the industrialized capitalist countries, had to concede the increasing power of the producing governments over that of the companies for their daily oil supplies and price stability. Moreover, the agreement underlined the growing effectiveness of OPEC as a bargaining cartel, and its use of "collective resource diplomacy," through which it could achieve what the producers had failed to achieve individually in the past. This encouraged many other less developed nations with nonoil raw material resources to follow OPEC's example, in order to exert themselves against what they saw as Western domination and exploitation of their resources, at the cost of their own national development. They regarded the Tehran agreement not only as an economic and political victory for OPEC, but also as a moral victory for themselves.[50] The Shah and his country held an important position in this victory. The Iranian government press hailed the agreement as a consequence of the Shah's relentless striving against the forces of domination in support of the less developed countries, which struggled to free themselves from such domination. Even some Arab oil ministers, after leaving Tehran, acknowledged the instrumental role played by the Shah in leading OPEC to victory.[51]

The Tehran agreement, however, by no means fulfilled the Shah's ultimate objective: to put into practice the 1951 nationalization. It took him another two years to secure a more solid basis for achieving this objective. During this period, the Shah's government indulged in no individual direct action against the companies. But it did a great deal, in conjunction with either OPEC or its other individual members, to adjust its oil revenue to world monetary changes, increase Iran's production, and further weaken the position of the companies. It supported Algeria's nationalization of 51 percent of French oil concessions on February 24, 1971, and endorsed the Venezuelan Hydrocarbons Revision Law, July 13, 1971, which required the companies "to cede . . . their unexploited concession areas by 1974" and "all

their residual assets" by 1983.[52] Iran joined **OPEC** in protecting
Iraq in its decision to nationalize the Iraq Petroleum Company's
concession (Kirkuk area), June 1, 1972, after an eleven-year dispute between the Iraqi government and the British-operated
company, and supported OPEC's Resolution 146 at the Twenty-
Eighth Conference to this effect, in order to prevent the companies from compensating for their losses in Iraq by increasing their
production elsewhere.[53] Moreover, in the context of the worsening monetary situation in the West and the devaluation of the
American dollar, Tehran advocated that because of the fluctuations in the world monetary situation **OPEC** should press the
companies to index to monetary changes their revenues paid to
producing governments. OPEC passed two important resolutions
to this effect at its twenty-fourth and twenty-fifth conferences.
It reached one agreement with the companies in Geneva, January
20, 1972, to increase posted prices by 8.94 percent to offset the
decline in the value of the U.S. dollar; and another agreement on
April 1, 1972, for an increase of 7.5 percent in the posted prices.[54]
These were, in effect, two amendments to the Tehran Agreement, under which the producing governments had agreed not to
ask for further price rises until 1975.

Meanwhile, the companies had been pressed hard by the Gulf
members of **OPEC** to meet another demand of the Caracas Conference: the expansion of the producing states' participation in
their oil industries. As a result, a participation agreement between the companies and Gulf states, excluding Iran, was final-
ized on November 6, 1972. This agreement provided for 25 percent government participation from January 1, 1973, rising to
51 percent by January 1, 1982.[55] The Shah fully supported other
Gulf states in this, but conducted separate negotiations with the
companies, on the grounds that Iran had already nationalized its
oil industry and did not need such a participation agreement.
In order to justify such a move, the Shah drew on the 1954
agreement itself and announced, on January 23, 1973, that one
of the terms of the 1954 agreement with the consortium was that
the operating companies would protect Iran's interests in the best
possible way, but that "we have evidence that this has not been
the case." Therefore, although the agreement provided for three
extension periods, each of five years, "we have ample grounds . . .
for not renewing the agreement with the Consortium in 1979,"
when it was due to run out.[56] He proposed two courses of action.

One was, as he said, to let the companies continue their operation up to 1979, provided that Iran's oil export capacity was increased to 8 million barrels and the country's earning per barrel was no less than those earned by other regional producers. After 1979, the consortium companies had to join other customers in "a long queue to buy Iran's oil . . . without any privileges over the other companies." The other was to sign a new contract with the consortium companies, whereby they would return to Iran all the policy-making and operational responsibilities that were not yet in Iran's hands. "The present operating companies could then become our long-term customers and we would sell them oil over a long term, in consideration for which we would give them good prices and the kind of discounts which are always given to a good customer."[57] In this, the Shah made it plain that he wanted the second alternative to be implemented, within the framework of his regime's close political, economic, and military links and alliance with the West. The major problem with implementing the second proposal, however, was the fact that Iran lacked sufficient technical know-how and trained manpower to operate the Iranian oil industry on its own. For this, the Shah proposed that Iran would still seek help from the consortium companies. When faced with the choice, there is no doubt that the second proposal was also the more attractive of the two to the companies. While freeing them from the responsibilities and hazards of domestic operations, the proposal assured them of not only continued oil supply for the next twenty to twenty-five years at favorable terms as Iran's "privileged customers," but also an important stake in the operation of the Iranian oil industry through their technical help. Moreover, the companies could still market a major proportion of Iranian oil at retail prices that benefited them.

Senior oil company officials discussed the Shah's proposals with him directly in St. Moritz, Switzerland, on February 26, and it was disclosed that a "satisfactory understanding" had been reached between the two sides. However, on March 16, the Shah announced that the oil companies had "totally surrendered," and had agreed to hand over "full control" of oil operations. He declared: "They have handed over to us total and real operation of the oil industry . . . with ownership of all installations." Furthermore, on March 20, the Shah announced that the Iranian takeover would take effect on the same day, and that both the installations—production and refining facilities—and the 17,827 employees of the consortium would be controlled by the National Iranian Oil Company.[58] Thus the "St. Moritz Agreement," replacing the 1954 Agreement, was concluded between Iran and the consortium companies. In view of the Shah's pronouncements, at first it appeared that the terms of the new agreement would be very different from those the Shah had outlined in his second proposal. It subsequently became clear, however, that the St. Moritz Agreement was formulated very much in line with that proposal, except that it came into force six years before the expiration of the 1954 Agreement in 1979.

The St. Moritz Agreement was to be valid for twenty years. Under this agreement, while the NIOC was entrusted with all the policy-making and management responsibilities, and the "control of all oil operations" and installations, including the Abadan and Mahshahr refineries and all related establishments, the former consortium companies were turned into Iran's long-term and privileged customers, with an important stake in running the country's oil industry because of their expertise. Upon submitting the agreement to the Majlis on July 19, 1973, however, Prime Minister Hoveida stressed that the NIOC would need the companies' expertise only for that part of the oil operation related "to exploration and exploitation." The companies' services would be contracted according to the laws of Iran, and would "be utilized temporarily for a period of five years." Moreover, he emphasized that under the agreement arbitration of any dispute with a contractor company would be based on Iranian laws, and the agreement's provisions "will be interpreted in accordance with the laws of Iran." Iranian oil would be sold to the companies at prices "no less than those earned by the Persian Gulf states." He characterized Iran's relationship with the companies, under the new agreement, as one between "seller and buyer." He hailed the agreement as an "historic document," implementing the Nationalization Act of 1951 "in its fullest sense after a lapse of twenty-three years, thus realizing our long-cherished national objective."[59]

The agreement did not pacify the Shah's critics, however, who branded it as yet another manifestation of the Shah's collusion with the West. A Tudeh party commentator in exile stated that although the companies were weakened in international politics and could no longer impose their will, the Shah's government, "as a result of behind-the-scenes deals," made them "privileged, long-term" purchasers of "our crude oil." This enabled them to hold on to their monopoly of the sale of a major part of Iran's oil "against the interests of the Iranian people" and contrary to "the spirit of the oil nationalization law (1951)." It recommended that "Iran should be free to sell its oil in world markets in any way that would secure its interests to the utmost."[60] In spite of all its encouragement and support for Iran and OPEC against the international companies, Moscow also criticized the new agreement. In a commentary, it pointed out that under the terms of the agreement Iran was not only committed to a long-term oil sale to the consortium companies, but also "Iran gets only four per cent of the oil production for its internal needs and for independent export. This share will only increase gradually, which means that the Consortium will, as before, retain the (increasing) role of middle-man between Iran and the oil buyers of the market of the capitalist world. As before, the member monopolies of the International Consortium will export large quantities of crude oil from Iran and sell these at a huge profit."[61]

Although the critics were partially justified at the time, the new agreement was a great improvement over the one concluded in 1954. But it clearly reflected the two facts that Iran still did not have the necessary capability to run its oil industry and market its oil on its own, and that Tehran was still deeply committed to close links and alliance with the West. One thing that the new agreement specifically failed to achieve was to entrust Tehran with the power to fix the price of its oil unilaterally according to its own interests, and curb the excessive profit made by the companies at the cost of Iran and consumers. This formed the Shah's next major oil objective: to put into effect what subsequently became known as OPEC "oil-price politics." This essentially aimed at empowering the producing governments to fix the posted prices on their own with reference to their own interests and their perception of the changing world economic and oil market situation, and, conversely, to influence the world market situation, should the producing governments' interests necessitate it.

After the conclusion of the St. Moritz Agreement, the Shah's government increased its complaints about the lack of correlation between oil prices and the world inflation, which had continuously devalued Iran's real oil income since the Tehran Agreement. It also pointed to the growing discrepancy between the prices of oil and other energy resources in terms of the former's high quality and capacity to produce hundreds of important by-products, particularly petrochemicals, and the companies' bias in influencing the oil prices on the basis not of the real value of oil in the world market, but of their own profits. Tehran prompted OPEC to consider this matter urgently, launching a vigorous campaign, and supporting any statement or action by other OPEC members. In a communique on July 27, 1973, OPEC declared that member countries not only should obtain an adequate price for their oil, but should also negotiate with a view to attaining conditions that would foster permanent and diversified sources of income within their territories. At its thirty-fifth conference, in Vienna on September 15-16, OPEC agreed that the six Gulf states should negotiate either collectively or individually to obtain substantial price increases, in view of the fact that the existing posted prices and annual increases were "no longer compatible with prevailing market conditions as well as galloping world inflation."[62]

Meanwhile, taking advantage of its increased control over Iran's oil industry, NIOC followed the example of a number of non-Persian Gulf OPEC members, and offered some of its surplus oil to international bidding. Given the world panic about a prospective energy shortage, and the heavy dependence of Japan on the Persian Gulf in general and Iran in particular, Japanese companies offered the highest bids for Iranian oil: $17.80 a barrel. This showed the value of Iranian oil in the world market, though the price was artificially enhanced by the prevailing circumstances. It provided the Shah's government, along with other Persian Gulf producers, with a solid base for bargaining against the companies in the forthcoming negotiations over the implementation of the thirty-fifth OPEC Conference's resolution. Although the companies at first resisted any further price increase, and regarded it as violation of the Tehran Agreement, they finally opened negotiations with six Persian Gulf members of OPEC on October 8. The Gulf states' position, according to press reports, was that posted prices for the Gulf states should be increased from the current average level of about $3 per barrel to $4.20.[63] The companies were reluctant to accept such a price, and when the fourth Arab-Israeli War broke out on October 6 and Iraq nationalized U.S. interests in the Basrah Petroleum Company, talks between the two sides broke down on October 12.

This breakdown marked the beginning of a period in oil politics during which the Shah skillfully took advantage of the Middle East war and its consequences to lead OPEC in asserting the sovereignty of producers over price fixing, and taking away any power that the companies exercised in this respect once and for all.

The use of oil as a political weapon by Arab producers in a forthcoming Arab-Israeli war had been in the cards for some time. President Sadat of Egypt had hinted strongly at such a possibility as early as April 1973.[64] This had subsequently added to growing speculation by the press and certain political and economic quarters in the West about a possible Arab embargo, and the question of whether the West could cope with it effectively.[65] The Iranian official reaction to all this was, however, cautious silence. The Shah's government issued no specific statement clarifying its position on a possible Arab embargo. In light of the Shah's refusal to participate in the Arab boycott in 1967 and his repeated disapproval of the use of oil for political purposes, as well as his strong assurances to the West and Japan of continued Iranian oil supply, the silence seemed not very important. It could have been safely assumed that Iran would not take part in any future Arab embargo measures. But if the silence was considered in view of the dramatic improvement of relations between Tehran and Cairo since the two sides reestablished diplomatic ties in 1970, and in view of Tehran's growing friendship and cooperation, at least at OPEC level, with other Arab states except Iraq, it can be seen that it benefited Tehran to remain silent. On the one hand, silence helped Tehran maintain its cooperative relations with the Arab states; on the other, it made the West uncertain as to what Iran's decision would be in case of an Arab embargo. There were no solid grounds for the Western consumers or Japan to assume that Iran would not respond favorably to Arab embargo measures. This gave Tehran the benefit of the doubt, which strengthened its position further against the companies. Tehran maintained its silence right up to the outbreak of the fourth Arab-Israeli war.

The war broke out on October 6, 1973. In order to retaliate against Western, particularly U.S., support for Israel, Iraq and Libya nationalized certain U.S. oil interests in their respective oil industries. Moreover, King Faisal of Saudi Arabia, a close ally of the West, had warned that Arabs might use their oil in concerted actions against the West.[66] Certain joint Arab embargo measures now seemed inevitable. At this point, however, the Shah's government reiterated its past policy of noninvolvement in the Middle East conflict, giving two reasons: Iran was a non-Arab state, though a Muslim country; and Iran did not believe in the use of oil as a "political weapon." But this time Tehran was very careful not to condemn the use of oil as a political weapon, nor to question its effectiveness in the context of the Middle East conflict. On the contrary, Tehran assured the Arabs that it would do nothing that could undermine their embargo measures.[67] Subsequently, Tehran refrained from increasing its production by an amount sufficient to offset the embargo's effect.

This dual approach enabled Tehran once again to maintain, at least on the surface, a balanced and central position between the West and the Arabs. Taking advantage of this position and the growing world panic about an energy crisis, as well as the Western world's preoccupation with the Middle East war itself, the Shah took the lead in urging other Persian Gulf members of OPEC to take unilateral actions to implement OPEC's thirty-fifth Conference resolution, even though talks between Gulf producers and companies on this subject had broken down at the start of the war. The Iranian delegation put the Shah's proposal to OPEC at its conference in Vienna on October 12, and received their unanimous approval.[68]

On October 16, one day before the Organization of Arab Petroleum Exporting Countries (OAPEC) announced its decision that the Arab producers would cut their production by 5 percent monthly until Israeli forces withdrew from the Arab territories they occupied during the 1967 war, the six Persian Gulf producers, led by Iran, unilaterally announced a 70 percent increase in the posted prices of their crude.[69] The increase in the posted prices was approximately $2 per barrel (from about $3 to $5), with an effective increase in payments by the oil companies to the producing governments of about $1.25 per barrel (from approximately $1.75 to $3).[70] In effect, the producing governments' share of the posted prices increased from the 40 percent agreed in Tehran in February 1971, to 60 percent. In the case of Iran, the government raised its posted prices to $5.09 per barrel, from which its share was to be $3.05 per barrel. The Iranian oil minister, Amuzegar argued, however, that since the posted prices no longer affected the actual market price of oil in the Persian Gulf, the increase in the latter amounted to only about 17 percent. Either way, in real terms government income increased by about 70 percent per barrel. This virtually nullified the formula endorsed by the Tehran Agreement, which had been modified twice, in January and June 1972. Meanwhile, Amuzegar warned the companies that if they, either individually or in a group, refused to transport Persian Gulf oil on the basis of the new prices, then the Gulf producers "would be unanimously prepared to offer their oil," at the new prices, "to any customers who want to buy." Amuzegar stressed that the Persian Gulf price increase, in which Iran played the leading role, must not be associated with the embargo measures adopted by OAPEC on October 17, and thus Iran must not be implicated in the Arab embargo actions.[71]

One cannot overlook the importance of Iran's actions in relation to the Arab embargo, however. There are several reasons to suggest that in many ways Iran helped and participated, at least indirectly, in the Arab embargo. It must be remembered that the Arab producing states of the Persian Gulf, which Iran led in the move for the price increase, were members of OPEC and OAPEC at the same time. Exactly one day after they had unanimously approved the Shah's proposal for a unilateral price increase, they endorsed a 70 percent increase in OAPEC oil prices, and committed themselves to OAPEC's embargo measures, which consisted of 5 percent monthly production cuts and, subsequently, a total oil embargo against the U.S. and the Netherlands. Moreover, the Iranian-led Persian Gulf price increase was decided on at an OPEC meeting held at the same time and place (Kuwait) as OAPEC's meeting to formulate its embargo. There is no doubt that the embargo measures were entirely decided by OAPEC, but the leadership for the price increase was initially provided by Iran, which had a fair knowledge of what OAPEC was about to decide the next day. In view of this, and of the fact that the Shah stood by his assurance to Arab producers that Iran would do nothing to undermine their embargo measures, Iran cannot be totally divorced from the Arab actions and their consequences. At the time, Iran's role was disguised by its public disassociation from Arab embargo measures, and reassurance to the West and Japan of an uninterrupted oil supply from Iran. Its role was also overshadowed by the world's preoccupation with the Middle East and Arab producers' militancy, and so received little publicity and analysis in the West.

Once OAPEC's embargo measures took effect, however, the oil shortage in the world market became very acute, and the West and Japan were forced to value Iran more than ever before as their only major OPEC supplier. The prevailing circumstances thus shifted once more to favor the Shah's policy of price increase and price control. In the next meeting of OPEC, in Vienna on December 20, the Iranian delegation, speaking on behalf of the producers, recommended "that oil be priced at $12 to $15 a barrel."[72] Although this was sharply criticized by the companies and the American government,[73] the oil ministers of six Gulf member countries decided at another OPEC meeting held in Tehran from December 22 to 23 to set the "take" of the "host" or producing governments at $7 per barrel of Arabian light 34-degree API (the standard quality), as against about $3, which had been fixed in accordance with the October price increase. This meant that for such oil the posted prices would be increased from January 1, 1974, to $11.65 per barrel, from the level of about $5.11 in force since November 1, 1973. Moreover, OPEC announced that it would hold an extraordinary conference on January 7, 1974, to discuss the basis for a long-term pricing system, replacing the posted prices mechanism, and to "review the possibility of establishing a dialogue between oil-producing and oil-consuming countries in order to avoid entering into a spiral increase in prices and to protect the real value of [its member countries'] oil." It also stressed that since "the government take of $7 per barrel is moderate," the consuming countries should refrain from further increases in their export prices.[74]

In a press conference in late December, the Shah hailed the price increase as a great success in establishing the producers' sovereignty over oil pricing, and eliminating the companies' influence in this respect once and for all. He also spelled out for the first time in a detailed and coherent fashion his regime's objectives in pressing for such rapid price increases. First, despite the price increases in 1971 and 1972, the Shah said that the producing states did not earn as much as their oil was valued at in the world market, and the producers' price increases were not keeping up with the galloping global inflation. Second, oil was undervalued in relation to other available sources of energy, particularly coal. Third, oil was "too precious" to be just burned away. It should be used more efficiently from now on, because no other sources of energy produced hundreds of important byproducts, especially petrochemicals, which one day could substitute for oil itself as a source of both capital formation and industrial development. Fourth, oil was a nonreplenishable commodity, which in the case of Iran would run out by the end of this century. Before it ran out, the Shah stressed that there was a definite need for Iran to diversify its process of economic development so as not to be entirely dependent on oil. For this, Iran needed to use its oil with great care, so that the country could extract enough capital out of it over as long a period as possible, in order to create other bases for its economic development and other sources of energy, such as atomic stations. Fifth, despite the expansion of the producing states' control over their respective oil industries in the last few years, the companies still influenced the pricing of oil and, as a result, made excessive profits at the cost of producing and consuming countries. One important consideration that the Shah failed to list was the high cost of his military program, which he saw as necessary for the emergence of Iran as an oil-producing and regional power.

The Shah also stressed that the $7 "take" per barrel was not going to be final. He described it as "a commercial price," which would be subjected to periodic reviews. "It is almost a price that we [OPEC] have fixed out of kindness and generosity for you [the West]." He hoped that the "real price" of oil would be fixed in consultation with the OECD countries, "so that we could see what the real value of other sources of energy are and what the prices of oil should be in view of its preferential advantage over other sources of energy. Then the price of oil would be tied to world inflation." The Shah noted with pleasure that the companies, in their relationships with Iran, had effectively become nothing "more than simple buyers." "The last thing in their hand was the price mechanism and that also we have wrested from them. It is now we who govern the oil prices." He wished that OPEC's decision concerning $7 as "take" or "base" price would lead to replacement of the posted price mechanism, which he described as complicated, unnatural, fictitious, by a more defendable and equitable pricing system. He said that from now on the producer would take its share of $7 per barrel, no matter how much profit the companies made out of customers; controlling the companies' profit was the responsibility of the consuming governments.

The Shah warned that the industrialized capitalist countries

"will have to realize that the era of their terrific progress and
even more terrific income and wealth based on cheap oil is fin-
ished, they will have to find new sources of energy. Eventually
they will have to tighten their belts." However the Shah was very
careful neither to undermine his policy of accommodation and
alliance with the West, nor alienate the support of many less
developed nations. He was fully conscious of the fact that his
regime was deeply committed to the West and that Iran's progress
had become tied to the capitalist world and depended on its
continuous prosperity and well-being. Therefore the Shah sought
to separate his hard-line oil diplomacy against the West from
Iran's overall special relationship with the West. He declared,

> We do not want to hurt the industrial [capitalist] world at
> all, not only because we are going to be one of them our-
> selves . . . soon, but what good will it bring anybody if the
> present known industrial world and its civilization is crushed
> and terminated? If the present world has deficiencies they
> could be remedied, gradually, wisely. But if it is destroyed
> what solution do we have? And what is the interest of mak-
> ing the poor countries even poorer and only a few countries
> getting all the money in the banks? If the world economy
> crumbles down the value of these paper monies will not be
> more than the sheet of paper on which they are printed.[75]

Although the Shah stressed that Iran needed most of its oil
revenues, which increased from about $4 billion in 1973 to over
$17 billion in 1974,[76] for its own development, he undertook that
Iran would help the capitalist countries in any way possible to
sustain their economic progress (though perhaps not at the past
rate), and offset any deficit in their balance of payments caused
by spiraling oil prices. He subsequently proposed that the capitalist industrial nations could pay for oil partly in cash and partly
in some sort of bonds, which would in effect permit them to buy
now and pay later. He also showed keen interest in some kind of
barter trade with the industrial countries, whereby these countries could exchange their capital goods, military arsenals, and
know-how for a secure Iranian oil supply.[77]

The Shah now once again found it timely to break his non-
committal attitude toward the Arab embargo measures, and call
on Arab producers to end their measures against the West. He
stressed that although the Arabs "played a good game with the

oil card during the [Middle East] war," the continuation of this game during peacetime would be "very dangerous."[78] He therefore urged them to stop their "game," which had immensely helped the Shah in fulfilling his oil objectives, but was no longer in the interest of Iran. During 1974, Tehran not only refrained from pressing for further substantial increases in oil prices, but also urged intensive cooperation between the oil-consuming and oil-producing countries. To this end, Tehran supported President Nixon's call, in January 1974, for a dialogue between consuming and producing countries, promised financial help to the West for developing alternative sources of energy, agreed with the U.S. call for a worldwide campaign against energy waste. Most importantly, Iran concluded a number of bilateral multi-million-dollar oil and trade agreements with the United States, Britain, France, Japan, West Germany, and many other West European countries, though not at the cost of Iran's growing commercial ties with the Soviet Union and other communist countries.[79] Meanwhile, Tehran made it clear that from now on it would not cave in to any Western pressure against maximizing Iran's benefit from its resources. For example, Tehran firmly rejected two suggestions by U.S. Treasury Secretary George Schultz and President Ford in January and October 1974, respectively, that Iran, along with other OPEC members, should reduce its oil prices by about 50 percent so that the world economy could avoid a major dislocation.[80] While President Nixon was organizing a consuming countries' conference to consider the "energy crisis" and adopt a unified position in a forthcoming dialogue with producing countries in early 1974, the Shah personally warned Washington against organizing a "consumers cartel."[81] The Shah also strongly condemned Kissinger's hint, on January 13, 1975, of possible military action against oil-producing countries in case they pressured the capitalist world to the point of "actual strangulation." The Shah warned that he would do everything in his power to resist such an action against any oil producer whatever.[82]

With regard to the less developed countries, which had supported OPEC at first, but by 1974 had begun to express their unhappiness over OPEC's reluctance to give them oil at discount prices and support them financially,[83] the Shah made several proposals to help. He urged the oil-producing states, particularly those with large surpluses (Saudi Arabia, Kuwait, and Libya, which had smaller populations than Iran) to aid the less developed countries either through bilateral agreements or through regional and international organizations. One idea that attracted the Shah was for oil-producing states to "create some kind of international bank or fund . . . and put this at the disposal of an international body which is going to finance all the wise projects that could be carried out in . . . developing countries." He also recommended that the oil producers should invest directly in the developing countries to benefit those countries, and to "keep inflation away" from their own countries—inflation as a result of surplus revenues.[84] Tehran subsequently claimed that it had devoted 6 percent of Iran's GNP to aiding the less developed countries in 1974-1975. The major recipients were listed as Pakistan, India, Egypt, Jordan, Turkey, and Afghanistan. The extent to which Tehran was influenced by political and strategic considerations in extending aid to these countries, and to what extent it fulfilled its initial undertakings, will be discussed in Part II.

* * *

It took the Shah's regime more than twenty years to achieve Iranian ownership and control of Iran's potential as an oil power. The regime's progress in this respect corresponded with its emergence from a position of heavy dependence on the United States and international oil companies in the 1950s to a position from which it could conduct its domestic and foreign affairs with more flexibility, but in convergence with the interests of the West, in the second half of the 1960s. The major factor in helping the regime to achieve this stature was the Shah's White Revolution, which aimed at mobilizing the masses and centralizing political power in support of the Shah's rule. The White Revolution created a degree of economic and political stability in Iran that strengthened the Shah's hand in the conduct of Iran's foreign relations. The Shah's regime was thus relatively successful in developing friendly and cooperative relations with all its regional neighbors except Iraq. But in both this and its drive to maximize Iran's benefits from its oil resources, the regime was immensely aided by the changes in regional and international situations, including the formation and activation of OPEC as an effective cartel, and the two Middle East wars of 1967 and 1973 and their consequences, which the regime skillfully exploited in order to achieve its own oil policy objectives.

The realization of Iran's oil potential in the interests of the country brought the Shah's regime not only enormous and unprecedented wealth, but also diplomatic strength, with increasing influence in regional and world politics. It could not escape the fact that it was deeply committed to the West, however, and it could act only within the limits set by this commitment. Its new power nevertheless gave the regime strong leverage in its relationship with the outside world, particularly the West, which suddenly found itself more dependent than ever before on Iranian oil and, for that matter, on Iranian oil money under the control of the Shah's regime. The capitalist countries, more than any others, found it necessary to acknowledge the influential position of the Shah's regime, and set out to win its favor in whatever way possible in order to recycle to the West the money that had been transferred to Iran as a result of the oil price increases. The Shah, in turn, demanded increasing help from the West in achieving his broader goal of transforming Iran into a capitalist-oriented self-generating economic and military power before the country's exportable oil ran out.

PART TWO

The Emergence of Iran
as a Regional Power

THE PERSIAN GULF

INTRODUCTION

THE IRANIAN OIL achievements in the early 1970s greatly enhanced the country's emerging position as a regional power with global influence. The expansion of Iran's control over its oil industry and the unprecedented increases in the country's oil revenue provided the Shah with a viable, oil-based source of capital and the diplomatic power he needed to engage in intense "resources diplomacy." Hence, he could accelerate his drive to achieve his ultimate national goal: *Tamaddon-e Bozorg* (Great Civilization). This goal involved not only the building of a "just," "democratic," and "prosperous" Iran, but also the development of the country into a mighty, self-sufficient, and self-generating "economic and military power" capable of guarding its own region against what the Shah perceived to be regional subversion and instability as well as against outside powers' "hostile" and "hegemonial" interference.[1] He considered this to be a prelude to the emergence of Iran as a global power in its own right, before the end of this century. Although the Shah had sought to strengthen the Iranian economy and military capability systematically as part of his White Revolution since the early 1960s, in the 1970s, with the start of his new oil achievements, he greatly magnified the scope and intensity of his efforts for this purpose.

In building Iran's regional paramountcy, the Shah seemed to have been pursuing a pattern of regional behavior with two persistent and intertwined but conflicting aspects. On the one hand, he worked for regional political and economic cooperation. On the other, he was determined to prevent and uproot any force or development, whether it was inspired locally or externally—particularly by the Soviet Union and its regional clients—that he considered to be subversive and disruptive to the Iranian regional role, interests, and security. In line with these goals, the Shah seems to have sought to achieve two major objectives: to secure a regional market, fields of investment, and sources of raw materials, which were vital for the development of Iran's economic power; and concurrently, to modify, strengthen, and preserve the existing regional situation in favor of Iran without causing any major regional upsurge against Iran while the country was undergoing intense economic industrialization and militarization. However, he was trying to achieve his vision of Iran as the leading power within a region that, because of its sociological, political, and economic makeup, as well as its strategic location and significance to the outside world, was one of the world's richest but most volatile and unpredictable regions, and his very search for paramountcy was likely to destabilize its politics.

This second part of the book does not aim to provide a comprehensive description and analysis of all the issues concerning the emergence of Iran as a regional power nor does it enter the controversy surrounding the conceptual question: what is a regional power? The power and region of any state have to be understood in relation to its concrete situation, rather than on the bases of broad definitions and theoretical criteria, and every state that is recognized or claims to be recognized as a regional power provides its own case.[2] Thus I shall look at the Iranian case largely on its own, focusing mainly on certain issues: first, the Shah's vision toward which he was striving, what he perceived to be Iran's status within the Iranian region, and the factors influencing him in this vision; second, the Iranian resources capability and the economic and military measures undertaken by the Shah to realize his vision; third, the Iranian pattern of regional behavior while the Shah was engaged in pursuing his vision; and, fourth, the repercussions of his policies in his bid for regional paramountcy.

CHAPTER V

The Shah's Vision

THE SHAH'S VIEWS concerning the status of Iran as *qodrat-e mentaqe'i* or regional power were complex, if not altogether original. They were based on his own beliefs, experiences, desires, expectations, interpretation of Iranian history, and perception of Iranian needs for stability and security in a changing and insecure world. He expressed his views in small fragments that have little coherence or consistency, which makes the task of systematically outlining and analyzing his views quite difficult. However, it is reasonably clear that by "regional power" the Shah meant the transformation of Iran into a strong, prosperous, and stable monarchical state with the ability to fulfil two major functions: to guard and influence its region according to its own political and economic interests, and to regulate and conduct its relations, particularly with its neighbors, from a position of strength. The Shah considered this, together with the simultaneous development of what he called "political, economic, and social democracy" inside Iran, to be essential if his absolute dynastic monarchy was to remain pivotal to the operation of Iranian politics, and if Iran was to preserve and develop itself effectively, and conduct an "independent national foreign policy" with maximum regional security and stability.[1]

He claimed that by achieving this, Iran would reach the frontiers of what he called *Tamaddon-e Bozorg* (Great Civilization), his ultimate goal. Although he was never very clear about what *Tamaddon-e Bozorg* would be in its achieved form, or when it would be realized, his fragmentary remarks provide some clues. It seemed that *Tamaddon-e Bozorg*, if accomplished, would have meant that Iran had become a prosperous industrialized and welfare state, and a formidable world economic and military power in its own right; it would have achieved greater economic and conventional military strength than that deployed by Britain and France.[2] In the late 1960s, the Shah set the early 1980s as the probable date for achieving this goal, but a decade later, he spoke about the end of the century.[3]

The emergence of Iran as a regional power had to precede the country's success in achieving world power, however. The Shah believed that Iran's status as a regional power had to be based mainly on his own firm national leadership, the Iranian oil potential, and economic and military power.[4] To him, it seemed necessary to strengthen the civilian and military sectors of national life simultaneously, under the direction of a strong and resolute leadership: the developing civilian sector provided technology, know-how, expertise, and economic infrastructure, on the one hand, and the military sector safeguarded the Iranian oil potential, the backbone of Iran's national development, against disorder, subversion, and aggression, on the other.[5] It was largely due to the weakness of Iran in these respects that during the first decade of the Shah's rule the country had a low regional standing and credibility, and was vulnerable to regional pressures, particularly from the Soviet Union and "radical" Arab forces. By becoming heavily dependent on the United States, the Shah had successfully launched his White Revolution and progressively built his domestic resources in the context of a changing regional and international situation. By the late 1960s, as a result, Iran was reasonably strong both domestically and regionally, though it had neither obtained full control over its oil, nor become assertive in its "region." Before discussing the Shah's endeavors to exploit the new Iranian oil gains to enhance the country's regional position, we must consider what regional factors prompted the Shah to build the Iranian resources for regional paramountcy, and what he considered to be the Iranian region. These questions can be examined in relation to three major areas: the Soviet Union, the Persian Gulf, and Iran's eastern flank—the Indian subcontinent and the Indian Ocean.

The Soviet Union

The Shah was always distrustful of Moscow's intentions toward his country. This was partly because of his anticommunist convictions and his belief that his type of monarchy was the right form of regime for Iran, but was largely based on historical reasons. He constantly reminded the Iranians and the world that the Soviets not only forcibly occupied the Iranian northern provinces in the 1920s and 1940s, but also actively aided the outlawed Iranian Communist party (Tudeh) and other hostile groups against his regime whenever it had the opportunity. He claimed that although Iranian-Soviet relations had improved considerably, largely because of Iran's growing domestic strength and regional importance, Moscow was still pursuing a "backdoor" policy with the aim of weakening his regime by helping regional dissension, furthering regional tensions, and supporting hostile governments and groups against it.[6] As evidence, the Shah could cite Soviet support for the radical Arab Ba'th government of Hasan al-Bakr in Iraq, with which Iran had longstanding political and border disputes, and the Arab nationalist revolutionary groups in the Persian Gulf, of which the Shah regarded the Popular Front for the Liberation of the Arabian Gulf (after 1974, the Popular Front for the Liberation of Oman) as most threatening to Iran. Moscow also supported the Marxist government of the Peoples Democratic Republic of Yemen, which advocated and helped revolutionary actions contrary to the Iranian interests in the Gulf; the Popular Front for the Liberation of Iranian and Pakistani Baluchistan; and the Afghani and Indian governments in their territorial disputes with Iran's regional CENTO ally, Pakistan, whose possible further dismemberment (after the creation of Bangladesh in 1971) the Shah saw as detrimental to the security of Iran, and therefore intolerable.[7]

The Persian Gulf

The Shah came progressively to regard the Gulf as both vital and troublesome to Iran, for several reasons. The waterway provides Iran with its only strategic outlet to international waters and the outside world; it is through this outlet that over 90 percent of Iranian oil export and about 60 percent of the country's nonoil trade are handled. Moreover, the Gulf's bed holds sizable mineral resources, of which Iran, like any other littoral state, is eager to have a reasonable share. But the Gulf is also of great economic importance to the outside world. Although Iran holds the world's fourth biggest reserves (about 60 billion barrels), after Saudi Arabia, the USSR, and Kuwait, the other Gulf states—all Arab nations—hold about 50 percent of the world's proven oil reserves, and produce about 30 percent of the world's present oil consumption.[8] This economic significance is complemented by the strategic importance of the Gulf because of its central location between the Mediterranean and Indian Ocean, and between central Western Asia and the Horn of Africa. It is no wonder that the Shah referred to the Gulf as the "jugular vein" of Iran.[9] The major powers have competed for political and economic influence in the region, especially since World War II, though it was largely under the British protectorate until 1971. The stability of the area has meanwhile been undermined by serious internal tensions and conflicts. This has been partly because of outside infiltration and interference, but largely due to a number of differences within and between the political units of the Gulf region.

The population of the region is divided into two main groups: the Persians, with a majority in the Gulf's most populous state, Iran; and the Arabs, who predominate in the rest of the Gulf states. The two groups are distinct from one another on ethnic, cultural, historical, and even religious bases. Each has claimed primacy over the other whenever it has felt threatened by each other's dominance.[10] This has been complicated by long-standing political disputes as well as territorial claims and counterclaims. In the past, the most outstanding disputes between the two sides concerned the island of Bahrain, an Arab emirate with a Persian minority; and the strategically important Shatt al-Arab waterway between Iran and Iraq. Tehran claimed Bahrain as part of its territory after Britain extended its protectorate over the island about one and a half centuries ago.[11] Tehran also rejected the traditional Iraqi claim of sovereignty over Shatt al-Arab, demanding that the waterway should be controlled jointly by Iran and Iraq on an equal basis.[12] The first dispute constrained Iran's relations with most of the Arab world. The second dispute, in conjunction with other border and ideological disputes continuously strained Iranian-Iraqi relations.

In turn, the Arabs' claims and counterclaims included their support for the secession of the Iranian southern province of Khuzistan (as "Arabistan"), which was once ruled by an Arab family and has a sizable Arab population; the Iraqi policy of aiding and sheltering many anti-Shah groups and movements, including the Tudeh and the Popular Fronts for the Liberation of "Arabistan" and Baluchistan;[13] and the Arab states' constant reference to the Persian Gulf as the "Arabian Gulf" in order to assert Arab dominance there.[14]

Iranian-Iraqi differences were exacerbated after 1967, when the pro-Moscow Ba'th party rose to power under the leadership of Hasan al-Bakr in Baghdad. The Shah perceived this as a major change in the regional status quo, and as threatening to Iranian security and stability. The Ba'th government's attempt to exploit Iraqi differences with Iran for domestic purposes reinforced the Shah's perception. As a result, Tehran stepped up its financial and military support for the Kurdish secessionist movement in Iraq, under the leadership of Mostafa Barzani, and Baghdad increased its support for the anti-Shah groups and sought to rally Arab support for them.[15] This led to open conflict between the two sides. Although a full-scale Iranian-Iraqi war was avoided, relations between the two countries continued tense until the early part of the 1970s.[16]

The volatility of the political situation in the Gulf has been further increased by the rapid socio-economic changes within the Gulf states, activities of the Gulf's dissenting "revolutionary" groups, and intra-Arab tensions. All the Gulf states, although to a lesser extent than Iran, have been undergoing intensive socio-economic transformations from traditional, centralized, and absolute feudalistic or semi-feudalistic societies to economically more diverse and sophisticated, politically more bureaucratized and educated, and socially more flexible ones.[17] The growing wealth of the region from its oil seems to have played the most important role in this process. All the states have been, and are, at different stages of socio-economic development, but they have one feature in common: new political and social groups that are imbued with ideas of domestic reform and structural change. While many of these groups have been content to press their demands within existing systems, a few have opted to bring about fundamental changes from outside the system through revolutionary methods.

One of the most active and publicized groups of the latter type in the Gulf area has been the Popular Front for the Liberation of the Arabian Gulf (PFLOAG), which in 1974 changed its name to the Popular Front for the Liberation of Oman (PFLO). After carrying out sporadic actions against pro-Western conservative governments in the Gulf, the PFLO, by the start of the seventies, succeeded in turning Dhofar, the southernmost province of Oman, into a center of its revolutionary activities. In this, it was backed by the radical Arab governments of Iraq,

Syria, and the Peoples Democratic Republic of Yemen, as well as the Soviet Union, China, and the Popular Front for the Liberation of Palestine.[18] The PFLO thus constituted a serious threat not only to the Gulf's conservative Arab regimes, but also to that of the Shah, who considered the PFLO and other similar groups very dangerous. They could extend their activities to the Strait of Hormuz, the strategic passage connecting the Gulf with the Indian Ocean, and to the Iranian coastline. Hence they could sabotage the Iranian sea lanes and other vital lines of communication, as well as the Iranian coastal oil installations. They could weaken the Gulf's conservative Arab regimes, counteracting the Shah's endeavors to expand and preserve the conservative status quo in the Gulf in the interest of his own regime and policies. And they could enhance the position of the Iranian dissident groups and stimulate them.

Giving further cause for concern in the region have been intra-Arab differences between the "radicals," led by Iraq and the Peoples Democratic Republic of Yemen, and the "conservatives," led by Saudi Arabia. This division has manifested itself in ideological, political, and territorial disputes.[19]

Another factor that increased the Shah's concern for the situation in the Gulf was the British announcement of its decision in 1968 to withdraw its protectorate forces from the Gulf as part of its overall withdrawal from "east of Suez" by 1971. The Pax Britannica had for more than a century been a constant irritant to Iran, but it had also been a protective shield against encroachment by other powers and serious subversive activities in the Gulf. The British decision to withdraw posed the problems of a power vacuum and raised the question of the fate of the small emirates and sultanates, hitherto British protectorates, in the Gulf. The withdrawal induced the Gulf's "radical" and "conservative" forces to become active against each other in relation to these problems, and invited outside powers, particularly the United States, the Soviet Union, and the People's Republic of China to increase their activities in order to advance their own positions.[20] Meanwhile, Britain proposed the creation of an Arab federation of the so-called Trucial States and other sultanates and emirates, on the one hand; and supported Iran, as the West's biggest and most capable and trusted ally, to play a leading role in filling the "vacuum," on the other.[21] By the end of 1971, however, further dissension between Iran and many of the Gulf Arab states, induced the latter to reject the Iranian bid for paramountcy in the Gulf.

The Eastern Flank

Another region that caused anxiety for the Shah from time to time lies in an arc from southeast to southwest of Iran. The region comprises Afghanistan, the subcontinent, and the Indian Ocean, particularly those parts that flank the approaches of the Persian Gulf and Horn of Africa, and form the Iranian sea lanes or what the Shah called "the Iranian life lines."[22] Over the years, there were a number of developments in this region that the Shah perceived as threatening to Iran.

One such incident was Afghanistan's border dispute with Pakistan. Afghanistan not only shares a long border with Iran, but also a common language, culture, history, and similar form of government—until Afghanistan was declared a republic in July 1973. Apart from some differences over the distribution of water from the Helmand River, which has its origins in Central Afghanistan and flows through the Afghan land into southeast Iran,[23] the two countries had enjoyed steady and friendly relations from the inception of the Shah's rule. Afghanistan, however, unlike Iran, developed close ties with the Soviet Union, which were largely manifested in extensive Soviet economic, technical, and military aid after 1956.[24] Meanwhile, Afghanistan's relations with Pakistan, Iran's regional ally, often suffered from a serious border dispute between the two countries. While successive Afghan governments were pressing for the self-determination of Pushtuns, who form an Afghan minority in Pakistan, within a territory that Kabul called Pushtunistan, the Pakistani governments refused to respond to Afghan pressures, and regarded the matter as internal. Moscow supported Afghanistan on the issue explicitly during Khrushchev's leadership, and afterwards implicitly, by stating its support for "self-determination of peoples" in general.[25]

The Shah viewed Afghan-Soviet friendship and Soviet support for Afghanistan in its dispute with Pakistan with suspicion and ill-feeling. He suspected Soviet motives in trying to weaken Pakistan and find direct access to the Indian Ocean through Afghanistan. The Shah therefore gave Iran's full support to Pakistan; after the signing of a twenty-year treaty of friendship between New Delhi and Moscow and the creation of Bangladesh in 1971, he declared that Iran would not tolerate further dismemberment of Pakistan.[26] The Afghan coup in July 1973, which replaced the traditional monarchy with a republican regime headed by President Mohammad Daoud, increased the Shah's concern. During Daoud's premiership (1953-1963), Afghan-Soviet friendship flourished and Afghan-Pakistani relations deteriorated over the "Pushtunistan" issue.[27] At first Tehran, like Peking, suspected Moscow of being behind the coup.[28] But it soon found out that the coup was purely an Afghan internal matter, that Daoud would pursue the Afghan traditional policy of nonalignment, and that he was eager to strengthen Iran-Afghan relations.[29] This did not alleviate the fact, however, that the Afghan coup constituted a severe blow to the cause of monarchy in the region, and provided a source of inspiration for thousands of Iranian intellectuals and activists who opposed monarchy as a dictatorial and repressive institution in Iran.[30]

Meanwhile, the Shah was concerned about Pakistan's chronic domestic instability and dispute with India over Kashmir, on the one hand, and the growing Indo-Soviet friendship before the change of government in India in early 1977, on the other. Pakistan has been suffering from acute tensions both domestically and in its relations with Afghanistan and India since its creation in 1947. Domestically, the country's troubles have manifested themselves in frequent changes of government, military takeovers, communal riots, industrial unrest, mob violence, and, of greatest concern to Iran, secessionist movements. The most important of these have included the Bengali movement for independence, culminating in the creation of the independent state of Bangladesh in December 1971; and the Baluchi and Pushtun movements for independence or autonomy in Baluchistan and the North-West Frontier province of Pakistan. The Bengali movement was actively supported and aided by India, and finally realized its aim with Indian military assistance. The other movements, which are still alive, have been encouraged and at times helped by Afghanistan in support of the latter's stance on the issue of "Pushtunistan."[31] This situation has been further complicated by the long-standing Indo-Pakistani dispute over Kashmir, which has led to two major wars between the countries, and by the Indo-Soviet, Afghan-Soviet, and Indo-Afghan friendships, as well as the close ties between these three countries and Iran's western neighbor, Iraq. This, together with the failure of successive Pakistani governments to find an appropriate solution for Pakistan's problems, and the fact that Iran shares a common border and coastline with Pakistan and has its own Baluchi minority, were influential in shaping the Shah's regional perceptions.

By the start of the 1970s, the Shah perceived a Moscow-Kabul-New Delhi-Baghdad axis as a distinct possibility; such an alliance could not only weaken Pakistan, but also help Moscow to develop a chain of bases of influence from Delhi to Baghdad and Aden, and increase its capability against Iran as far as the Persian Gulf and Indian Ocean. At a time when the United States was suffering from isolationist tendencies, largely as a result of its involvement in Indo-China, and London had decided to withdraw from the Persian Gulf, this could ultimately, as far as Tehran was concerned, lead to the Soviet encirclement of Iran. The Shah's perception of these regional developments prompted him to expand his regime's regional goal and redefine the Iranian region of security and interests. He began to seek new ways of strengthening Iran's capability to pursue a more assertive but "proper" pattern of regional behavior.[32] In doing so, the Shah brought to maturity his conception of Iran as a "regional power."

In expanding the Iranian national goal, as it appears from the sequence of developments, the Shah resolved to achieve various major objectives. First, Iran must continue to pursue an anti-communist policy. That is, it must continue to strengthen its own national resources, in convergence with the Western interests, against possible Soviet hostile action, direct or indirect. But this, meanwhile, should not harm the development of a normal, peaceful, and symmetrical relationship with the Soviet Union at official levels.

Second, Iran should vigorously seek and prepare itself to replace Britain in its traditional role as stabilizer and protector in the Persian Gulf after the British withdrawal from the region, and rebuff any attempt by outside powers, particularly the Soviet Union, to take over some of the British responsibilities in the Gulf.[33] In this, the Shah sought to safeguard Iran against internal subversion sponsored by any hostile government or group from the Gulf region; ensure uninterrupted passage through the Strait of Hormuz, Shatt al-Arab, and the Gulf as a whole; protect the Iranian oil resources and facilities on and offshore in the

Gulf against deliberate sabotage or disruption; and boost the psychological stability of the Gulf's smaller states, sultanates, and emirates, which in the past had relied on British protection against regional threats.

Third, Iran must seek to acquire the capability to undermine the rise of any Soviet-backed or left-wing force in the region south and southeast of the Iranian borders. Iran should conduct balanced relations with all the three regional countries: Afghanistan, Pakistan, and India. In doing so, it should strive to strengthen its alliance with Pakistan, and support that country to preserve its sovereignty and territorial integrity; it should mediate between Pakistan and its neighbors, and encourage and help Afghanistan and India to reduce their dependence on Soviet aid.[34] Otherwise, the Shah considered that Pakistan's weakness and regional tensions could only assist Moscow to entrench its influence in the region.

In sum, Iran's regional objectives developed in line with the Shah's overriding goal of transforming Iran into a paramount power that would maintain the regional status quo under the leadership and guardianship of Iran.

By the early 1970s, the Shah defined the changing Iranian region of security and interests well beyond the geographical perimeters of West and Central Asia and the Persian Gulf. He stated,

I must confess that three or four years ago I only thought of the defence of the Persian Gulf because most of our wealth was obtained from Bandar Abbas and from the Hormuz Strait at that time, so we only wanted to preserve this wealth and to maintain free access to the outside world. But events were such that we were soon compelled to think of the Oman Sea and Iran's shores on the Oman Sea as well. And again world events were such that we were compelled to accept the fact that the sea adjoining the Oman Sea—I mean the Indian Ocean—does not recognise borders. And now, as far as our thoughts are concerned, we are no longer thinking only about guarding Abadan or Khosrowabadan or Bushire or even Bandar Abbas or Hormuz. We are not even thinking only of guarding Jask and Chah Bahar. [As for] Iran's security limits—I will not state how many kilo-meters we have in mind, but anyone who is acquainted with geography and the strategic situation, and especially with the potentials of air and sea forces, knows what distances from Chah Bahar this limit can reach.[35]

In order to achieve these regional objectives and build and sustain Iran's position of leadership, the Shah resolved that Iran should achieve the necessary "power."

CHAPTER VI

Resources Capability

THE ABILITY of a state to act successfully largely depends on the resources—including political, social, human, economic, and military potential—that it can draw on.[1] Iran's greatest resource strength, oil, became effectively available to it in the early 1970s, enabling the Shah to pursue, with the utmost speed and vigor, his process of building up Iran as a regional power. In the 1970s, the Shah found himself suddenly in possession of enormous petro-dollar revenue and great resource bargaining power. He was able to engage in intensive "resources diplomacy" to trade off the Iranian oil and surplus petro-dollars for the best, and even for scarce, capital goods, expertise, technology, skilled manpower, and arms; to sell Iranian products in suitable markets and on favorable terms; to give aid to and invest in countries that were useful in helping him to promote his national and regional goals; whenever necessary, to buy off relevant and influential individuals, companies, institutions, organizations, and governments around the world; and to promote his own leadership both at national and international levels. In this context, the Shah accelerated his drive to increase the Iranian economic and military potential, and resolved that Iran must achieve a maximum degree of nonoil-based economic industrialization and military sophistication within the next two decades.[2]

ECONOMIC PROGRAM AND OBJECTIVES

The Shah began a systematic build-up of the Iranian economy with his White Revolution. The measures adopted in the context of the Revolution and featured prominently in Iran's Third and Fourth Economic Development Plans (1962-1973) proved effective in stabilizing and stimulating the Iranian economy, and developing a modern industrial infrastructure.[3] By 1971, before the huge oil price increases, Iran claimed to be enjoying one of the highest rates of economic growth in the world and to be moving fast toward becoming a highly industrialized state in comparison with all its neighbors except the Soviet Union and India.[4] To establish this conclusively would require a comprehensive analysis of the Iranian economy at the time. For our purpose, however, it suffices to indicate that some of the major economic indicators support such a claim. During the Iranian year of 1349 (21 March 1970-20 March 1971), Iran achieved an economic growth rate of 10 percent at constant prices, with its GNP estimated at $10.9 billion. In this, the oil and service sectors contributed 3.3 and 3.1 percent, respectively; the shares of industries and mines, water and power, agriculture, and construction were, respectively 1.8, 0.9, 0.6, and 0.2 percent. The rate of growth of the value added in oil was 12.5 percent, increasing the total oil revenue for the year to $1,136 million; in the service sector the rate of growth was 9 percent, within which the public and private sectors services grew by 12 and 6 percent, respectively; in industries and mines it was 13.2 percent; in water and power, 39.9 percent, with electricity alone counting for a growth rate of 41.5 percent; and in construction it was 5.4 percent. The labor force and productivity recorded a growth rate of 2.8 and 7.3 percent, respectively. These rates of growth either met or exceeded the target set by the Fourth Economic Development Plan.[5]

The agricultural sector, however, recorded a decline of 3 percent, as against the Fourth Development Plan's target of 4.4 percent growth. The production of foodstuffs, tobacco, and cotton was less than that in the previous year. This was largely attributed to a decline in the labor force in agriculture, mainly on account of the relatively higher money wage rates and productivity in other sectors, and increasing immigration from rural to urban areas. As a result, agricultural exports and imports registered very unbalanced growth rates of 4.2 and 60.9 percent, respectively, over those in 1969-1970. But this was generally in line with the government policy of giving priority to industrial development over agriculture.

During the same year, while investing about Rls. 6 billion in agriculture (well below the target of about Rls. 13 billion envisaged by the Fourth Plan), the government invested about Rls. 30 billion in the industrial and mining sector. The proportion of the active population in agriculture declined by about

0.9 percent; but the number of people active in industries and mines increased by 8 percent; 19.5 percent of the working population was involved in this sector. Value added increased by 13 percent and productivity rose by 5 percent. Apart from the traditional industries, such as textiles, carpets, and packaging, major new industries that recorded a high growth rate included steel, machinery, and petrochemicals. The items contributing to the rise in industrial productivity included vehicles, petrochemicals, electric appliances, and radio and television, which together accounted for 57 percent of the rise. The growth rate in mining production was largely caused by the exploitation of mines—especially of chromite, lead, and zinc—for which the world demand was growing.[6]

Meanwhile, the value of Iran's foreign trade, other than oil, was $1.95 billion in 1970-1971, and had a 9.3 percent growth rate, as against 11.3 percent in 1969-1970. The fall in the rate of growth in foreign trade was largely due to a slower growth in imports, because a number of projects requiring capital goods had already been completed. Iranian economic growth, however, still remained heavily dependent on a growing level of imports. As a result, while Iran's nonoil exports amounted to $277.9 million, the country's imports were valued at $1,676.6 million, though the former grew by 13.6 percent and the latter by 8.7 percent in 1970-1971 as against 12.8 and 11.0 percent, respectively, in the previous year.[7] This discrepancy was rectified to a large extent by the Iranian oil exports. Although the leading Iranian oil customers were Japan and the West, in particular the EEC countries, which were the major suppliers of Iran's imports, the country's major foreign customers of nonoil exports were the socialist states, led by the Soviet Union ($100.3 million, with a 4.3 percent rate of increase). In this, the socialist countries were followed by the EEC countries ($60.1 million, with a 16.7 percent rate of increase), the United States ($24.2 million, with a 4.7 percent rate of decline), the ECAFE countries ($27.5 million, with a 59 percent growth rate), the United Kingdom ($9.8 million, with a 1 percent rate of increase), and finally Turkey and Pakistan, members of the Regional Cooperation for Development ($1.7 million, with a 21.4 percent rate of growth). The emerging trend was clearly in favor of Iran's growing trade with the regional countries. The conclusion of "clearing agreements" between Iran and the socialist countries was an important factor in the growth of trade between the two sides.[8]

The rate of growth in the social services sector—education, health, and welfare—was also considerable, but not as high as in many other sectors. This was largely because of the lower priority accorded by the government to investment in this sector. Although the government claimed a literacy rate as high as 37 percent,[9] there is serious doubt about the accuracy of this claim. The term "literacy" is difficult to quantify, and according to the government's own admission, most of Iran's estimated 67,000 villages suffered from an acute shortage of teaching staff and poor educational facilities. About 50 percent of school-age children were still not receiving an education.[10]

The government also claimed a great improvement in the field of health. But this improvement was limited by the number of physicians and dentists, totaling 8,950, of whom physicians constituted 87 percent. The officially reported ratio of physicians to the population was 1 to 3,700 persons, but most of the doctors were in the major cities, particularly Tehran. For example, in the governate of Zanjan and province of West Azerbaijan, the ratio was one physician to over 15,000 and 9,000 persons, respectively. There were also about 35,000 hospital beds in the country, most of them in Tehran. A government report admits that "the major portion of health facilities was confined to Tehran and the Central Province." The government's total expenditures on education and health amounted to Rls. 3.2 and Rls. 2.5 billion, respectively. These figures were much lower than the government expenditures on defense or on administrative services in the same year.[11]

The government's welfare measures were limited to basic pension, superannuation, and some social insurance schemes, and the relegislation of workers' sharing in the factory profits. These all suffered extensively from administrative incompetence, corruption, and lack of proper enforcement. The government's disbursements on social welfare services amounted to Rls. 898 million, though this represented a rise of about 60 percent over the corresponding figure in 1969-1970.[12]

It needs to be stressed that the Shah's economic policy, embodied in the Third and Fourth Plans, aimed mainly at economic growth rather than economic development. The latter would have required comprehensive political and social changes, and schemes for redistribution of wealth on a nationwide scale—measures that the Shah's regime, given its nature, did not want and could not cope with at this stage.[13] Nevertheless the rate of Iran's economic growth and industrialization did reach an impressive stage by 1971. The new oil achievements of the early 1970s, moreover, enabled the Shah to multiply his government's expenditures and intensify his diplomatic activities to pursue his goal of economic growth and industrialization at a more ambitious and accelerated rate. During the period 1971-1974, the Iranian oil revenues increased from Rls. 152.1 billion to Rls. 1,297.4 billion, with annual growth rates of 74.4, 20.2, 161.1, and 171.7 percent, respectively. At the same time, Iran's GNP grew from Rls. 1,036.3 in 1971 to Rls. 2,270.0 (1972 prices), representing annual growth rates of 10.1, 14.2, 34.2, and 43.0 percent, respectively.[14] As a result, government expenditure, the Iranian economy, and foreign trade experienced a phenomenal rate of growth. In the light of changing circumstances, the Shah ordered a revision of Iran's Fifth Economic Development Plan (1973-1978), which took effect in late 1974. He declared that this Plan would be "equal to all four previous plans combined. By the end of the Fifth . . . Plan, we will be in quite a distinguished and unprecedented position. However, we are already thinking about the Sixth Plan and even beyond, which we call the period of our grand civilization [*Tamaddon-e Bozorg*]. We hope to find the Iranian society on the threshold of this grand civilization by the end of the Sixth Plan."[15]

Explaining the over-all objective of the Fifth Plan, the Shah declared that it was "to achieve a stage at which the Iranian society, enjoying utmost privileges of social and economic development, could be transferred into a strong society enjoying culture and learning." In order to realize this objective, the Plan was to: "provide maximum public welfare"; "maintain the country's economic growth rate and to adopt serious measures to control the effects of inflationary tendencies" due to the world economic situation and the government's high expenditure; expand the agricultural and industrial sectors with "a rapid transformation toward the most advanced industries of modern times"; "establish access to the latest scientific and technical achievements in the industrialized countries and their application to advance Iran's technological standard as rapidly as possible, as well as bringing about the effective participation of research institutes and studies necessary for industrial and agricultural growth"; achieve a high growth rate in the services sector; and promote "culture and mass media" according to the needs of Iran. Moreover, the Shah stressed that the plan placed emphasis "on cooperation with other countries, participation in investment and activities, expansion of the economy on the basis of mutual interests and extension of aid to countries which are taking steps toward expansion."

The Plan envisaged an annual GNP growth rate of 25.9 percent at constant prices—more than double what it was during the Fourth Plan—and the GNP was to increase from Rls. 1,165 billion in the final year of the Fourth Plan to Rls. 3,686 billion during the corresponding year of the Fifth Plan. Considering the estimated rate of 2.9 percent annual growth of population, the per capita GNP was to rise from 37,523 in 1972-1973 at constant prices, to 106,650 rials in 1977-1978. The Plan projected a total capital investment of Rls. 4,698 billion, annual growth rates of 29.7, 19.3, and 27.2 percent in gross domestic investment, consumption, and public sector consumer expenditure at constant prices, respectively. Of the total capital investment, Rls. 3,118 billion was to be public (government) investment, and Rls. 1,580.2 billion private investment, representing a rise by 38.1 and 17.7 percent, respectively, over the corresponding figures of 12.9 and 14.6 percent during the Fourth Plan. Excluding the oil sector, gross domestic production was to rise at the rate of 15.0 percent per annum; the value added of agriculture was to grow by 7.0 percent, of manufacturing and mining by 18.0 percent, and services by 16.4 percent.[16]

The total government receipts during the Fifth Plan period were projected to amount to Rls. 8,296.5 billion, of which 79.8 percent would come from oil and gas, and the rest from direct and indirect taxes, small foreign loans, and other government revenues. The total revenues from oil and gas during the Plan period were estimated to be Rls. 6,628.5 billion, representing a twelvefold increase compared to the Fourth Plan period. Total government allocations were projected to amount to Rls. 6,241.4 billion, of which 13.3, 31.5, 21.0, and 34.2 percent were allocated for public affairs, defense, social affairs, and economic affairs, respectively. These percentages were to comprise both current and development expenditures. An estimate of Rls. 745.1 billion for foreign investment was also included in the total government payments. During the Plan period the volume of Iran's foreign trade was expected to increase manyfold, with stress on expanding transactions with regional states for reasons of both political and economic expediency. Given the scope and direction of its social welfare programs, the Plan also gave some attention to economic development as against economic growth, which had largely characterized the previous Plans.

It was an underlying intention of the Plan to diversify Iran's economic development and industrialization from their heavy dependence on the Iranian oil resources to becoming more self-dependent, self-generating, and independent of oil, which was expected to lose its export potential by the end of this century. But the Plan was very ambitious in both its scope and objectives. For its successful implementation, Iran had neither the necessary capital goods nor the trained manpower, expertise, technological and scientific know-how, and infrastructural facilities. As a result, its implementation was foreseen to require heavy importation.[17] This will be discussed in Chapter VIII.

The Plan was designed to strengthen Iran's position as not only an economic power but also a military power. The Shah believed that the one could not be achieved without the other. He stated, "In view of the regional and international problems, the strengthening and consolidation of the country's defence power will enjoy special priority in the Plan, so that it should act as the main factor in safeguarding the country's stability and independence, maintaining the precious fruits of economic and social expansion and securing Iran, as before, as an area of peace and reliance in today's turbulent world."[18]

Military Capability

Military capability can be approached, defined, and measured in various ways, depending on one's choice and interpretation of the variables that constitute its components. In the following discussion, the term will be used to mean the sum aggregate of Iran's national "putative military power," or "capacity for taking or defending objects forcibly as well as . . . means to exercise coercion." A state's putative military power may be evaluated in relation to its ready military forces and their functions, military potential (from which additional military capabilities can be

derived), and military reputation, that is, the known and expected disposition of a society to resort to military strength if
national interests are crossed by other societies.[19]

The military traditionally fulfilled a variety of significant and
interrelated functions in Iran. These ranged from providing the
Iranian rulers with an effective power base and instrument of
coercion and policy implementation, to policing the domestic
order and acting as a deterrent against external threats and
infiltration. It has therefore played a central role in the shaping
and conduct of Iranian politics. The Shah, like his predecessors,
was determined not only to control the military but also to
expand, reorganize, and modernize it as much as possible, so
that it could perform its functions more efficiently and successfully. During the 1950s and 1960s he succeeded in transforming
the Iranian armed forces into an expanded and well equipped
modern army, navy, and air force, with paramilitary, special task,
and intelligence forces. During the year 1970-1971, when the
British withdrawal from the Gulf was imminent, Iran's GNP
was estimated at $10 billion, and Iran's defense budget
amounted to over $1 billion. The Shah commanded armed forces
totaling 221,000 men. Their armaments included M-60 A1 tanks,
escort destroyers, patrol vessels, coastal minesweepers, F-40 all-
weather fighter-bombers, F-5 tactical fighter-bombers, F-86 all-
weather interceptors, and an advanced radar system, as well as
ground-to-ground and ground-to-air missiles and a variety of
armor. Most of these arms had been supplied by the United
States.[20] They did not include any of the world's most advanced
weapons; and the Iranian military had not acquired a capacity
either to challenge a possible direct Soviet operation or match
India's military potential. It had, however, attained a putative
capability to outclass the varying military strength of other
regional forces (though Iraq may have maintained a higher
number of combat aircraft).[21] It was an effective driving force
behind the Shah's autocratic rule, on the one hand, and his
domestic policy of socio-economic reform, on the other; and it
was strong enough to aid the Shah in promoting Iran as the
most logical and capable successor to Britain in the Gulf.

On the basis of this capability, the Shah engaged in a number
of what may be regarded as forward military actions. They included military aid to and training of the Kurdish secessionists
against Baghdad, particularly in the late 1960s;[22] logistic support

for Pakistan during the Indo-Pakistani war in 1965, and the
transfer to Pakistan afterwards of 90 F-86 Sabre fighters, which
reportedly took part in the air war with India in 1971;[23] support
for North Yemen and an expression of readiness to aid the
Sana'a government against the Peoples Democratic Republic of
Yemen after the latter became independent in 1967;[24] and above
all, the military take-over of the strategic islands of Abu Musa
and the Greater and Lesser Tumbs in the Persian Gulf, on the
mouth of the strategic Strait of Hormuz, just before Britain
formally withdrew its forces at the end of 1971. Moreover, the
Shah was prepared to commit Iranian forces, comprising 3,000-
5,000 men with special counterinsurgency units and air cover, in
Oman in support of the pro-Western conservative Muscat government against the Popular Front for the Liberation of Oman,
in 1971-1973.[25]

The Iranian military capability before 1972 was not achieved
by increased economic strength, productivity, industrialization,
technological and scientific advancement, foreign trade and capital holdings abroad, or political and administrative efficiency—
which are generally considered as the basis for a state's increased
putative military power.[26] In fact, Iran's progress in these fields
was very modest. The military capability was attained largely
due to an increased Iranian GNP, which was mainly a result of a
steady rise in the country's oil revenues, and foreign aid, notably
from the United States. As a result, Iran's military potential
(which must not be misunderstood as military capability), as
well as its economic potential, was limited by dependence on
supplies and expertise from outside, the quantity of capital
inflowing from oil, and the extent of the country's economic
capability. The oil achievements of the early 1970s, however,
strengthened the Shah's position so that he could make spectacu-
lar increases in his government expenditures for improving the
Iranian economic-military potential at a more ambitious and
accelerated rate. This potential, determined by the size and
composition of a state's military and nonmilitary resources,
stresses the interdependence between these resources in such
areas as expertise, scientific and technological know-how, trained
manpower, and infrastructure. The development of economic-
military potential is often regarded as the most effective way to
increase and safeguard the domestic and regional stability and
security, as well as the self-sufficiency and autonomous strength of

a given state.[27] Now, along with expanding investment expenditures for economic development and heavy industrialization, the Shah embarked on a massive military build-up, which was rare in the history of less developed countries.

During 1972 and 1973, when Iran's income from oil began to rise steeply and amounted to $2,380 and 4,100 million, respectively,[28] the Shah wasted no time in increasing the Iranian defense budget by 29 percent in 1972 and 11 percent in the following year (or $1,375 and 1,525 million respectively).[29] He immediately sought to strengthen, above all, his army and air force for short-range, particularly counterinsurgency, operations against possible hostile groups, mainly in the Gulf area. He was able to bargain for the best and most advanced nonnuclear weapons for his armed forces. They included 202 Bell AH-IJ assault and 287 Bell 214A "Isfahan" utility helicopters, at a total cost of $430 million, as well as 141 Northrop F-5E Tiger 11 fighter aircraft, costing $377 million, and a variety of missiles.[30]

The year 1974, during which the Iranian oil income quadrupled, reaching a record level of over $17 billion, and the country's GNP rose to over $40 billion, marked a turning point in the Shah's drive for military build-up.[31] He declared,

> At present, Iran has a certain military potential . . . to the extent that so far no one has managed to trifle with us (in spite of a number of regional hostilities against Iran). I promise . . . that within the next four or five years Iran's armed forces will be such that no one had better entertain any evil thoughts about Iran. . . . Obviously, to have weapons and an army is not something which can be had free of charge, but thank God, today we can afford to purchase as many of the best weapons in the world as we can absorb, without any favours from anybody, for we pay cash. Of course, we are grateful that the producer provides us with the best weapons.[32]

In order to fulfil this promise, "defense affairs" were given almost as much priority as "economic affairs" in the revised Fifth Economic Development Plan. The government undertook to spend a total of Rls. 1,968.7 billion (about $28 billion at constant prices) on defense during the plan period. This was to account for 31.1 percent of its total allocations, only 2.7 percent less than what the government pledged to devote to economic development. From the total defense allocation, Rls. 1,967.4 and Rls. 1.3 billion were to be for military and civil defense expenditures, respectively.[33] Even so, the Shah found the Plan's defense allocations smaller than what he could actually spend. He consequently did not abide by the Plan, and his defense spending exceeded the Plan's target by the beginning of 1978, the Plan's final year. Between 1974 and 1977, the government defense spending rose from $3,680 billion to $9,400 billion—an increase of 141 and 650 percent over that of 1973, respectively. Meanwhile, the government's total defense disbursement amounted to over $28 billion.[34] The Iranian budget for the fiscal year of 1978-1979 (the final year of the Plan period), which provided for a record $59.2 billion expenditures, allocated $9.9 billion for defense. With this, the government's total defense expenditures, during the Plan period, was to be over $10 billion more than what was originally envisaged in the Plan.[35] During the first four years of the Plan, defense consumed an average of 27 to 29 percent of the government budget.[36]

Iran thus became not only a big military spender, but also a leading arms purchaser in the world after 1974. Iranian officials guarded the Shah's military purchases and orders with strict secrecy. But according to outside sources (particularly U.S. Congressional hearings and reports and the Stockholm International Peace Research Institute) the total cost of the Shah's arms purchases and orders between 1973 and 1977 alone exceeded $15 billion.[37] In 1977, Iran was the world's largest single purchaser of U.S. arms, buying about $5,700 million worth; this accounted for more than half of the entire U.S. arms sales to foreign countries.[38] The Iranian military procurement consisted of a variety of the most advanced and sophisticated weapons, both defensive and offensive, for all branches of the country's armed forces. They included Chieftain MK5 "Shir Iran" tanks and Victor armored recovery vehicles (both British); F14A Tomcat fighter/interceptor, F-4E and RF-4E Phantom aircraft, a Phoenix air-defense system, "Spruance"-class destroyers, renovated "Tang"-class submarines, fleet tankers, Lockheed P-3C Maritime aircraft, and a wide range of antitank, antiaircraft, and guided missiles (all American). Moreover, as the Shah was impressed by the effective performance of SAM missiles, used by Egypt and Syria, in the Middle East War of October 1973, Iran planned to buy an undisclosed number of such missiles from the Soviet Union. To this

effect, the Iranian war minister, General Tufanian, concluded a
$414 million arms deal with the Soviet authorities during his
visit to Moscow in November 1976. The deal provided for the
Soviet supply of SAM-7 and SAM-9, and a number of antitank
and antiaircraft guns to Iran, starting in 1977.[39] This was the
second deal of its kind between Tehran and Moscow. It was significant not so much for what it may have offered to Iran militarily as for its political implications in terms of strengthening
the Shah's position in his arms dealings with the West. Not all
the above-mentioned arms were in the possession of Iran by 1978,
of course, but their deliveries were expected to be completed by
the mid-1980s.

The Shah's military purchases and orders were mainly of two
types: cash payment and oil-for-arms deals. The first type was
predominant until late 1975, while Iran's oil income was continuing to increase. However, with a temporary downward fluctuation in the world oil market in early 1976 and the Saudi
Arabian decision to restrain OPEC from huge oil price increases,
the Iranian oil revenue dropped by 2-4 percent against an expected rise of 5 percent.[40] As a result, the Shah urgently sought to
trade Iranian oil for arms directly. Iran concluded the first such
deal with Britain in November 1976, whereby the latter undertook to provide Iran with the most advanced ground-to-air missiles (worth £400 million) for a long-term oil supply.[41] It was
soon reported that Iran was trying to negotiate similar deals with
Britain and the United States with regard to Victor armored
recovery vehicles and F16 fighters.[42]

Meanwhile, the Shah was seeking eagerly to develop Iran's
own arms industry. By the late 1970s, Iran produced only pistols
and machine guns, but the government had undertaken a number of programs to expand the production of such small arms.
After 1974, Tehran concluded several agreements with the
United States and Britain to assemble Bell 214 Utility and Bell
209 AH-IJ armed helicopters, Hughes Tow antitank missiles,
electronics, and BAC Rapier SAM missiles, as well as to produce
part of the total order of 1,600 Chieftain tanks under licence.[43]
On March 17, 1978, Britain agreed to expand the existing repair
shops for some 1,000 Chieftain tanks already at the disposal of
Iran, and set up a mini-assembly line for the tanks on order in
Iran in 1979.[44] Major Iranian arms assemblage and production
plants had already become operative in Shiraz. But the country's

success in this field, as in many other military and economic fields, was limited by the lack of a solid nonoil economic/industrial base, sufficient trained manpower, and scientific/technological know-how and infrastructural capacity.

The Shah's massive military build-up, irrespective of whether it had self-generating potential and whether it was in the interest of the Iranian people, had provided Iran with such a large numerical or theoretical military capability that the country had come to be regarded not only by its own leadership but also by concerned foreign quarters as the dominant military power in the Persian Gulf. As a U.S. Congressional Staff Report put it, "upon delivery between now [July 1976] and 1981 of equipment ordered to date, Iran, on paper, can be regarded as a regional superpower."[45] This military strength had become an effective driving force behind the Shah's aims both at home and in the Iranian region and international arena. Its usefulness was increased by the fact that the regional countries in particular, and the world in general, were aware of the Shah's military build-up, but were largely uncertain of what it could do if it were used. As long as the sizable military inventory remained and continued to grow, the Shah and his regime had the putative instruments to guard and exert themselves against the regional countries (whether weak like Qatar or strong like the Soviet Union) that seemed to be watchful of the Shah's military build-up but unsure of its potential effectiveness.

It must be stressed that the Shah's military program was a non-nuclear one, though Iran had concluded agreements with the United States, France, and West Germany to build over twenty nuclear reactors for "peaceful purposes" before the Iranian oil wells were expected to run out of their exporting potential.[46] In fact, the Shah had demanded that the Persian Gulf and Indian Ocean be declared a "zone of peace."[47] Iran, a signatory to the Non-Proliferation Treaty, had made several motions to this effect in the United Nations in the previous few years.[48] But this had not prevented the Shah from stating that Iran's conventional military capability enabled the country to fulfil several vital objectives: to deter Moscow from carrying out any direct or indirect action against Iran, or, if this failed, to put up an effective resistance to any Soviet action until Iran's Western allies came to its aid; to guard the Iranian economic development and its regional security and interests against forces of disruption and

sabotage in the region; to influence and possibly control developments and events in the politically volatile areas of the Persian
Gulf and Iran's eastern flank; and to enforce the traditional prestige of the Shah as "the king of kings" and of Iran as a country
that was once a mighty imperial power in its own right.[49]

CHAPTER VII

Pattern of Regional Behavior

THE SHAH'S GOAL of developing Iran into an effective regional power was clear, but his regional policy behavior in pursuit of this goal did not have a totally coherent pattern. It was changing, complex, and often inconsistent. There were, however, two consistent themes: the Shah's search for what he called "regional cooperation," and his opposition to what he considered "communist/subversive" forces and activities within Iran and its region. The former theme lay behind his search for regional consensus and support for Iran's aspirations to a position as a regional power; the latter led Iran into limited regional military interventions. In these respects the regime's actions ranged from settling some of Iran's major disputes with its neighbors, offering sizable capital aid and investment to certain regional countries, and pressing for the formation of a regional "common market" and "collective security," to deploying Iranian combat forces in Oman and offering military aid to Somalia against Ethiopia.[1]

REGIONAL COOPERATION

The Shah's search for "regional cooperation" as a means to enhance Iran's regional stability and security, and enable the country to benefit from regional resources for its own socio-economic development, dates back to the early years of his rule. Although he used the term in different ways for rhetorical and practical purposes, an outline of his changing understanding of the term can be drawn on the basis of his policy statements and actions. During the 1950s, he believed that "the system of alliances and mutual aid" between states with common interests was the most effective way to ensure the stability and security of the world in general and of Iran in particular.[2] In this period he pursued a foreign policy that opposed Soviet communism and Arab revolutionary nationalism, but aimed at strengthening Iran's alliance with the West. At the regional level, this narrowed his options to seeking alliance and cooperation with those "friendly regional countries" that shared with him similar foreign policy convictions. These countries included Pakistan, Turkey, and Iraq, with which Iran forged an alliance through the Western-sponsored Baghdad Pact and its successor, CENTO, though Iraq dropped out of the latter in 1959. Although the alliance provided for economic and technical cooperation between member states, it failed to help the Shah's regime either to build a solid long-term basis for its own continuity or to strengthen the Iranian regional position. On the contrary, it aggravated Iran's relations with the Soviet Union and the Arab world, and caused anxiety for Afghanistan and India, which were engaged in serious border disputes with Pakistan.

By the beginning of the 1960s, the Shah began to deemphasize the military significance of CENTO in favor of its potential to promote regional economic cooperation. And during the next decade, the Shah succeeded in improving Iran's regional relationships. The Regional Cooperation for Development (RCD) was established with Pakistan and Turkey in July 1964; commercial ties with the Soviet Union were expanded, and the Soviets extended economic and technical assistance to Iran; economic and cultural ties with Afghanistan and India were improved; an effective working relationship with the conservative Arab states, led by Saudi Arabia and Kuwait, and even Iraq, was developed, at least at OPEC level; and Iran's relationship with the West, particularly the United States was to some extent brought into balance.

By the late 1960s, particularly in the wake of Britain's announcement of its intention to withdraw its forces from the Gulf, the Shah remained concerned about Soviet penetration and "communist subversion" in the vicinity of Iran. He resolved that Iran should assume the role of a leading guardian and deterrent power in its region, maintaining the stability of the status quo, and relying largely on its own strength.[3] The Shah now needed, more than ever before, not only a period of regional peace and stability but also increasing support from such regional resources as markets, raw materials, technology, and trained manpower, as well as considerable consensus and recognition for the status he wanted for Iran. This made it all the more pressing for him to pursue his policy of regional cooperation with increased vigor and on a larger scale. He thus found it expedient, while the Iranian-Soviet relationship was at its strongest, to seek better ties with the Arabs, on the one hand, and to strengthen Iran's relations with its eastern neighbors, on the other.

The Iranian-Arab Relationship

There were several major problems that had chronically strained Iran's relations with the Arab world in general and the radical Arab states in particular. They centered on Iranian policy concerning the Middle East conflict, the country's claim over Bahrain, its dispute with Iraq over Shatt al-Arab, and the Shah's general dislike for the Arab revolutionary regimes, and vice versa. Any improvement in the Iranian-Arab relationship depended on the two sides' success in overcoming these problems. The Shah initiated the process as early as 1967 when, in the wake of the third Arab-Israeli war, he reappraised his regime's Middle Eastern policy, and demanded Israeli withdrawal from Arab-occupied territory, though he condemned the use of oil as a political weapon by Arab producing states.

In 1968, when Britain announced its intended withdrawal from the Gulf, the Shah felt it expedient to resolve the problem of Bahrain once and for all. In a surprise statement in New Delhi on January 4, 1969, the Shah pledged, for the first time, that his government would "never resort to the use of force to oblige" the people of Bahrain to join Iran.[4] This statement was subsequently elaborated to mean that Iran was prepared to accept a referendum or plebiscite in Bahrain under United Nations auspices to decide the future status of the island. Britain and the U.N. acted swiftly, and on May 11, 1970, the U.N. Security Council adopted unanimously a resolution approving the finding of its Secretariat that "the overwhelming majority of the people of Bahrain wish to gain recognition of their identity in a fully independent and sovereign state." The Iranian Majlis endorsed this resolution with little opposition on May 14, 1970.[5]

Iran thus abandoned its traditional claim over Bahrain and resolved the problem amicably through quiet diplomacy with the U.N. and Britain in the year following the Shah's original statement. Lord Caradon, the British representative at the U.N. Security Council, praised the Shah's initial statement as "an act of statesmanship . . . which opened the door to settlement," and credited Iran with "magnanimity." Tehran rejoiced at the fact that the problem was solved "in such a manner as to contribute to creating a climate of peace, friendship and stability in the Persian Gulf." The Arab world's reaction to the solution, in general, was one of satisfaction, though Baghdad claimed the settlement to be a victory for the Arabs against the Shah's design for territorial expansion.[6] Tehran could not, in fact, have hoped for either a peaceful or forceful takeover of Bahrain: an overwhelming majority of the people of Bahrain did not want to join Iran, and Tehran could not undertake a military operation without risking a war with the Arabs.

In broad terms, the settlement proved to be in the interest of Iran's regional position and the Shah's search for regional cooperation. It put an end to a major dispute between Iran and its neighboring Arabs, which had caused the conservative Arab states to have reservations about developing close ties with Iran, and the radical Arab forces to be antagonistic to the Shah's regime and to denounce it for its imperialist ambitions.[7] It is possible that there were behind-the-scene dealings between London and Tehran in bringing about the Bahrain settlement. But the effect of the settlement was to remove a major restraining factor in Iranian-Arab relations, provide the Arab world with some evidence of Tehran's desire for regional peace and cooperation, and enable Tehran to concentrate on its other urgent objectives in the wake of British withdrawal.

In the meantime, the Bahrain settlement was complemented by Tehran's success in settling some of its other important differences with the Arabs. Tehran reached separate agreements with Kuwait, Saudi Arabia, and Qatar on the division of the continental shelf in the Persian Gulf in January and August 1968 and September 1969, respectively.[8] And although Iran at first refused to accept the formation of a British-sponsored confederation of the Gulf's small sheikdoms, which up to that point had been under British protection, because of the fear that such confederation could strengthen the Arabs' position against Iran, in 1971 Tehran softened its position by favoring the creation of the United Arab Emirates (UAE).[9] In return, however, it reached a behind-the-scenes understanding with Britain, allowing it to fulfil its traditional claim over the three strategic islands of Abu Musa and the Greater and Lesser Tumbs, near the straits of Hormoz.[10]

By the beginning of the 1970s, when Iran and the Arab oil-producing states jointly succeeded in turning OPEC into an effective cartel, Iran had settled many of its differences with the Gulf's Arab states. This had contributed effectively to promoting better regional understanding, based on common interests, and to expanding trade between Iran and these states as well as with Egypt, the leading member of the Arab radical camp.

But Iranian-Iraqi relations, meanwhile, had taken a turn for the worse. The dispute over the Shatt al-Arab had led to a breakdown of diplomatic relations and increasing border infiltrations and skirmishes between the two sides.[11] This was despite the fact that Tehran appeared very eager to negotiate its differences with Iraq following the solution of the Bahrain problem. Addressing the U.N. General Assembly in October 1970, the Iranian foreign minister, A. Zahedi, declared:

> We do not demand exclusive domain over it [Shatt al-Arab]. We seek no more than is accorded to us by the practice of nations under well established rules of international law, as shown in the case of Danube, the Rhine and the Scheldt rivers. [And that his government was] . . . ready at any time, at any hour, at any moment, anywhere, to start negotiations with the Government of Iraq, for the purpose of reaching a peaceful settlement of the Shatt al-Arab dispute, on the basis of boundary to be set at mid-channel on thalweg and freedom of navigation for all countries—throughout the entire river, in accordance with the accepted principles of international law.[12]

This eagerness did not pay off immediately for several reasons. First, the foreign policy of the Iraqi Ba'th government was still heavily influenced by nationalist-ideological values that sought an "Arab common policy" to preserve the Arab character of the Persian Gulf against Iranian claims, on the one hand, and stressed the strengthening of Iraq's relations with "the socialist camp and the third world," on the other. As a corollary to this, Baghdad opposed "pro-capitalist" forces, whether Iranian or Arab, in the Gulf. Second, the Ba'th regime was facing growing domestic opposition, and it was, therefore, in its interest not to press for an immediate settlement of its dispute with Iran. Third, the Baghdad-Moscow relationship was being cemented rapidly, particularly in the Friendship Treaty of 1972, and as a result Baghdad was feeling more confident of Soviet support for its regional stance. On the other hand, the Iranians were not yet strong enough to be effective in persuading the Ba'th regime to move toward a negotiated settlement. Thus, the Iranian-Iraqi dispute over Shatt al-Arab and its side-effects, such as Iranian support for Iraqi Kurdish secessionists and Iraqi backing of anti-Shah groups, continued to strain relations between the two countries.[13] It was not until 1975 that changing domestic and regional circumstances made it more urgent and desirable for both sides to negotiate a comprehensive agreement. Before evaluating this, it is necessary to look at the concurrent and rapid friendly developments in Iranian-Egyptian relations.

The transformation of the Iranian-Egyptian relationship from one of hostility during the 1950s and 1960s to one of friendship and close cooperation in the 1970s began with the change in Iranian policy on the Middle East conflict and the weakening of Egypt as the leading radical pan-Arabist force following the 1967 Arab-Israeli war. This, with the strengthening of Iran's regional position, led to the restoration of diplomatic relations, after a ten-year break, between the two countries shortly before President Nasser's death in 1970. The emergence of Anwar al-Sadat's regime as a moderate force with growing pro-Western and anti-Soviet behavior fostered the development of ties between Egypt and Iran. Besides, Egypt badly needed outside capital aid and investment to supplement the annual subsidies from Arab oil-producing states, led by Saudi Arabia and Kuwait, to rebuild its war-torn economy, cities, and defence forces. Egypt's relative technological and industrial advancement in the Arab world made it an attractive source of support for Iran, and its strategic location, with the Suez Canal, made it a viable gate to markets and resources in Africa and Europe. Iran's fast-growing economy gave it an expanding interest in securing access to wider markets, industrial raw materials, agricultural products, technology, and fields of investment. Above all, the Shah was always searching for regional political influence. The result of all this was a growing coincidence of interests between Cairo and Tehran in regional and international politics.[14]

Tehran and Cairo were thus able to strengthen their political and economic relations very rapidly after 1970. At the political level, Sadat's increasing opposition to Arab "extremism" and Soviet influence, as well as his search for peace with Israel and friendship with the United States, had particular appeal to the

Shah, who supported Sadat in all these respects. The Shah rejoiced over both the increasing closeness of Egyptian ties with the conservative Arab states as against the radical ones and Sadat's expulsion of the Soviet military advisors in 1972, and he expressed solidarity with Egypt during the 1973 Arab-Israeli war.[15] He supported Egypt's war effort and offered relief aid.[16] He was subsequently more persistent in supporting Israeli withdrawal from the occupied Arab lands and the right of the Palestinian people to self-determination, even if this would involve the establishment of some form of Palestinian entity adjacent to Israel.[17] Moreover, he praised Sadat for his peace initiatives; he was the second world leader, after President Carter, to support Sadat's historic peace mission to Jerusalem in December 1977. He subsequently described Sadat's mission as "dignified" and "manly," and expressed Iran's "warmest feelings of friendship and support . . . for [the Egyptian leader's] efforts to bring peace and stability" to the Middle East region. In return, Sadat shared and supported the Shah's concern for the security and stability of the Persian Gulf against Soviet penetration and "subversive" actions, as well as his resolution that the Gulf's security must be a responsibility of its littoral states.[18] Similar concerns led to the coincidence of the two sides' interests and involvement even beyond the Persian Gulf-Middle East region. This was exemplified in their common political and material support of Zaire against the alleged Soviet-backed mercenary invasion of the country in 1977, and to Somalia against the Soviet and Cuban-backed Ethiopian government in the conflict in the Horn of Africa from late 1977 on.[19]

The development of political friendship and cooperation between Iran and Egypt was complemented by a rapid expansion of economic ties between the two countries. Drawing on its growing oil income, Iran concluded a major economic protocol with Egypt on May 27, 1974. The protocol was valued at $1 billion, the aim being to "expand economic and trading cooperation" between the two countries. Iran undertook to help finance reconstruction of the ruined towns in the Suez Canal area, particularly Port Said; the widening of the canal; the establishment of numerous joint industrial, mining, and agricultural ventures in Egypt; and the expansion of certain existing Egyptian industries. Moreover, Egypt agreed to offer Iran a free zone at a port on the Mediterranean as an outlet for Iranian commercial and industrial activities in Africa and Europe, and Iran agreed in principle to participate in a multinational project to construct a pipeline to transport oil from Suez to Port Said.[20] Subsequently, in September 1975, the two countries also agreed to improve their air links and develop a joint shipping line; and in June 1976, Egypt agreed to grant Iran oil terminal facilities.[21] These fast-growing economic ties resulted in a manyfold increase in the volume of trade between the two sides, favoring Iran, from 1972. During the first nine months of 1354 (March 21, 1975 to March 20, 1976), Iran's imports from Egypt amounted to over Rls. 64 billion, but its nonoil exports to Egypt exceeded Rls. 788 billion; Egypt ranked ninth in the world among importers of the Iranian goods.[22]

The Iranian-Egyptian friendship was significant in terms of the Shah's search for regional political and economic influence. It helped the Shah to secure access to economic outlets, and it also gave him important political leverage, which helped him to improve Iran's relations with certain other radical Arab states, particularly Syria and Iraq, strengthen the country's ties with the conservative Arab states, and isolate the Arab "revolutionary" groups, especially in the Persian Gulf. In the past, it had largely been the Tehran-Cairo hostility that had impeded the Shah from seeking better ties with Egypt's close ally, Syria, and exploiting the traditional rivalry between Cairo and Baghdad to strengthen Iran's position against Iraq and other radical Arab forces. After 1973, however, the development of Tehran-Cairo friendship left Syria and Iraq in a vacuum, and reduced the latter's capacity to influence the conservative Arab states against Iran. This, together with Iran's growing regional strength and Syria's realization of this strength, helped Tehran and Damascus to exchange ambassadors in March 1974; conclude an economic protocol in June 1974, whereby Iran agreed to supply Syria with $150 million worth of credits for joint ventures, and sign a trade agreement promising further economic transactions and cooperation between the two sides.[23] The Tehran-Cairo friendship and Tehran-Damascus rapprochement, as well as Iran's strengthening ties with the conservative Arab states, particularly those in the Persian Gulf, and U.S. and Israeli support for Iran's position, by late 1974 were not only putting pressure on Iraq through fear of isolation, but also coincided with certain changes in the behavior of the Ba'th government.

By now the Ba'th regime, like Iran, had drawn on its growing oil income to begin certain ambitious domestic socio-economic reforms, for the successful implementation of which it needed continuous domestic stability, regional peace and security, support from regional resources, and better relations with the West. This meant that it could no longer afford to continue its fight against the Kurdish secessionists indefinitely or isolate itself from the Arab world altogether. It could not overlook the changing balance of forces in its region, where Iran was clearly in the ascendent; and it was not in its interests to pursue an anti-Western policy and deprive itself of alternative markets and sources of capital goods and technological know-how.[24] Meanwhile, the Shah was concerned that the Iranian-backed Kurdish struggle with Baghdad was enlarging, and could eventually involve Iran in a full-scale war with Iran. He was also aware that the Iranian oil zones were very vulnerable to possible Iraqi artillery and air strikes. Iran was at the time undergoing a very crucial period of its economic development and military build-up, and it would not be in its interest, in any way, to engage in a war with Iraq.[25]

Thus both sides found it beneficial to negotiate their differences as soon as possible. They entered serious discussions in late 1974, without much success. However, while attending the OPEC summit in Algiers in March 1975, the Shah and the strong Iraqi vice-president, Sadam Husain, held an unprecedented meeting, with the Algerian president's mediation. The two leaders signed a historic communique, which provided for the settlement of the Shatt al-Arab dispute. It was agreed that the two parties should demarcate their land frontiers under the terms of the long-inoperative 1913 protocol.[26] Moreover, Iran pledged to end its support for the Kurdish movement, and Iraq undertook to end its support for anti-Iranian groups. Subsequently, both sides agreed that if either knew of any subversive individual who was seeking to infiltrate the other's territory for the purpose of causing "disorder," it would make such an individual known to the other immediately.[27] A joint communique issued at the end of Premier Hoveida's official visit to Iraq in late March 1975 declared: "They [Hoveida and Sadam Husain] emphasised their resolve to develop relations in all fields, to the mutual interest of the two countries. The two sides further reaffirmed that the area [Persian Gulf] should be free from any foreign intervention."[28] With the implementation of most of the provisions of the agreement and its subsequent protocols, the Shatt al-Arab dispute and its side-effects were settled for the present; and in the course of the settlement, Iraq endorsed the Shah's original resolve that the security of the Persian Gulf must be the responsibility of its littoral states and that outside powers must be kept out of the region.

This further strengthened the Iranian regional position and created, as the Shah felt, a regional atmosphere in which he could fruitfully increase his efforts to persuade the Gulf states to cooperate with Iran in its regional anti-"subversion" campaign, and join Iran in forming a Persian Gulf "collective security," in which Iran would assume a dominant position.[29] The Shah attempted to complement his Gulf policy by adopting similar behavior toward the states in Iran's "zone of security" to the east.

The Iran-Eastern Zone Relationship

The most important problems perceived by Tehran in its relations with countries on its eastern flank included Pakistan's chronic domestic instability and its inability either to avoid dismemberment in 1971 or to solve its problem of Baluchi-Pushtun movements; Afghan-Pakistani and Indian-Pakistani disputes over Pushtunistan and Kashmir, respectively; Afghan-Soviet-Indian friendship (at least until the change of government in India in early 1977), and the Soviet interest in securing a direct access to the Indian Ocean; and India's growing economic and military strength as an Indian Ocean power, which had expanding ties with the Arab world and an interest in securing some stake in the wealth of the Persian Gulf.

All these factors were in opposition to the Shah's search for status as a regional power. Therefore, he adopted a policy that aimed to keep Iran's alliance with Pakistan alive and support that country's domestic stability and prevent its further dismemberment. In order to check Soviet influence in the zone, he sought to reduce Afghan and Indian dependence on Soviet economic aid. He used Iranian capital aid and investment in Pakistan, Afghanistan, and India to further these goals. To restrain the disputes between Pakistan and its neighbors from causing security problems for Iran, he offered Iranian mediation. He used resources diplomacy to undercut Indian ambitions for influence in the Persian Gulf at the cost of Iran's interests, and to safeguard Indian Ocean approaches to the Persian Gulf and the

Iranian sea lanes in the ocean. His goal always was not only to settle potentially dangerous quarrels, but to increase Iran's access to the markets and the mineral, agricultural, technological, and industrial resources of India, Pakistan, and Afghanistan.[30]

A major and long-standing difference between Iran and Afghanistan, before the 1970s, was over the distribution of water from the Helmand river, which rises in central Afghanistan and flows into southeastern Iran. After discussions in 1972, Tehran agreed that Afghanistan was entitled to take a greater proportion of the river's water in years of low flow—a condition that Tehran had rejected in the past. The two countries concluded an agreement in March 1973 whereby the Helmand river problem was settled amicably, and a major constraining factor in Afghan-Iranian relations was removed.[31] Similarly, Tehran attempted to resolve its political differences with India over Iran's traditional support for Pakistan over Kashmir. It did so by refraining from making public statements on the issue in support of Pakistan after the second half of the 1960s, and by giving combat support to Pakistan during the Indo-Pakistan war in 1971.[32]

The Shah's interest and role in mediating the Afghan-Pakistani and Indian-Pakistani disputes date back to the early 1960s. He played a crucial role in the restoration of diplomatic relations between Afghanistan and Pakistan in 1963 (they had been broken off two years earlier over the issue of Pushtunistan), and in opening a dialogue between the two sides to resolve their differences peacefully.[33] This start eventually led to the exchange of official visits between King Zahir of Afghanistan and President Ayyub of Pakistan in 1966, and an understanding between the two sides not to let the Pushtunistan issue undermine their relationship.[34] But with the change of regime in Afghanistan in July 1973, President Mohammad Daoud, a strong supporter of the Pushtunistan claim during his prime ministership (1953-1963), singled out Pakistan as the only country with which Afghanistan had a major political dispute, and declared his regime's full support for the right of the people of Pushtunistan for "self-determination."[35] Afghan financial and military aid to the Pushtun-Baluchi movement increased, and relations deteriorated, with border skirmishes between Afghanistan and Pakistan.[36] This alarmed the Shah, particularly in the wake of initial widespread speculation that Moscow was behind the coup in Kabul. He promptly declared that Iran would not tolerate any further disintegration of Pakistan after the creation of Bangladesh. He promised to help Bhutto's government suppress Baluchi and Pushtun secessionist activities; in this, he was also deeply concerned about the effect of such activities on the Baluchi population of Iran. Once the Shah was assured of Daoud's determination to continue the traditional Afghan policy of non-alignment, and Daoud had pledged to honor the Helmand agreement of March 1973 and had stated his desire to strengthen Afghanistan's friendly relations with Iran, however, the Shah reembarked on a mediating role in urging Kabul and Islamabad to negotiate their differences. In support of this, he promised a considerable amount of capital aid and investment to both sides, as well as access to Bandar Abbas and Chah Bahar ports on the Persian Gulf for Afghanistan.[37] Thus, he made a major contribution to the resumption of talks between Kabul and Islamabad, which eventually led to direct discussions between Daoud and Bhutto in 1976. Although the problem of Pushtunistan remained unresolved, the two leaders agreed to pursue peaceful negotiations and improve their relations in their mutual interests.[38]

In a similar fashion, the Shah consistently stressed negotiation as against confrontation as the only way to resolve the Indo-Pakistani disputes. He offered mediation between the two sides several times. Although during the Indo-Pakistani war of 1965, Iran supported Pakistan's "just" claim over Kashmir, it confined this support to political statements and limited logistic aid, though it gave extensive relief support.[39] Following the war, the Shah offered to mediate, and during separate visits to Islamabad and New Delhi he urged both sides to settle their differences peacefully. In the late 1960s, Tehran transferred to Pakistan a number of Sabre fighters, which were reportedly used against India in the war of 1971. But during the war, the Shah followed his past policy of nonmilitary involvement in support of Pakistan. Subsequently, he contributed importantly to bringing about the Simla "peace summit" between Bhutto and Mrs. Gandhi in 1973. He regarded the Simla settlement as a welcome step in creating peace and normalizing the situation in a zone that was of great significance to Iranian regional security and stability.[40]

In the most important example of the Shah's search to stabilize the zone to his east, he offered economic ties to the countries involved, with a promise of oil at discount prices, as well as sizable capital aid and investment. During the 1960s, Iran's economic relationship with the three countries experienced a steady expansion. With Pakistan, this took place largely within the framework of Regional Cooperation for Development (RCD), but with Afghanistan and India it was arranged on a bilateral basis. Between 1965 and 1970, the volume of Iran's trade with Afghanistan was not much less than that with Pakistan, and with India it was five times greater.[41] Although during the same period Iran was a junior partner in RCD, in comparison with the more industrially advanced Turkey and Pakistan, its economic relationship with India increased significantly, as exemplified by the joint Indian-Iranian development of the Madras refinery in India.

The economic relationship, between Iran and the three countries entered its most expansionist phase in the early 1970s, however, with the sudden rise of Iran as a financial power. During 1974-1975, Tehran reportedly promised Afghanistan about $2 billion aid, committed itself to $647 million for Pakistan, and extended $133 million to India, particularly for joint ventures.[42] The overall Iranian commitment up to 1978 included actual or potential participation in a number of agricultural and industrial projects in the Afghan provinces of Herat and Kandahar, near the Iranian border, and the Hajigak iron ore mine, north of Kabul; development of petrochemicals and shipbuilding in Pakistan; and in India a refinery at Madras, an iron ore mine at Kurdramukh, and an irrigation canal to help grow foodgrains in the Rajasthan Desert.[43] The promised Iranian aid to Afghanistan was to finance the first Afghan railway, joining the country with the Iranian railways in the west and the Pakistani railways in the east. Upon the completion of the Afghan railway by 1983, as planned, Iran and its major ports on the Persian Gulf would be directly connected overland, not only with Afghanistan but also Pakistan and India—an important substitute for the unrealized ECAFE highway.[44] In return, Tehran sought both economic and political gains. At the economic level, it endeavored to widen its access to the markets and resources, particularly iron ore, agricultural products, technology, and trained manpower, especially of India. Iran also expected to use these countries as an outlet to several other "riparian states" of the Indian Ocean—Burma, Thailand, Indonesia, Malaysia, and Singapore—as well as Australia.[45]

At the political level, it was the Shah's objective to reduce Afghan and Indian dependence on Soviet aid and stimulate the two countries to lean more toward the West, and to persuade them to respect the territorial integrity and stability of Pakistan. He also wanted to secure the approval of the three states for his Persian Gulf policy and for his concern for the safety of the Indian Ocean against what he saw as Soviet penetration and local subversion. Although Prime Minister Bhutto and President Daoud, during separate visits to Tehran in 1974 and 1975, respectively, endorsed the Shah's Gulf policy indirectly, and supported him in his view that the Persian Gulf and Indian Ocean should be declared a "nuclear-free peace zone," Mrs. Gandhi, during her visit to Tehran in 1974, avoided giving her approval in these respects, except that she agreed with the Shah on the question of a "peace zone." Mrs. Gandhi's reluctance stemmed largely from India's growing fear of the Shah's military build-up and his aspirations toward domination of the Indian Ocean, on the one hand, and her country's friendship with the Soviet Union, on the other. Her successor, Morarji Desai, did not go much further than Mrs. Gandhi in his approval of the Shah's policies, though the Indian prime minister asserted during the Shah's visit to India in early 1978 that "a constructive relationship [between Iran and India] based on political understanding and enriched with economic cooperation would make for real stability and lasting tranquility in our region."[46]

In order to establish a structure for his policy of regional cooperation, the Shah proposed the formation of a "regional common market." He first put forward this proposal for an Indian Ocean economic union in 1974. It was to include not only Iran and the countries of the Indo-Pakistan subcontinent, but also Burma, Thailand, Indonesia, Singapore, and Australia.[47] The idea was rejected at that time by India, on the ground that such a union would be dominated by Australia. The Shah revived his proposal, however, during his visit to New Delhi in early 1978, without including Australia in the scheme.[48] India agreed in principle with the new proposal, but Pakistan rejected it on the grounds that "the setting up of the common market at this stage by the countries having different economic patterns will [not] serve any useful purpose." Nevertheless, the Shah was anxious to see the establishment of such a scheme in which Iran would have a dominant role, as an extension of RCD, as soon as possible. For this purpose, Iranian Foreign Minister 'Abbas 'Ali Khalatbari declared after a meeting of RCD in June 1977 that Iran would welcome "with open arms" requests by regional countries to join the Regional Development for Cooperation.[49] The Shah's proposal for this "regional common market" was closely linked with his proposal for similar economic and defence plans for the Persian Gulf. If realized, these schemes would have provided mechanisms within which the Shah would have sought regional legitimacy and support, not only for his political and economic aspirations but also for another major aspect of his regional behavior: Iranian military intervention against regional "subversion."

ANTI-SUBVERSION

The Shah persistently sought to combat what he called "the forces of subversion, destruction, sedition and treason," not only inside Iran but also in the Iranian region.[50] He was always very broad and subjective in defining these forces, and as a result, he maximized his discretionary power in identifying and categorizing them. In general, he included all those who opposed, either in part or whole, his rule and his domestic and foreign policy objectives, whether for pragmatic, or ideological, or religious reasons. On the political spectrum, these forces ranged from nationalist critics and religious extremists to Arab and Marxist revolutionaries (some of whom may have been both Arab and Marxist). The Shah branded these forces as "Marxist," "Islamic-Marxist," or "terrorist," and their actions against his regime, whether direct or indirect, as "terrorism." He declared that communism was outlawed in Iran, and there was no place for the activities of these forces in Iranian politics. It was, he said, his regime's national duty to contain and possibly eliminate such forces not only in Iran but also in its region, south of the Soviet borders, as well as opposing them at the international level.[51]

In this, the Shah sought to achieve three major regional objectives: to weaken the regional bases of support for the opposition forces inside Iran; to immunize the Iranian oil industry installations, sea lanes, and expanding regional political and economic interests against hostile actions; and to strengthen the regional conservative forces and boost Iran's search for regional cooperation in support of its rising power. The Shah stressed, however, that this antisubversion/anticommunist aspect of his regional behavior did not have to restrain Iran from developing friendly relations with the Soviet government or, for that matter, with any other government that supported Soviet or communist-inspired groups and developments in the Iranian region. He said: "the Russian Government is one thing and the international Communist Party is another. That is why we have cordial relations with the USSR, but fight communism at home."[52] The "subversive/communist" forces that the Shah saw as most dangerous regionally mainly included the Popular Front for the Liberation of Oman, the Marxist-Leninist government in the People's Democratic Republic of Yemen, and the Popular Front for the Liberation of Baluchistan. These forces were supported, in one way or other, by the radical Arab countries of Iraq, Syria, and Libya, as well as the USSR and China, although the policy of China changed dramatically after 1974 in favor of the Shah against Soviet influence in the region. The Soviet-backed, Marxist-Leninist government in Ethiopia was more recently added to the list of the "subversive" forces.[53]

The Shah sought to enforce his antisubversion policy with sanctions from, and in support of, his policy of regional cooperation. In this, he attempted to exploit the antiradical attitude of the conservative and moderate states, particularly in the Persian Gulf, which also felt threatened by what the Shah referred to as "forces of subversion." The Shah's proposals for a regional common market and collective security aimed at achieving, among other things, a structural framework that would provide Iran with a carte blanche for intervention in pursuit of the Shah's antisubversion policy. Conversely, he used the threat of "subversion" to justify the continuous Iranian military build-up in defence of regional cooperation and the status quo. Although the Shah attempted to enforce his antisubversion policy largely by acting upon formal requests from "friendly" governments, except in the case of Iranian support for Kurds against the Baghdad government and Iran's military takeover of the Tumbs in the Persian Gulf in 1971, he made it clear that, should he deem it necessary, he would not be restrained by the lack of such a request. In an interview in January 1974, in reply to a question about what Iran would do if one of the Persian Gulf sheikdoms were occupied by an extremist force, the Shah said, "It's very difficult to envisage it if [we] were not asked to intervene by these countries themselves. I have proposed a regional pact, an agreement, a treaty . . . for the security of this region. So far we [have] got no answer. The entrance of the Persian Gulf is a question of life and death for us. To keep it open, with or without the cooperation of others, is another answer to your question why do we spend money on defence."[54]

From the beginning of the 1970s, the Shah's antisubversion actions intensified, largely parallel with the increasing Iranian resources capability. There were a number of limited Iranian regional military actions, both direct and indirect. The best examples of direct aid—the deployment of the Iranian combat troops—were the Iranian military occupation, in November 1971, of the small islands of Greater and Lesser Tumbs, and the deployment of the Iranian forces in the Sultanate of Oman since 1973. Tehran had a long-standing claim over the strategic islands of Abu Musa and the Tumbs. In the case of Abu Musa, Tehran reached an accord with the sheikdom of Sharjah, which agreed to the extension of Iranian control over the island, in return for some political and economic rewards, before the British departure from the Gulf.[55] But in the case of the Tumbs, Tehran failed to reach an agreement with Ras al-Khaimah. Tehran declared that with the impending departure of the British from the Gulf, the return of the islands was imperative to Iran's security, since they commanded the entrance to the Persian Gulf.[56] Thereupon, it resorted to its military power and occupied the islands forcibly, resulting in fatalities on both sides, just prior to the British departure. The direct Iranian military action, the first of its kind, took place largely because of the Shah's fear that if Iran did not take over the Tumbs, then they could easily have been dominated by Soviet-backed "subversive" Arab forces, among which PFLOAG had, by now, caused a great deal of anxiety for the Shah.[57]

By 1971, the PFLOAG had become fully operative in a "people's war" in the Omani southern province of Dhofar against Sultan Qabus' regime. The initial successes of the PFLOAG in extending its control over Dhofar had gravely concerned not only Sultan Qabus and other conservative Arab governments in the Gulf, but also the Shah, particularly in the light of increasing guerrilla activities inside Iran by certain radical groups that the

Shah later called "Islamic-Marxists."[58] Upon a request from Sultan Qabus, the Shah joined Saudi Arabia, Kuwait, Jordan, and Britain in sending military aid to the Omani government in early 1972. Within two years of this, as the overall military capability of Iran was growing fast, Tehran deployed about 2,000-3,000 of its special counterinsurgency forces, backed by fighter-bombers, heavy artillery, and helicopter troop carriers, against the PFLOAG in Oman. The Iranian forces operated independently of the Omani forces, and they formed the largest foreign force on Omani soil. They started their major offensives in December 1973, and played a decisive role in weakening the stronghold of the PFLOAG in Dhofar.[59] On December 12, 1975, Sultan Qabus declared "the final destruction" of the PFLOAG.[60] This declaration was premature to some extent; the PFLOAG continued its activities at least until 1977, and the Iranian troops were still in Oman in 1978. Nonetheless, the Shah succeeded in winning the friendship of Sultan Qabus as a close ally, who praised the Shah for his "heroic role" in defending Oman against the "communist-backed rebels," and committed his regime to work together with Iran in order to ensure the stability and security of the Persian Gulf. In line with his aid to the Muscat government, the Shah declared Iran's readiness "to assist any Persian Gulf country needing and requesting it to maintain its security and stability."[61] He made it clear that such Iranian assistance was also available to "friendly" governments beyond the Gulf, and he subsequently gave military aid to the Pakistani and Somali governments against the Baluchi Popular Front for Armed Resistance and the Ethiopian Marxist-Leninist government, respectively.

Iranian aid—without combat troops—to these two governments provide the best examples of the country's indirect regional military actions. In the case of Pakistan, the aid took place largely during 1973-1975, when the Baluchi Popular Front stepped up its activities against Bhutto's government. The Front, which reportedly commanded 6,000 to 8,000 men, received support not only from Pakistan's national opposition party and the National Awami League, based in the North-West Frontier Province, but also from Afghanistan, Iraq, the People's Democratic Republic of Yemen, PFLOAG, and the Soviet Union. Iranian military aid to Islamabad included the loan of ten helicopter gunships and heavy logistic support against the guerrillas, as well as direct action against the guerrillas whenever they tried to seek sanction among the Iranian Baluchis.[62]

In the case of Somalia, Iranian military aid to the government of Mohammad Siad Barre reportedly began in late 1977. It took place in the light of a number of developments in the Horn of Africa from 1974 on. Before the overthrow of Emperor Haile Selassie's traditional regime and its eventual replacement by a Soviet-backed Marxist-Leninist government, close ties of imperial comradeship had existed between the Shah and Haile Selassie. Somalia's growing ties with the Soviet Union and radical Arab states, and its revolutionary pronouncements under President Barre, had meanwhile become a source of worry for the Shah. However, the rise of the Soviet-backed regime of Mengistu in Addis Ababa in 1974, the development of a rift between Somalia and the Soviet Union, which became apparent as early as 1976, and the subsequent conflict between Somalia and Ethiopia resulted in a dramatic change from a Soviet-Somali to a Soviet-Ethiopian alliance. This changed the general situation in the Horn of Africa, and President Barre appealed to the West, the Arab world, and Iran for military and economic support to compensate for the loss of Soviet aid, and to strengthen his country's position in its conflict with the Soviet and Cuban-backed government of Ethiopia. In a common anti-Soviet/anti-communist cause, the Shah joined the conservative and moderate Arab states, led by Saudi Arabia and Egypt, in granting extensive military aid to Somalia against Ethiopia. By February 1978, Iran emerged as the major donor. During the first quarter of 1978, its aid was reported to consist of over ten shipments of mortars, heavy artillery ammunition, and ground-to-air missiles, as well as personnel.[63] Tehran, however, claimed only the shipment of "light arms," and denied any involvement of Iranian personnel in Somalia.[64]

The sudden growth of closer ties between Iran and Somalia was highlighted by Barre's official visit to Tehran in December 1977. The Somalian president praised the Iranian foreign-policy position as "positive," deserving his "commendation," and the Shah said he respected his former adversary as an "outstanding personality," and promised Iranian aid to Somalia against Ethiopian subversion. Both leaders agreed "on the need for the Indian Ocean to remain stable and secure." The Shah regarded the security of the Indian Ocean from communism/subversion as vital to Iran's sea lanes and stability of the Persian Gulf.[65] For this reason the Horn of Africa figured prominently in the Shah's overall security considerations, and Barre's friendship was very important to the Shah.

It was remarkable that up to 1978 the Shah had managed the antisubversion aspect of his regional policy behavior with a great deal of independence and self-interest. The general regional reaction was watchful and cautious, and none of the regional states had succeeded in deterring him from indulging in military actions as freely as he had. Even in the case of the Iranian military takeover of the Tumbs, the regional (particularly Arab) reaction was at the political level. While the conservative Arab states and Egypt expressed their guarded verbal disapproval of the Iranian action, and the Soviet Union maintained silence, Iraq and Libya retaliated only by breaking off diplomatic relations with Iran and nationalizing the British share in their oil industries for what they called the "Iranian-British collusion" against the Arabs—they suspected London to have been behind the Iranian takeover.[66] The fact that the Shah seemed to be successful in his quest for regional influence does not, however, negate the fact that his whole process of turning Iran into a guardian and deterrent regional power also had serious repercussions for both Iran and its region, or the fact that both his domestic and regional policies were self-defeating in many ways.

CHAPTER VIII

Repercussions of the Shah's Policies

THERE IS NO DOUBT that the Shah's efforts to increase Iranian economic and military capabilities, in conjunction with a regional policy that emphasized cooperation and antisubversion, were effective in enabling Iran to appear and act as a powerful and influential state in its region. Iran achieved a capacity to strengthen its bargaining position in the conduct of its regional relations, winning friends and pursuing a resolute stand against what the Shah regarded as "subversive/communist" forces. But the Shah's progress in strengthening and exerting Iran's position as an anticommunist, pro-Western power in its region failed to transform Iran into a self-generating industrial and military power. His policies were not only unsuccessful in fulfilling their original objectives, but also caused serious tensions within Iran and its region. This was largely because they were, on the one hand, over-ambitious in their objectives—poorly planned, badly coordinated, and mismanaged; and, on the other hand, they were based on a frail domestic political structure.

As we have seen, the Shah magnified the scope and accelerated the implementation of his economic and military policies during 1971-1975, mainly on the basis of increases in Iran's oil revenue, on the understanding that such revenue increases would continue for at least the next decade. He declared that the overriding objective of his policies was to transform Iran into a nonoil, self-generating industrial and military power by the mid-1980s. To achieve this, he directed his policies toward extensive and rapid industrialization and militarization of Iran largely through capital-intensive and technologically advanced programs. It was obvious at the time to Iranian planners that the achievement of the Shah's objective within the given period of time was beyond Iran's noncapital and nonforeign-exchange resources. But it was assumed that, given the availability of and continuous rise in the financial and foreign exchange resources from oil, Iran's limitations could be overcome by relying on imports. This reliance was to be phased out gradually as Iran continued to build its own self-generating capability.[1] As a result, Iran embarked on massive importation of highly advanced capital goods, including arms, technology, expertise and, to some extent, trained labor force in support of a rapid economic/industrial and military build-up. Meanwhile, the regime envisaged a number of measures to improve Iranian administrative efficiency, infrastructural capacity, and social services, which were contained in the revised Fifth Development Plan.

While encouraging both domestic and foreign private participation in the capitalist-oriented Iranian economic expansion, particularly in the industrial sector, and while calling for more social equality under the Fifth Plan, the Shah's economic policy still remained heavily centralized: it aimed largely at economic growth rather than economic development. Under the Fifth Plan, the social services sector, including education, was still given a low priority. Of the total government allocation, only 21 percent was projected for "social affairs," as against 34.2 and 31.5 percent for economic and defence affairs, respectively. However, as an official Iranian source stated, the Shah could not afford a more decentralized policy of economic development, given the nature of his rule. He could not handle more extensive socio-political reforms, including redistribution of wealth, than he had already instituted, despite warnings by some of his advisors that such reforms were basic to a successful and efficient implementation of his economic/industrial and military plans.[2]

As a result, the Shah's overall policies of accelerated economic/industrial and military build-up soon proved to be beyond Iran's capacity to absorb at the rate envisaged by the Shah. By the end of 1975, after two years of high government spending, heavy importation of advanced industrial and military capital goods, and increased foreign investment (particularly by multinational corporations, mostly in specialized and capital-intensive industries, led by petrochemicals and rubber), Iran was confronted with a serious shortage of trained manpower and an abundance of technological, infrastructural, and administrative bottlenecks, as well as a spiralling inflation, a drop in its agricultural production, and social imbalances. Corruption at all government and nongovernment levels, traditionally endemic in Iran, was now exacerbated by the injection of huge sums of money into the economy.[3] Since the cities, especially Tehran, were the major centers for the sudden increase in capital accumulation and economic/industrial activities, the rural population began migrating to the cities in search of better employment and wages more rapidly than had been expected. As the population of the cities swelled—Tehran's population alone rose from about 2.5 million in 1970 to about 5 million in 1977—Iran's agricultural production dropped steadily in relation to its rising national consumption.[4] By 1978, while the Iranian cities suffered from acute social problems of overcrowding and unplanned urbanization, the decreasing rural population was losing its incentive to increase or even maintain production, as the promise of success in the cities lured more and more people away from the land. Thus, despite the Shah's claims for successful land reform and for the effectiveness of incentives designed to encourage increased agricultural activity, after the early 1970s Iran had become a net importer of livestock and agricultural goods. During 1977 alone, Iran had to spend about $2,500 million (10 percent of its oil income) on importing food.[5] In the same year, it concluded an economic agreement with Brazil so that it could trade oil for food.[6] Meanwhile, in the absence of a comprehensive wealth redistribution policy, the standard of living of the rural masses continuously slipped behind that of their urban counterparts.[7]

The Shah also failed to achieve any major increase in the output of the nonoil industrial sector of the economy, although he heavily stressed the importance of nonoil industrialization. Massive public and private investment occurred under the Fifth Plan, but most of the major economic indicators show a relative decline in this sector. The economic growth rate in the nonoil sector declined from 14.4 percent in 1976/1977 to 9.4 percent in 1977/1978.[8] During 1970/1971, the sector's production made up 48.3 percent (valued at over $131 million) of total Iranian nonoil exports; the corresponding figure for 1974/1975 was only 1.3 percent higher, that is, 49.6 percent (valued at over $288 million at constant prices).[9] In terms of export-import relations, nonoil exports fell from 22 percent of imports in 1959 to 5 percent in 1975/1976.[10] Despite the development of modern industries— petrochemicals, pharmaceuticals, rubber, electrical appliances, automobiles and transport, and metallurgical industries—the Iranian traditional industries, led by textiles, carpets, and food packaging, still provided most of Iran's nonoil exports and absorbed most of the country's labor force. This was largely because the modern industries were relatively capital-intensive, with multinational corporations having important shares in them; and the multinationals were interested in those stages of production in the industries concerned that proved most beneficial to them. As two writers conclude, "by and large . . . it seems that only the final, or the very last few stages are undertaken in Iran. As a result, in most cases the multinational enterprises are involved in assembly activities, with a relatively small share of the total value added of the product being attributed to the Iranian economy."[11] Even so, the nonoil industries were heavily protected by considerable subsidies from the oil sector. This meant that the products of most of the nonoil industries had not yet been put to the full test of international competition, and should Iran run out of oil, the country's economy could be left in an extremely vulnerable position.

The Shah's efforts to build up Iran's military capability irrespective of its toll on economic development were also responsible for the slow progress and discouraging position of the nonoil sector. He justified his policy on two major grounds: first, he argued, the military build-up, apart from safeguarding Iran's sovereignty, stability, security, oil wealth, and economic development, necessarily complemented the country's economic development in acquiring trained manpower, technology, knowhow, and basic infrastructure (port and storage facilities, roads, rail networks, and so on). Second, he argued, the high defense expenditure had not restrained Iran's economic development, simply because the civilian sector of the economy could not absorb what was being spent on the defense build-up. These, however, were the very grounds on which the defense expenditures proved particularly costly to Iranian economic development. The Shah was attempting to create an extremely modern military establishment "in a country that lack[ed] the technical, educational and industrial [as well as infrastructural] base to provide the necessary trained personnel and management capabilities to operate such an establishment effectively."[12] As a result, the military sector, instead of helping the economic sector, became locked in a serious competition with the latter to attract and train the limited number of highly skilled people and to acquire access to the country's limited scientific and technological skills and infrastructural facilities for itself. In this, the military sector was helped by the priority given to it by the government.[13]

Moreover, the high military expenditure added significantly to Iran's rising inflation (about 30 percent in 1976/1977), and was funded at the cost of more rapid development of the social sector, which was essential for the economic development of the country. A majority of the population was still illiterate, and acute social inequalities and untreated diseases, particularly in the rural areas, were still major problems. For example, despite triumphant claims by the government since the mid-1960s, about 60 percent of the Iranian people still could not read or write. This was attributed largely to the low government investment in education and the poor educational system. An official Iranian report, released in September 1976, stated, "in the last seven years, some 3.3 percent of GNP and 6 percent of the national budget have been devoted to education. On an average, the world's developed countries spend 7 percent of GNP and 25 percent of their annual budgets on education. Thus, in Iran, education could have enjoyed a higher priority." It also complained that from what had been invested in education, Iran had not made an appropriate gain. It attributed this mainly to poor educational management, which "lacks the desirable levels of technical, administrative and executive skills" and its failure to create the "right conditions."[14] One does not need to go into further detail to understand some of the major reasons for the lack of rapid improvement in Iran's trained manpower and socio-cultural conditions so necessary for the execution of the Shah's industrial and military programs.

Furthermore, even the success of the military sector in meeting its objectives was limited, in light of its massive costs. By 1978 many of the Shah's ambitious defense programs had run into serious difficulties—which were attributable to the lack of sufficient progress in the economic/industrial and social sectors. A U.S. Congressional Staff Report of July 1976 concluded that, in implementing the Shah's military programs, Iran lacked not only the necessary technical, educational, and industrial base, but also the needed "experience in logistic and support operations and [it] does not have the maintenance capabilities, the infrastructure, . . . and the construction capacity to implement its new programs independent of outside support." Moreover, it stated, "Most informed observers feel that Iran will not be able to absorb and operate within the next five to ten years a large proportion of the sophisticated military systems purchased from the U.S. unless increasing numbers of American personnel go to Iran in a support capacity. This support, alone, may not be sufficient to guarantee success for the Iranian program: The schedule for virtually every major program except equipment deliveries to the point of entry into Iran has slipped considerably due to the limitations noted above."[15] All these factors cast serious doubts on the Shah's claim that, as a result of his massive military build-up, Iran had already achieved a military deterrent capability against what he perceived as direct and indirect threats from the Soviet Union and other radical forces of the region; and that, consequently, the country was marching firmly toward becoming a world military power by the second half of the 1980s.

By 1977, Iran's general economic and social situation appeared grim. The country was beset by numerous problems, including spiraling inflation, increasing corruption at all levels—involving some members of the royal family and top government officials—and mounting social and economic inequalities that were widening the gap not only between country and city people, but also between the privileged and wealthy minority and the unprivileged poor majority.[16] Although no reliable official statistics are available, by unofficial estimates a large elite of about 15 to 20 percent of the population who benefited most from the oil wealth, the Shah's policies and their consequent opportunities, and who formed the upper social strata, led an amazingly lavish and extravagant Western life style. The remainder, who made up the lower social strata, lived largely in impoverished conditions, envious of those with wealth, but struggling to improve their own social conditions and fulfil their rising expectations in whatever way possible.[17] While the poor became restless with the lack of social opportunities and the growing shortages and high cost of their basic needs, including food and housing, a majority of the rich felt increasingly frustrated with the overcrowding and industrialization and congestion of the cities. This was in the face of an imminent slow-down in the general level of economic activity, and the fact that oil income was proving insufficient to finance the government's lavish spending, particularly as the Shah was not prepared to moderate his costly military program. The rising frustrations, against the background of the people's growing expectations, caused the Shah not only to seek foreign loans,[18] but also to force a change of cabinet. He admitted that in the previous few years, Iran's high economic growth, which was directed by his own policies, had caused "dislocations and backlash."[19]

In August 1977, he replaced his trusted and longest surviving prime minister, Amir 'Abbas Hoveida, by his more technocratic and disciplinary internal affairs and oil minister, Jamshid Amuzegar. The latter immediately promised to curb inflation, government excesses, and corruption; institute measures necessary to achieve more social equality and justice; and ensure a proper process of social and economic development in the interests of all Iranians, particularly the poor and unprivileged. He called on the Iranians to give up their "luxurious and idle living" in order to save Iran's "oil wealth" for the sake of a better future.[20] His government undertook a thorough review of Iran's Sixth Five-Year Development Plan for 1978-1983, which was supposed to have been published in October 1977. The Plan was considered to create a turning point in Iran's national development. In a private interview, a high-level Iranian planner revealed as early as September 1976 that the Shah had been warned that unless the government succeeded in curing Iran's social-economic ills under the Sixth Plan, the country faced, indeed, a bleak future.[21]

It was clear, however, that these ills could neither be cured nor prevented from expanding merely by social and economic measures. There was an urgent need for reforming one of their very important root causes: Iran's chronically frail domestic political structure. The political system, which had been built largely to bolster the Shah's absolute rule, could not effectively cope with the capitalist-oriented social and economic changes to which the Shah aspired. It had denied Iranians the political "safety valves" that were necessary in order for them to cope with these changes, and to be able to express their consequent grievances, demands, and frustrations openly and legally.

The traditional institution of monarchy had not only remained intact as a source of legitimacy, authority, and power, but had also strengthened its position during the economic and social changes in the country. It ruled the country with absolute power on the basis of the support that it drew from the armed forces, SAVAK, the bureaucratic and administrative apparatus, the rising oil-based middle class, and a portion of uneducated peasants and workers, who supported the monarchy because of their low social-economic consciousness and their traditional loyalty to the Shah. Below the institution of the monarchy, the political system provided for the people's participation in the decision-making process mainly through their election of representatives to the lower house of parliament, the Majlis, and the execution of policies. But, as in the past, the elections were largely controlled by the government, and only government parties were allowed to contest them.[22] Until 1975, two controlled parties, Iran-e Novin and Mardom, contested all elections. The former was always the government party and the latter served as a token opposition. But despite the belief he expressed in 1960 that a one-party system was an absolute dictatorship and "communistic," and not to be permitted in Iran, the Shah proclaimed the Iranian system a "one-party system" in early 1975. He merged the previous two parties into one, which he called the Hezb-e Rasta-khiz-e Melli (National Resurgence party), and banned all other parties. He called upon Iranians to join and support this party, and participate in politics through either its "right" wing or its "left" wing. He called those opposing the party and its government nonpatriots, and asked them to cease their political activities or leave the country, or else to face the penalties.[23]

In enforcing such a centralized and absolute system, centering largely around his own personality, the Shah successfully drew on Iran's petro-dollar wealth and social divisions, as well as on SAVAK and its method of cultivating a "politics of distrust" among the Iranian people. The increasing oil wealth enabled him to finance ambitious economic and military programs, subsidize every basic commodity, and create an economic atmosphere in which the Iranian people became deeply preoccupied with their own personal pecuniary gains. This gave a new dimension to the acquisitive instincts of many Iranians, who from different points of the social scale, interpreted everything in terms of a status based on wealth. Money became the central theme of many Iranians' activities under "government-controlled capitalism." In this context, Iran became a society dominated by complex social stratification. Within the upper, middle, and lower classes, dozens of other sub-classes developed. The Iranian's position within this social system depended on his degree of attained wealth.[24] This divisive social structure was accentuated by the activities of the SAVAK, which shrewdly cultivated a politics of distrust so that the people were led to believe that they were being constantly watched by its numerous members— although the Shah claimed that the SAVAK commanded no more than 4,000 members.[25] All this held back even a majority of the politically conscious Iranians, let alone the uneducated masses, from assessing their political and social situation realistically and openly.

The Iranian people in general became hesitant to discuss the politics of their country freely and objectively, and they displayed a remarkable lack of interest in participating in politics. This was confirmed even by the findings of the Rastakhiz party. In conducting a survey among students of universities and institutions of higher education in the first half of 1976, the party found that only 5.5 percent of the students were interested in pursuing a political career, and "thought participation in the party could lead to dialogue and steps to find solutions for problems facing youth." Moreover, "only 2.7 percent expected it [the party] would provide an opportunity to express views on national questions, 2 percent that it would prepare them to play a role in society and 3.8 percent that it would facilitate continuation of education or improve their material welfare." A majority of students expressed their preference for education or engineering as a career. Although the Rastakhiz party interpreted the outcome of the survey as a recognition by the Iranian youth of Iran's growing need for trained personnel in more professional fields, the survey clearly manifested a general political apathy on the part of even educated Iranians.[26] This apathy seems to have been a result mainly of people's fear that involvement in politics could easily lead to their suppression, and an expression of the lack of trust both between the people and government, and among the people themselves. In this respect, the finding of an Iranian journal cited by Marvin Zonis in 1972, remained valid until 1977: "The people . . . are distrustful. If you want the truth, the people have lost confidence in everybody and everything. . . . This distrust begins with the people themselves. People are no longer sure of their own ideas, beliefs, attitudes, or even their decisions. This distrust in oneself, gained through actual experience, extends naturally, to others too. They no longer trust anyone. They have heard so many lies, have seen so much creeping and crawling . . . whom can they trust? The people do not even trust 'the people.' "[27]

In this situation, the people were insecure and divided; but the throne managed to become more secure, and stronger than ever before. The Shah succeeded in enforcing his virtually absolute dynastic rule by suppressing all viable alternatives to his regime, pressing for ambitious economic/industrial and military objectives without giving much priority to improving social conditions, and forcing both old and newly emerged socio-political and religious opposition groups either to join and support his system or cease to be active in Iranian society. In the absence of any other formal channels, some of the opposition groups moved into underground activities against his regime. Although these groups stepped up their urban guerrilla actions from the early 1970s on, they were small in number and, at that time, failed to pose any serious threat against the sanctity and continuity of the Shah's rule. The Shah simply dismissed and discredited their sporadic actions as works of "Islamic-Marxist terrorists" who were sponsored by hostile outside forces.[28]

The degree to which the Shah centralized politics and con-centrated political and military power in his hands obviously did not help either political stability or socio-economic develop-ment in Iran. The Shah could not stop the emergence of new social and economic groupings, who wanted to fulfil their rising expectations and channel their desires and grievances along broader, more flexible, and different avenues of political partici-pation. Nor could he continue to control the behavior of his subjects as he had been doing for much longer, particularly once the momentum for pecuniary gains slowed down as Iran's oil income and economic activity leveled off, as it did after 1977. The people then found the opportunity to assess their social and political situation more rationally and realistically.

By 1977, amid growing economic and social difficulties, the political structure became a major source of worry not only for his advisors and foreign allies, but even for the Shah himself. Under pressure from mounting foreign criticisms, and particu-larly President Carter's stress on human rights, the Shah found it necessary to make some moves in order to "liberalize" the political system to some extent. For example, he permitted a degree of guarded criticism by the government-controlled press, some members of the Majlis, and certain key officials, of the government's execution of his policies.[29] The SAVAK was instructed not to persecute and torture dissidents to the extent it had previously, as long as the latters' activities did not have the intention or the potential to cause mass uprisings. A number of political prisoners were pardoned after they expressed their support publicly for the Shah's regime, and some dissidents were given open trials by civil courts rather than being sentenced, as previously, by military tribunals. Moreover, a number of important public servants were delegated sufficient authority to discharge their responsibilities with increased efficiency and flexibility and, consequently, could talk about certain medium-level policies in terms of their own initiatives rather than those of either the Shah or his close colleagues.[30] The Shah's appointment of a new government under Amuzegar was widely regarded as a further step in his attempt to continue the policy of gradual "liberalization."

The Shah himself never clearly explained how far he was prepared to take his policy of "liberalization," particularly with regard to his own position in Iranian politics. One of his close advisors, however, argued that the Shah had, at last, felt the necessity to disperse political power to some extent; his leadership would remain centralized, but the political process underneath him would become decentralized enough to ensure wider public participation, and administrative efficiency and discretion in the execution of the government's policies. He elaborated further that this could ultimately result in the transformation of the Shah's position into that of a constitutional monarch. This, however, according to the advisor, could not be achieved at least until the late 1980s. By this time, it would be hoped that Iranians would have achieved a greater degree of political maturity and preparedness to understand and cope with increasing democratic reforms; and that Iran would develop into a more socially balanced industrial society, which would provide an effective counter to the armed forces, so that the latter could be restrained from taking over political control.[31]

The Shah and his advisors were overly sanguine, however, that their attempts to change the political system through gradual liberalization would ensure immediate political stability and steady socio-economic development. They underestimated the seriousness of the domestic situation, which was becoming ex-

plosive. The liberalization measures soon proved to be very limited and too late, and therefore ineffective in easing the situation.
If anything, the measures opened the way, for the first time in
twenty-four years of the Shah's autocratic rule, for the various
opposition groups that had hitherto been suppressed to rally
public support against the Shah's rule. By early 1978 a series of
demonstrations were held in the major Iranian cities. At first,
they were mainly spearheaded by the Shia leaders, the Shah's
major religious opponents, who had a firm hold over Iran's
predominantly Shia Moslem population. This group had been
a determining force in Iranian politics since the conversion of
the country to Islam in the eighth century. In modern times the
Shia leaders had grown progressively discontented with the increasingly autocratic and secular pro-Western modernization of
Iran, under both Reza Shah and his son. Since they disapproved
of the Shah's absolutism, his pro-Western behavior, and the
growing American influence with its social consequences in Iran
during the 1950s, they joined many other socio-political groups
in leading a violent popular uprising against the Shah's rule and
reforms—particularly the land redistribution, which affected
their religious holdings—in the early 1960s. As in the late 1970s,
their leader then was Ayatollah Khomeini. Although the Shah
succeeded in crushing the uprising, and exiled Khomeini in 1964,
he failed to cut off the latter's ties with the Iranian masses. In
fact, exile made Khomeini a martyr and a symbol of religious-
political opposition to the Shah's rule. His martyrdom was
sharpened by the death of his son which he believed to be at the
hand of SAVAK. It enabled him to advocate the extreme goal
of overthrowing the Shah and establishing an Islamic republic
free of what he called immoral Western influence.[32]

After fourteen years in exile, Khomeini found the right opportunity to call his followers out onto the streets against the
Shah. Contrary to the expectations of the Shah and the outside
world, the religious protests soon provided a cover for many
secular, intellectual, and ideological groups, to register their
grievances against the Shah's rule. The protestors included the
National Front, formerly led by Mossadeq and headed now by
Dr. Karim Sanjabi, which had hitherto remained weak and
suppressed, and the Tudeh. By mid-1978, the protests developed
into a nationwide anti-Shah movement, involving a large number of partisan and nonpartisan intellectuals, students, profes-

sionals, public servants, government and private industrial workers, shopkeepers, and craftsmen, as well as religious zealots. The
catch words of these diverse groups became "down with the
Shah and his oppressive and corrupt rule," and "long live
Khomeini, Islam, democracy, freedom, and equality," reflecting
not an alliance between the groups, but rather a coincidence of
their common opposition against the Shah.[33] As subsequently
became clear, the influential Khomeini and his orthodox followers wanted an Islamic Iran, governed by Islamic law, with
balanced socio-economic development but no foreign interference, and without what they regarded as the Western-based,
immoral aspects of the Shah's modernization. The intellectual
and secular groups, excluding Tudeh and certain other leftists,
who were very much in the minority and aspired for a Marxist/
Socialist system in Iran, wanted a Muslim but democratic Iran
with political freedom and civil liberties. And the poor masses
wanted more social justice and a bigger share of the oil wealth.
Although the opposition was thus very factionalized, and had
no common platform for governing Iran following the Shah's
departure, it maintained and strengthened its anti-Shah unity
over time despite heavy human and material losses.[34]

At first the Shah tried to dismiss the opposition's mass protests
as the work of a minority of "religious fanatics" and "communists," who had joined together in a "black and red reaction"
with foreign help against Iran's progress and independence. He
considered such a reaction to be inevitable in the course of
building a progressive and democratic Iran. While warning the
opposition against any excesses, and ordering his security forces
to contain the protests, he promised to persevere with his policy
of gradual "liberalization."[35] As it became evident that the
opposition had a broad popular support, however, and that its
massive demonstrations and strikes were successfully paralyzing
the government machinery, essential services, many industrial
plants and businesses, and were about to be extended to the oil
industry—the backbone of the Shah's rule—the Shah had to
concede that he was facing the worst crisis in the twenty-five
years of his absolute rule. In August, he replaced Prime Minister
Amuzegar by the conciliatory Senate president Ja'far Sharif-
Emami, who had been known for his religious puritanism and
connections with the Shia leaders. He promised Islamic-based
reforms, freedom of the press and of political activities, release

of political prisoners, and free elections with participation of all political parties except those serving foreign interests. He also said the government would punish all those responsible for killings, misconduct, and corruption, stop government excesses, and bring about more social equality and justice. He called upon Iranians to unite behind him for the good of Iran.[36] Sharif-Emami immediately sought to appease the religious opponents and weaken the opposition by closing down night clubs, gambling casinos, changing the Iranian calendar from imperial back to Islamic, abolishing the post of women's affairs minister in the cabinet, and banning public drinking and all forms of pornography.[37] These concessions, however, were seen by many Western-oriented Iranians, who had so far benefited from and supported the Shah's modernization measures, as damaging to the course of Iran's progress and as threatening to their interests. This made them suspicious of the extent of the Shah's commitment to them.

Once the opposition had broken the myth of the omniscience of the Shah and the invisibility of his secret police, the promises and measures of the new prime minister could not reduce the public outcry. The opposition rejected the concessions as insufficient, and demanded the unconditional abdication of the Shah; Iran's 37,000 oil workers began a partial strike, which soon developed into a prolonged full-scale one, and on September 8 the Shah imposed martial law on twelve major Iranian cities. This marked the end of the Shah's liberalization policy. In the face of a determined and emotional opposition, martial law only led to more clashes between protestors and troops, causing hundreds of casualties—which, in turn, increased public dislike for the Shah and violent protests against him. With the continuous loss of his credibility among the public, the Shah became increasingly dependent on his loyal armed forces, which he had trained and equipped to protect him and Iran as one, not only against a foreign enemy but now against the Iranian people. While the opposition was appealing to the feelings of brotherhood among the troops, and this was gaining the sympathy of some of the junior officers and conscripted soldiers, if not the middle- and high-ranking officers,[38] the Shah finally played a long-held card in early November. In a desperate attempt to stop the increasing bloodshed and the paralysis of government and economic life, he put Iran under a military government

headed by General Gholam Reza Azhari. Meanwhile, for the
first time, he publicly admitted his past mistakes and excesses,
both political and socio-economic. He stressed that such mistakes,
particularly political repression and brutality by SAVAK, would
not be repeated, and that all those responsible for those evils
and for Iran's socio-economic ills would be punished. He said
that the military government's prime task was to restore law and
order so that elections for a civilian government could take place
early in 1979.[39]

With this measure, however, the Shah made yet another
mistake. Military rule was not a viable alternative to a political
solution to the Iranian crisis. By imposing military rule, in fact,
he set the stage for a final but bloody confrontation between his
troops, who had had no experience in handling massive riots
since 1963, and the inflamed and persistent opposition. While
the troops dug in to enforce strictly military rule, the opposition
leaders—Khomeini and Dr. Sanjabi—rejected the military government and ordered their followers to increase their protests
and strikes.[40] Within five weeks, not only were hundreds of
people killed, but the whole Iranian economy came to a virtual
halt and on December 11, the opposition showed the extent of
its mass support by drawing about 2 million people to a peaceful demonstration in Tehran.[41] The oil production of Iran, the
world's second largest exporting country, dropped from about 6
million barrels a day early in the year to almost nil in December.
This caused serious concern not only for the Shah, but also for his
Western allies, who became extremely worried at the prospects
of another oil shortage and an oil price rise.[42] The crisis also
caused thousands of Iranians to leave the country and transfer
massive amounts of capital to foreign banks.[43]

By the end of 1978, amid increasing bloodshed and strikes, the
ineffectiveness of the military government, and the opposition's
persistent calls for the Shah's removal, Washington, which had
so far supported the Shah unequivocally, also began to doubt
whether the Shah could survive. On December 9, President
Carter expressed this publicly, and it soon became clear that
Washington had no option but to press the Shah to establish an
effective civilian government, transferring to it most of his
absolute power, and thus transform his position to that of a
constitutional monarch.[44] The Shah himself felt the urgency for
such action. He sought the support of his "moderate" political

opponents, led by the National Front, to form a government at the cost of much of his own absolute power. After a long search, he finally succeeded in persuading Dr. Shahpur Bakhtiar, a long-standing political opponent of the Shah and deputy leader of the National Front, to form a government, provided that the Shah transfer to it most of his power, leave the country at least temporarily, and never return as an absolute monarch.[45] The Shah accepted Bakhtiar's conditions, and after the Bakhtiar government was approved by the Iranian parliament, the Shah left Iran on January 17, 1979, for a holiday abroad.

The Bakhtiar government, however, was rejected by both Khomeini and Sanjabi as "illegal," for it was formed under the Shah and lacked popular support.[46] Although Bakhtiar initially had the support of the higher ranks of the armed forces, in the face of Khomeini's triumphant return from exile shortly after the Shah's departure, and the government's lack of support from the lower ranks of the armed forces, he could not survive more than a month. This opened the way for Khomeini to set up his promised Islamic Republic and end the 2,500-year tradition of monarchy in Iran.

The Shah's failures on the domestic front were accompanied by failures in his regional policies. He was largely unsuccessful in pursuing his regional goals, not only because of the traditional cultural, religious, and political differences between Iran and the countries of the region and among those countries themselves, but also because of the nature of his policies. His rapid build-up of Iranian resource capabilities and his search for regional stability and support for Iran's position as a paramount regional power had caused several developments contrary to his objectives. First, although many regional countries were cautious in not criticizing the Shah's policies openly, they were very worried lest his ambitions result in the establishment of Iranian economic and military dominance in the region. So although most of the regional countries consented to the Shah's Gulf policy and made use of his economic and, at times, military offers for their own national development and security, they declined to agree with proposals concerning the formation of a regional common market and Persian Gulf "collective security." This was a serious setback for the Shah's ultimate goal of establishing a regional structure in which Iran would hold the type of regional power he envisaged.

Second, the Shah's policies aimed primarily at strengthening Iran's relations with the conservative and moderate states in the region, and at bolstering their position. But it was some of these very states that reacted most sharply against the Shah's search for regional supremacy. They worked intensively to increase their own resources, particularly military capabilities, in order to counterbalance the Iranian military build-up, among other things. In this, Saudi Arabia took the lead. Given the Saudi oil wealth and consequent political leverage, the country's leadership had little difficulty in attracting Western support not only for accelerating its socio-economic development but also for building up its armed forces and equipping them with the most advanced nonnuclear weapons in the Western inventory.[47] The other smaller but oil-rich Gulf states, led by Kuwait, followed the Iranian and Saudi example and built up their defense capabilities; this provided justification for such "radical" countries as Iraq and the Peoples Democratic Republic of Yemen to increase their defence expenditures in order to guard themselves against possible consequences of the Iranian military build-up. As a result, the Shah's military policy played an important role in precipitating an intensive local arms race in the Gulf region and in prompting Iran's eastern neighbors, especially Afghanistan and India, to pay attention to their respective defense strengths more than ever before.[48] A competitive arms build-up at the cost of socio-economic development and political reforms could easily lead to instability and insecurity as well as interference by outside powers, rather than to the reverse, which was what the Shah claimed to be pursuing.

Moreover, the Shah's policies and the fear of possible Iranian regional hegemony were apparently a major consideration in the Saudis' continuous attempts, particularly after 1974, to influence OPEC politics against Iranian interests. The Shah needed increasing oil revenue in order to keep up the momentum of his ambitious economic and military programs, and was therefore interested in further oil price rises, which needed to be undertaken through OPEC. Saudi Arabia, the leading OPEC producer with the largest proven oil reserves, did not need further increases in its oil income, for its rate of earning was already more than sufficient to finance its extensive programs of national development and defense build-up, and give it one of the world's largest surplus revenues.[49] Using its strong position in OPEC, Riyadh sought to keep the primary source of the Shah's drive for regional paramountcy—oil revenue—in check by striving either to freeze or keep as low as possible further oil price increases. During 1975 and most of 1976, Riyadh resisted any major price increase. At the OPEC Conference of December 1976, where Tehran had taken the lead for a crude price increase of 15 percent, Saudi Arabia firmly opposed such an increase, and bargained for either no increase or a very small one. Finally, when Iran and most of the other OPEC members agreed on a 10 percent rise from January 1, 1977, with a further 5 percent at mid-year, Saudi Arabia, joined only by the United Arab Emirates, decided to permit only a 5 percent increase in its crude price. Announcing the decision, the Saudi oil minister, Sheikh Yamani, also stressed that his country was planning to increase its output by nearly 20 percent so that it could lessen the impact of the decision by other producers to charge higher prices for their oil.[50] In the short term, the Saudi decision resulted in the diversion of some of the Iranian customers to Saudi Arabia and a substantial drop in the country's oil exports. During January 1977 this drop amounted to 1,500,000 barrels a day.[51] To compensate for this drop, and to save the ailing Iranian economy from running short of funds, the Iranian cabinet agreed immediately to raise about $500 million in loans from American and European banks.[52] In the long term, the Saudi move meant that Riyadh clearly had the necessary leverage to check the rate of growth in Iran's oil income and, consequently, influence the Shah's economic and military build-up as well as his regional behavior in his search for regional supremacy. Moreover, it firmly established the fact that Saudi Arabia, not Iran, held the key to OPEC politics, and was most important to the West and the less developed countries as both oil and capital supplier. These considerations prompted Tehran to denounce Riyadh for seeking "to declare war against OPEC," and to denounce Yamani as "a stooge of capitalist circles."[53] This rift that developed between Tehran and Riyadh was obviously potentially very damaging to the Shah's efforts to achieve his national and regional objectives.

Another weakness in the Shah's conduct of his policy of regional cooperation was his financial overcommitment to a number of regional countries. During 1974 to 1976, when Iran's growing income from oil was at its peak, the Shah promised huge sums in foreign aid and investment to many states, particularly

Afghanistan, Pakistan, India, Egypt, Syria, Jordan, Sudan, and Lebanon. Most of these states therefore included important projects, for which finances were supposed to come from Iran, in their development plans. But as domestic economic difficulties pressed the Shah after 1975, he found himself largely unable to fulfil his financial commitments. He announced a major cutback in Iranian foreign aid in general, and the suspension or slow disbursement of agreed commitments. Some of the recipient governments, disillusioned with and distrustful of Tehran, turned for capital aid to those very sources that the Shah had sought vigorously to out-maneuver—Saudi Arabia, Iraq, Libya, and, most importantly, the Soviet Union.

Afghanistan provides a classic example in this respect. Tehran had promised the Daoud government about $1.2 billion in aid during 1975-1976 so that it could reduce its dependence on the Soviet Union for economic development.[54] Relying on this promise, Daoud included a number of important projects, most significantly the first Afghan railway network, in his Seven Year Development Plan (1976-1983), to be financed from Iranian aid. But by the end of 1977, Tehran had disbursed only $10 million to Kabul, and it had become clear to Daoud that the promised Iranian aid was not forthcoming on time, though he needed it badly in order to carry out his projects. In his quest for aid from alternative but non-Soviet sources, he undertook a trip to India, Saudi Arabia, Egypt, and Libya in early 1978. But amid serious economic difficulties and political unrest, Daoud's government was overthrown in a military coup, led by the Afghan underground left-wing People's Democratic Party, in April 1978. As *The Economist* argued at the time, the Shah's failure to fulfil his promise of aid may well have contributed to the overthrow of Daoud's regime and its replacement by what Tehran saw as a hostile pro-Soviet regime.[55]

Meanwhile, the Shah's determination to combat any force or development that he regarded as "subversive/communist," and therefore threatening to Iran's interests and security, seemed very self-defeating. It was almost inevitable that such forces and developments would arise frequently in the Iranian region. Apart from being of immense economic and strategic importance to outside powers, the region was composed of states that differed greatly from each other in terms of their socio-political systems, stages of socio-economic development, and national wealth. And they were changing states, undergoing rapid socio-economic and political development, which would necessarily stimulate both old and new groups with different socio-economic aspirations and political demands, and gave rise to movements causing disruptions contrary to the Shah's notion of regional stability and security. For example, the Popular Fronts for the Liberation of Oman and Baluchistan, which the Shah earnestly sought to eliminate, were primarily the products of such changes, though they were backed by certain outside powers with vested interests in the region. They largely represented groups that had opted out of their respective governmental systems for ideological, ethnic, and pragmatic reasons, and that sought to achieve structural changes for what they believed to be best in improving the social and economic conditions in their respective societies. The most effective way to deal with these groups was not to seek their elimination by the use of brute military force, as the Shah believed, but to help improve their political and socio-economic conditions, and so remove their prime motivations for "revolutionary" activities. For this very reason, despite the triumphant claims by the Iranian, Omani, and Pakistani governments, the military operations against PFLO and PFLB were not especially effective, and the resistance movements were not altogether suppressed.

In conclusion, it needs to be stressed that the Shah's domestic and regional achievements appeared more impressive on paper than they were in reality. His policies failed to achieve their own projected objectives. They were overambitious, poorly planned, badly coordinated, and mismanaged; and they were, therefore, unresponsive and counterproductive in relation to Iran's means and needs. On the domestic front, the military build-up took a great toll of economic and social policies, which achieved little in terms of creating the desired self-generating nonoil potential for Iran to be a viable and effective regional and, consequently, world power in its own right. In this respect, Iran's gains from its nonreplenishable oil resources were minimal. On the regional front, Tehran's economic and military policies caused anxiety and provoked serious reactions, particularly on the part of Saudi Arabia, and the Shah's regional behavior with its emphasis on "cooperation" and "antisubversion" was largely unproductive in terms of his domestic and regional objectives.

Conclusion

ONE STRIKING FEATURE of the Shah's rule was the similarity between the circumstances of his rise and his fall from power. His assumption of effective power in August 1953 was marked by bloodshed, popular discontent, and the belief that he was an American puppet. So was his downfall in January 1979. While in power, he largely succeeded in establishing his absolute rule throughout Iran, making his subjects succumb to his wishes and maintain silence about his leadership and policies, increasing Iran's control over its oil resources, undertaking a speedy process of capitalist-oriented development that focused on industrialization, and building up very sizable modern armed forces. He also succeeded in strengthening Iran's regional and international position, and cultivating global prestige for himself as the "king of kings" and "light of the Aryans." In all this, his major objectives were to strengthen the position of the monarchy as pivotal to Iranian politics, on the one hand, and to build a strong, prosperous, and independent Iran that could become a world capitalist power in its own right, on the other.

The Shah's goals and policies were, however, full of inherent contradictions and weaknesses. They could not ensure the continuity of his rule on a popular basis nor, ultimately, hold back an overwhelming majority of the Iranian people from rejecting him as the "enemy" of Iran and an "agent" of the United States. If anything, his goals and policies stimulated the very trends and forces that eventually caused the Shah's downfall. Despite all his efforts, the Shah never succeeded in establishing a process of balanced political and socio-economic development, through which he could build a sound domestic system and change Iran progressively according to the needs, resources, and rising expectations of a majority of its people. Nor did he ever manage to overcome the indignity of his initial reliance on the CIA for wresting power from Mossadeq, nor break free from his initial dependence on the United States, and thus balance Iran's rela-

tions with that country on the basis of a symmetrical relationship.

The Shah's dual objectives that he pursued throughout his
rule, to strengthen the monarchy and to transform Iran into a
strong modern pro-Western state, were constantly in conflict
with each other. So were the policies that he adopted in realizing
these objectives. The Shah continuously sought to make his
position indispensable to Iranian politics by centralizing power
as much as possible. Perhaps like any other absolute ruler, he
pursued a policy of severe political repression and manipulation
of political, economic, and social processes. Thus he successfully
denied Iranians not only the basic political freedoms and civil
liberties, but also the rights and opportunities to fulfil themselves to the best of their abilities and to participate creatively
in building a modern society. The end result was an expanded
and costly but, as in the past, very top-heavy, incompetent, and
corrupt state machinery and a repressed nation, which was
dominated by increasing class consciousness and socio-economic
inequalities and injustices. This nation, where the people were
forced to respect the Shah and his policies, and where the cost
of the administrative, security, and military apparatus exceeded
the amount spent on social welfare by a large margin, was largely
governed by the Shah's notorious secret police, SAVAK. The
government was dominated by the personalization rather than
the institutionalization of politics. The country lacked the necessary safety valves whereby its people, individually or collectively,
could lawfully voice their grievances, demands, and expectations.
By 1977, a national tragedy had occurred: SAVAK had become
so pervasive that a majority of Iranians could not even trust
each other, let alone the government. They had become increasingly resentful of the Shah's system, with which they could not
identify themselves.

Meanwhile, in order to build a strong, modern Iran and, of
course, to support his throne, the Shah was pursuing a capitalist-
oriented process of socio-economic development. This process,
however, unleashed forces opposite to those the throne required
for its centrality in politics. In order to prove productive and
serve the cause of stability, the development process needed, most
of all, a governmental system that would allow increasing political and economic decentralization, public participation, and in-

dividual initiative, and thus put more stress on social development and the progressive redistribution of wealth. In the long run, only such a system could have proved to be effective in coping with the socio-economic changes and consequent public demands and expectations unleashed by the process of development. There was thus a basic conflict between what the Shah wanted for his own position and what he desired for Iran. He had, indeed, created a fundamental dilemma that he could not resolve without eventually either abandoning his absolute power, or else reverting to a strictly centralized development policy, more compatible with the needs of his throne.

By 1977, he had evidently become conscious of the dilemma, and began what he called a process of gradual "liberalization" of the Iranian system. This process, however, proved to be too slow and too late, particularly in view of the fact that the Shah's economic and military policies had proved to be beyond Iran's nonoil and noncapital resources, had failed to achieve their objectives, and had produced an extremely unbalanced socioeconomic environment. This situation was no longer acceptable to a majority of Iranians, including some of those who benefited most from the Shah's policies. Thus, the grounds were ready for the 1978 mass movements, and eventually for the people to force the Shah from his throne. There is no doubt that the religious leaders, led by Khomeini, played an instrumental role in attacking the Shah's pro-Western, corrupt, and "immoral" dictatorship. Their role, however, must not be overestimated, for the mass movements were not essentially religious. In fact, a large number of people who followed Khomeini were not necessarily practicing Muslims. Nor did they agree with Khomeini's idea of an Islamic Republic. They followed him because they shared a common opposition to the Shah's rule. But because the Islamic message had a wide appeal to the Iranian masses, who had been imbued with it for centuries, Khomeini and his supporters were ultimately able to seize political power.

The Shah never succeeded in freeing his regime from its early dependence on and close identification with the United States. He was continuously suspected by a majority of his people of being an American agent. Although in the 1960s he tried to diversify the sources of dependence, he could not reorient Iran's mode of development and foreign policy interests to the point of breaking with the United States or the international capitalist market. Nonetheless, he succeeded in normalizing Iran's relations with the Soviet Union, improving the country's regional position, and eventually realizing, in conjunction with OPEC, Iran's potential as an oil power. As a result, by the early 1970s the Shah was in a fairly strong position. He could bargain effectively not only with his adversaries but also with his allies; he was in a position to use his oil strength to balance his relationship with the United States without necessarily breaking away from the capitalist camp.

However, he resolved instead that upon the British withdrawal from the Persian Gulf, Iran act as the "guardian" of the region. He therefore embarked on an enlarged and accelerated industrial and military build-up. In order to implement these programs, which were beyond Iran's noncapital resources, he resorted to a policy of accelerated importation of highly sophisticated capital goods, military arsenals, technology, expertise, and trained personnel from the West, particularly the United States. This meant, in essence, the reinforcement of Iran's early dependence on the United States in a different form. The dependence was now based more on Iran's needs for noncapital and nonoil resources for its rapid transformation into a regional and eventual world power than on the political, economic, and military needs of the Shah's regime for its survival, as in the 1960s.

The United States played a determining role in strengthening this dependence within the framework of the "Nixon Doctrine." The doctrine, formulated in 1969-1970, underlined America's new desire, in the wake of its humiliation in Indo-China, to construct a world system in which the United States, the central power, would help generate strong regional actors, who would secure their own and American interests in their respective regions.[1] Washington chose Iran as one of the test cases for the application of the doctrine.[2] During a state visit to Tehran in May 1972, President Nixon personally assured the Shah that the United States was ready to sell him any conventional weapons system that he wanted. This decision of the president, which was confirmed in instructions to the American bureaucracy, "was unprecedented for a non-industrial country; there were apparently no major interagency review of arms sales to Iran prior to the visit. . . . The decision not only opened the door to large increases in sales to Iran, but also effectively exempted sales to Iran from the normal arms sales decision-making processes in the State and Defence Departments. In so far as is known, the May 1972 decision . . . [was] never formally reconsidered, even though the large oil price increases in 1973 enabled Iran to order much more than anyone anticipated in 1972."[3]

Moreover, the United States supported the Shah's economic policies, and met almost all of his requests in this area. Together with the arms sales, this resulted in a dramatic increase in the volume of trade between the two sides, which was overwhelmingly in favor of the United States. This was manifested in the U.S.-Iranian agreement of August 1976. Under the agreement, commercial trade between the two sides was to rise from $10,000 million between 1974 and 1976 to $40,000 million during 1976-1980; and their military trade, which had totaled about $10,000 million between 1973 and 1976, was to be extended by another $15,000 million during the same period.[4] The change of the U.S. administration from Republican to Democrat under Jimmy Carter did not alter the basic spirit of the Nixon Doctrine governing U.S.-Iranian relations. Despite his stress on human rights and the strict control on arms to countries other than U.S. Western allies, in November 1977 President Carter pledged support for the Shah's leadership and policies, and praised him as a "strong leader"; he declared, "we look upon Iran as a very stabilizing force in the world at large."[5] He therefore responded favorably to virtually all military and nonmilitary requests made by the Shah, even though the Congress had become increasingly critical of this attitude.

As a result, the State Department continued to point to Iran as a successful case of the application of the Nixon Doctrine. Washington talked in terms of applying the doctrine within a "twin-pillar" policy—referring to American support for Iran and Saudi Arabia as twin powers on either side of the Persian Gulf. This policy was based on the assumption that the two countries shared common "basic objectives of peace, stability and economic development," and that they were both "responsible" pro-Western actors in the region who had, therefore, ample grounds for building a harmonious and cooperative relationship in support of their own regional interests and those of the United States. In this, however, as it turned out, Washington underestimated the potential for conflict of interests between the two countries that was inherent in their traditional differences and varying national and regional objectives. In the mid-1970s, this was manifested not only in their competitive arms race but also in their differences within OPEC over oil price increases. In the context of applying the Nixon Doctrine, the U.S. government sought to strengthen its special alliance with Iran and to preserve what Under-Secretary of State Philip Habib called America's "important national interests there."[6] The United States also wanted to "recycle," as other Western countries were doing, the money that it had paid and was going to pay to Iran for its oil, and thus help the worsening U.S. balance of payments. In the process, the other major beneficiaries were American multinational corporations and entrepreneurs dealing with Iran, as well as the American arms dealers and companies. In 1976, Anthony Sampson found that "nearly every arms company now looked towards the Shah. . . . The Shah seemed to be lurking everywhere, under every balance sheet, inside every projection of future earnings."[7] From the beginning of the 1970s, therefore, there was a dramatic upsurge in the number of American civilian and military personnel involved in different fields in Iran. At the start of 1978 they numbered about 37,000, and this number had been predicted to reach 50,000 to 60,000 by the early 1980s.[8] Their long-term presence was considered to be essential for the implementation of the Shah's programs of industrial and military build-up.

The overall result was that Iran in the 1970s became more dependent on the United States, and thus more open to American political, economic, and social influence than ever before, though the nature of this dependence was different from that in the past. Particularly in view of a fast-growing number of Americans with influential positions in the Iranian administration, economy, armed forces, and social services, many Iranians became increasingly convinced that the Shah was essentially an American puppet, who had sold their country to the United States. They felt that their cultural identity, traditional beliefs, and values, as well as traditional yearning for freedom and justice were being seriously threatened, and that their natural resources were being exploited to benefit foreigners more than Iranians. A frequent complaint heard in Tehran was that while many working-age Iranians (about 30 percent) were either unemployed or could not find work matching their qualifications, thousands of foreigners were brought in at high wages to do the jobs for which Iranians could have been trained locally and employed at much lower wages. They felt that the country had been led in a direction that was not of their own choosing, and that was contrary to their needs and expectations. They could not help but to implicate the United States continuously in what the Shah was imposing on them.[9]

Given this situation, the Shah could not rightly claim that he had, or was about to have, a sound basis for achieving his "Great Civilization," that is, transformation of Iran into a mighty, prosperous, and "democratic" world power. In fact, at the time of his fall, the Shah's vision of Iran had not developed in reality beyond what may be called a "dependent regional power," power that had achieved certain economic and military capabilities based on its oil income, but that lacked the necessary self-generating potential to sustain itself and function effectively without heavy long-term reliance on the United States.

In evaluating the years of his rule in terms of both his domestic and foreign policy objectives, it must be concluded that at the end the Shah was largely the victim of his own behavior and policies, which were contradictory in themselves and incompatible with the needs of the Iranian society. And the degree of support that he received from the United States was in the long run counterproductive.

* NOTES *

INTRODUCTION

1. B. Lewis, *The Middle East and the West*, p. 68-69.

2. For a discussion of the "dependencia tradition," see T. Dos Santos, "The Structure of Dependence"; S. Budenheimer, "Dependency and Imperialism: The Roots of Latin American Underdevelopment"; A. Emmanuel, *Unequal Exchange*; A. G. Frank, *Latin America: Underdevelopment or Revolution*; J. Galtung, "A Structural Theory of Imperialism"; J. L. Richardson, "World Society: The 'Structural Dependence' Model," unpublished paper; J. A. Caporaso, "Dependence and Dependency in the Global System: a Structural and Behavioral Analysis"; R. Higgott, "Competing Theoretical Perspectives on Development and Underdevelopment: A Recent Intellectual History."

3. See D. Vital, *The Inequality of States: A Study of the Small Power in International Relations*; D. Vital, *The Survival of Small States: Studies in Small Powers/Great Powers Conflict*; W. E. Paterson, "Small States in International Politics"; R. L. Rothstein, *Alliances and Small Powers*; C. Holbraad, "The Role of Middle Powers"; M. Leifer, *The Foreign Relations of the New States*.

I · IRAN AND TRADITIONAL WORLD POWERS RIVALRY

1. For detailed discussion, see W. M. Shuster, *The Strangling of Persia*; M. Mahmud, *Tarikh-e Ravabet-e Siyasi-e Iran ba Englis dar Qarn-e Nuzdahom-e Miladi*; F. Kazemzadeh, *Russia and Britain in Persia, 1864-1914: A Study in Imperialism*; M. M. McCarthy, *Anglo-Russian Rivalry in Persia*; R. K. Ramazani, *The Foreign Policy of Iran: A Developing Nation in World Affairs, 1500-1941*.

2. G. N. Curzon, *Persia and the Persian Question*, I: 3-4.

3. The text of the agreement is summarized in Kazemzadeh, *Russia and Britain in Persia*, pp. 105-108. The northern provinces of Azerbaijan, Gilan, Mazandaran, Astarabad, and Khorasan, which were regarded as the sphere of Russian influence, were not covered by the concession.

4. The text is in J. C. Hurewitz, *Diplomacy in the Near and Middle East—A Documentary Record, 1535-1914*, pp. 249-51.

5. For details of the British decision and its negotiation on the Anglo-Persian Oil Company, see M. Jack (now Kent), "The Purchase

of the British Government's Shares in the British Petroleum Company, 1912-1914."

6. J. Amuzegar and M. A. Fekrat, *Iran: Economic Development under Dualistic Conditions,* pp. 18-19.

7. For example, despite some of the adjustments made under the Armitage Smith award in December 1920, the Iranian government's royalty, which in 1919 amounted to £469,000 on a production of just over 1 million tons, and compared with the company's net profit of just over £2 million, had by 1939 increased to £1,288,000 on a production of 5,460,000 tons, and compared with the company's net profit of £5,206,000. B. Shwadran, *Middle East Oil and the Great Powers,* pp. 33-37. Also see: B. Nirumand, *Iran: The New Imperialism in Action,* pp. 26-34; L. P. Elwell-Sutton, *Persian Oil: A Study in Power Politics.*

8. For the parts of the agreement concerning Iran, see J. C. Hurewitz, *Diplomacy in the Near and Middle East,* pp. 266-67.

9. For the details of the "capitulation rights," which gave immunity to British and Russian subjects against their criminal and civil offenses in Iran, see A. Sa'id-Vaziri, *Nizam-e Kapitolasiyon . . . Iran.* For details of the treaties, see C. R. Markham, *A General Sketch of the History of Persia,* pp. 527-52.

10. For a critical review of the constitution see M. Ravandi, *Tafsir-e Qanun-e Asasi-e Iran.*

11. In Khuzistan, the British had given protection to a local chief, Sheikh Khaz'al, as an independent ruler to safeguard the British interests in the province, though the sheikh was nominally acknowledged as a subject of the Shah of Iran. For details of this and the Anglo-Russian activities in Iran during World War I, see J. Marlowe, *The Persian Gulf in the Twentieth Century,* pp. 42-53; Kazemzadeh, *Russia and Britain in Persia,* pp. 426-47.

12. The text of the treaty is in R. Sanghvi, *Aryamehr: The Shah of Iran,* pp. 337-38.

13. For details of this and the Iranian communist movement, see G. Nollan and H. J. Wiehe, *Russia's South Flank: Soviet Operations in Iran, Turkey and Afghanistan,* pp. 21-28; S. Zabih, *The Communist Movement in Iran.*

14. L. Fischer, *The Soviets in World Affairs,* I: 430.

15. For excerpts of the treaty, see G. Lenczowski, *Russia and the West in Iran, 1918-1948: A Study in Big-Power Rivalry,* Appendix 1, pp. 317-18.

16. For details see A. Banani, *The Modernization of Iran, 1921-1941,* pp. 112-45.

17. This Iranian dissatisfaction reached its climax when the company announced in 1931 that the Iranian government was to receive no more than £307,000, as against £1,288,000 in the previous year. B. Nirumand, *Iran: The New Imperialism in Action,* p. 31.

18. The text of the agreement is in: J. C. Hurewitz, *Diplomacy in the Near and Middle East*, pp. 188-96.

19. For the views of the Iranian government on the 1938 Agreement, see "Iran Presents Its Case for Nationalisation," *The Oil Forum*, March 1952, pp. 83-86.

20. For excerpts of the pact, see G. Lenczowski, *Russia and the West in Iran*, pp. 305-306, n. 16.

21. P. Avery, *Modern Iran*, pp. 336-37.

22. Meanwhile the Soviet share in Iran's trade fell from 34 to 11.5 percent. Lenczowski, *Russia and the West in Iran*, p. 95; also see pp. 145-66.

23. W. Churchill, *Triumph and Tragedy*, p. 90.

24. Mohammad Reza Shah Pahlavi subsequently criticized Britain bitterly for not being honest with his father, and for not making a second attempt to persuade him to peaceful cooperation rather than undertaking a joint military invasion of Iran with the Soviet Union. M. R. Pahlavi, *Mission for My Country*, pp. 72-74.

25. Churchill, *Triumph and Tragedy*, pp. 97-99.

26. For details see E. Abrahamian, "Factionalism in Iran: Political Groups in the 14th Parliament (1944-46)"; H. Kayostovan, *Siyasat-e Movazene-ye Manfi dar Majles-e Chahardahom*, esp. pp. 285-308; P. 'Alanur, *Hezb-e Tude-ye Iran Sar-e do Rah*; P. Mobarez, *Dar Piramun-e Hezb-e Demokrat-e Iran*.

27. In fact, the traditional aristocracy, a heterogeneous body that was largely composed of elements from among the large landowners, the tribal leaders, and remnants of the Qajar family, still dominated the government. For details, see K. Tabari, "Iran's Policies toward the United States during the Anglo-Russian Occupation, 1941-1946," Ph.D. dissertation, pp. 35-36, 57-58, and 62-65; S. Zahra, *Namayandegan-e Majles-e Showra-ye Melli dar Bist va yek Dowre-ye Qanun-Gozari: Motala'ai az Nazar-e Jame'a-Shenasi-ye Siyasi*, p. 178.

28. H. Arfa, *Under Five Shahs*, pp. 374-76.

29. The Tripartite Treaty of 1942 was concluded between Iran, Britain, and the Soviet Union. For the text of the treaty, see Hurewitz, *Diplomacy in the Near and Middle East*, pp. 232-34. The last paragraph of the Tehran Declaration stated: "The Governments of the United States, the U.S.S.R., and the United Kingdom are at one with the Government of Iran in their desire for the maintenance of the independence, sovereignty and territorial integrity of Iran." R. H. Magnus, comp., *Documents on the Middle East*.

30. They used the tribes, who were relatively stable and, "imbued with conservativism, resented radical change. The Soviet policy of Tudeh stood for change. Hence the tribes were naturally inclined to be hostile to communism." Lenczowski, *Russia and the West in Iran*, p. 253. For details, see *ibid.*, pp. 235-62.

31. For Sayyed Ziya al-Din's anticommunist and pro-Western stance, see his important and coherent declaration of December 20, 1944, in H. K. Kermani, *Az Shahryar-e 1320 ta Faje'e-ye Azerbaijan* II:604-22. Excerpts of the declaration are also in Lenczowski, *Russia and the West in Iran*, Appendix IV, pp. 323-25.

32. Lenczowski, *Russia and the West in Iran*, p. 245. The following section is based largely on Lenczowski.

33. *Foreign Relations of the United States, Diplomatic Papers: The British Commonwealth, the Near East and Africa*, III: 374-82.

34. T.H.V. Motter, "The Persian Gulf Corridor and Aid to Russia," pp. 288-90.

35. D. Lohbeck, *Patrick J. Hurley*, pp. 195-96.

36. The U.S. military advisors included Colonel H. Norman Schwarzkopf, the former director of New Jersey's state police, who was respected as a "leading American authority on rural police," and who subsequently played a prominent role in the CIA-backed operation overthrowing Mossadeq's government in favor of the Shah's rule in 1953. On Schwarzkopf see *U.S. State Department Bulletin* 11, no. 265 (July 23, 1944), 91. On the U.S. military advisors see *Foreign Relations of the United States, 1943, Diplomatic Papers*, IV: 550-51.

37. A. C. Millspaugh, *Americans in Persia*, pp. 47-48.

38. For the text of the bill, see Kermani, *Az Shahryar-e 1320 ta Faje'e-ye Azerbaijan*, II: 600-601. Mossadeq's main objective in securing the bill was to stress the urgent need for reexamination of the oil concession held by Britain, on the one hand, and prevent any more concessions similar to that given to Britain at the cost of Iran's benefits from its resources, on the other. For parts of Mossadeq's view concerning this matter, see *ibid.*, pp. 577-600.

39. Lenczowski, *Russia and the West in Iran*, pp. 219-21.

40. On the role of the Tudeh and the Red Army, see *Foreign Relations of the United States, 1945, Diplomatic Papers*, VIII: 480-83, 490-91.

41. J. C. Campbell, *The United States in World Affairs, 1945-47*, pp. 85, 90.

42. H. S. Truman, *Memoirs. Vol. 2, Years of Trial and Hope, 1946-1952*, pp. 94-95.

43. In March 1946, in an interview with the American ambassador to Moscow, Walter B. Smith, Stalin said, "You don't understand our situation as regards oil and Iran. . . . The Baku oil fields are our major source of supply. They are close to the Iranian border and they are very vulnerable. Beria [the head of the M.V.D.] and others tell me that saboteurs—even a man with a box of matches—might cause us serious damage. We are not going to risk our oil supply." W. B. Smith, *Moscow Mission, 1946-1949*, p. 40. Stalin reportedly also stressed to the ambassador "how important it was for the Soviet Union to get a larger share

in the exploitation of the world oil deposits and [Stalin] maintained that first Britain and then the United States had laid obstacles in her [Soviet] way when she entered to obtain oil concessions." Cited in L. Landis, *Politics and Oil: Moscow in the Middle East*, p. 4.

44. For details of the text, see *Foreign Relations of the United States, 1946, Diplomatic Papers*, VII: 414-15.

45. See A. B. Ulam, *The Rivals: America and Russia since World War II*, p. 117. Qavam subsequently argued that he signed the agreement "in the best interests" of Iran and in order to save the country from "the dangerous situation." For excerpts of his speech, see R. K. Ramazani, *Iran's Foreign Policy, 1941-1973*, p. 142.

46. G. Lenczowski, "United States' Support for Iran's Independence and Integrity, 1945-1959," pp. 50-51. Millspaugh had served Iran in a similar capacity once before, in 1922-1927. For details of Millspaugh's mission and his difficulties in Iran, see his book, *Americans in Persia*; Avery, *Modern Iran*, pp. 359-61; Ramazani, *Iran's Foreign Policy, 1941-1973*, pp. 76-85, 186; D. Acheson, *Present at the Creation: My Years in the State Department*, p. 501.

47. About the background and aims of the Democratic party, see Mobarez, *Dar Piramun-e Hezb-e Demokrat-e Iran*.

48. Amuzegar and Fekrat, *Iran: Economic Development under Dualistic Conditions*, p. 28.

49. S. H. Longrigg, *Oil in the Middle East: Its Discovery and Development*, p. 157.

50. Henry Grady, U.S. ambassador to Iran at the time, believed that at least 95 percent of the Iranian people were behind Mossadeq on the issue of oil nationalization; see his article, "Tensions in the Middle East, with Particular Reference to Iran," 554. For an account of the strong Iranian sentiments against foreign influence at this time, see Philip Toynbee, "Behind Iran's Seething Nationalism." The text of the "supplemental agreement" is in: *Correspondence between His Majesty's Government . . . February 1951 to September 1951*, pp. 19-22, and the text of the recommendation, p. 25. Hereafter cited as *Correspondence Concerning the Oil Industry in Persia*.

51. Feda'iyan-e Islam was an underground extreme religious group, which was supporting Mossadeq's nationalization and had been involved in a number of killings and assassination attempts in Iran since the early 1940s.

52. The text of the bill is in *Correspondence Concerning the Oil Industry in Persia*, pp. 29-31.

53. Cited in M. Fateh, *Panjah Sal-e Naft-e Iran*, p. 525.

54. Cited in Ramazani, *Iran's Foreign Policy, 1941-1973*, pp. 192-93.

55. A. Sampson, *The Seven Sisters: The Great Oil Companies and the World They Shaped*, p. 138.

56. The other six companies, under their present names, were Exxon, Shell, Gulf, Texaco, Mobil, and Socal. Before the 1960s, these companies, including BP, were responsible for virtually all oil production in the world outside the Communist countries and North America. They operated very much as an international cartel and acted as instruments of Western governments' foreign policies. For details see P. R. Odell, *Oil and World Power*, pp. 13-14, 24-25.

57. For the initial British rejection of the nationalization, see the text of a telegram, dated May 2, 1951, from British foreign secretary to the Iranian government in *Correspondence Concerning the Oil Industry in Persia*, pp. 31-32.

58. Henry Grady was, however, reflecting the initially favorable attitude of the U.S. government toward Iran's attempts to maximize its benefit from its oil. In a press release on May 18, 1951, the State Department announced, "In our talks with the British Government we have expressed the opinion that arrangements should be worked out with the Iranians which give recognition to Iran's expressed desire for greater control over and benefits from the development of its petroleum resources." *U.S. State Department, Bulletin*, 14, no. 621 (28 May 1951), 851.

59. *The Economist*, July 18, 1953, p. 189.

60. F. Kazemzadeh, "Soviet-Iranian Relations: A Quarter Century of Freeze and Thaw," p. 67. Also see W. B. Ballis, "Soviet-Iranian Relations during the Decade 1953-64," pp. 9-11.

61. Acheson, *Present at the Creation*, p. 506.

62. A. Eden, *Full Circle*, p. 201.

63. Acheson, *Present at the Creation*, p. 602.

64. By now Acheson believed that "Iran was on the verge of an explosion in which Mossadeq would break relations with the United States, after which nothing could save the country from the Tudeh Party and the disappearance behind the Iron Curtain." *Ibid.*, p. 603.

65. D. D. Eisenhower, *Mandate for Change, 1953-1956*, p. 166.

66. *Ibid.*, pp. 161, 166.

67. For a more detailed account of these developments, see Avery, *Modern Iran*, pp. 416-39; Nirumand, Iran: *The New Imperialism in Action*, pp. 73-86. For royalist accounts of the development, see Pahlavi, *Mission for My Country*, pp. 93-110; and Arfa, *Under Five Shahs*, pp. 396-410.

68. Eisenhower, *Mandate for Change*, pp. 161, 162. The full text of the reply is in Magnus, *Documents on the Middle East*, pp. 122-23.

69. Secretary John Foster Dulles disclosed to the House Foreign Affairs Committee that "At this time [mid-1953], non-communist forces, encouraged by our aid and friendly interest over the past two years, took measures to ensure that Iran would turn toward the free world—

The fact that during the preceding two years, the United States had kept alive the confidence of patriotic Iranian elements in our ability and willingness to help contributed to tipping the balance in favour of loyal non-communist Iranians." U.S. Congress, House Committee on Foreign Affairs, Hearings, *Mutual Security Act, 1957*, p. 1,215. For further account of the CIA involvement see *idem, The Mutual Security Act of 1954*, 2nd Session, pp. 503, 569-70.

70. Loy Henderson, the American ambassador to Tehran during the nationalization crisis, in a private interview with the author in October 1976, confirmed the central role played by the CIA and American embassy in toppling Mossadeq. He put the cost of the operation at "millions of dollars." He denied, however, Bahman Nirumand's allegation (*Iran: The New Imperialism in Action*, p. 85) of a conspiracy between the CIA's director, Allen Dulles; Princess Ashraf, the Shah's twin sister, who had been exiled by Mossadeq; and Henderson himself, forged in Switzerland, where Ashraf was staying, in plotting the overthrow of Mossadeq a week before the event.

In his interview with the author, Henderson also confirmed the direct and crucial involvement of these personalities in creating an atmosphere whereby the royalists could achieve an easy victory against Mossadeq. For the royalists' claim of spontaneity of the uprisings against Mossadeq, see Pahlavi, *Mission for My Country*, pp. 396-410; Arfa, *Under Five Shahs*, pp. 82-106.

71. Arfa, *Under Five Shahs*, p. 84.

II · IRAN'S DEPENDENCE, 1953-1963

1. This concept is used here in the context of the explanation in the Introduction.

2. Cited in F. Kazemzadeh, "Soviet-Iranian Relations: A Quarter-Century of Freeze and Thaw," p. 69.

3. To this effect the Shah subsequently wrote, "In our experience it is the new imperialism—the new [Soviet] totalitarian imperialism—that the world's less-developed countries today have most to fear. Advancing under false colours, the new imperialism pretends that it supports the genuine nationalism of each newly developing country; works its way into native nationalist movements; and then proceeds to subvert them. It concentrates on negative, destructive nationalism and thrives on the chaos that follows." M. R. Pahlavi, *Mission for My Country*, p. 139.

4. *U.S. State Department, Bulletin* 29, no. 742 (September 14, 1953), 349. For definitions of the basic American interests and objectives in the Middle East in this period, see J. C. Campbell, *Defense of the Middle East; Problems of American Policy*, pp. 162-63 and 34. J. C. Hurewitz, "Regional and International Politics in the Middle East," pp. 81, 105.

5. D. D. Eisenhower, *Mandate for Change, 1953-1956*, pp. 165-66; Pahlavi, *Mission for My Country*, p. 107.

6. For the text, see J. C. Hurewitz, *Diplomacy in the Near and the Middle East: A Documentary Record*, pp. 348-83. See also *History and Text of Iranian Oil Agreement*, in Persian. On April 29, 1955, however, the five U.S. companies turned over one-eighth of their shares to some smaller American companies, which became known as the Iricon Group of companies. During the 1960s, the Iricon Group consisted of American Independent Oil, Atlantic Richfield, Continental Oil, Getty Oil, Sagnal Companies, and Standard Oil of Ohio.

7. Cited in address by Amir 'Abbas Hoveida, prime minister, on the occasion of the presentation to Majlis of the Bill of the Agreement of 1973 for the sale and purchase of petroleum (Tehran, July 19, 1973), p. 2.

8. This will be discussed in detail in Chapter V.

9. A. Sampson, *The Seven Sisters: The Great Oil Companies and the World They Shaped*, p. 157.

10. *Bank Markazi Iran Bulletin*, July-August 1963, pp. 240-41.

11. J. Amuzegar and M. A. Fekrat, *Iran: Economic Development under Dualistic Conditions*, p. 43.

12. Eisenhower, *Mandate for Change*, p. 166.

13. *U.S. Office of Statistics and Reports, International Administration, Foreign Assistance and Assistance from International Organizations*, July 1, 1945 through June 30, 1966, p. 12. Hereafter cited as *U.S. Office of Statistics and Reports*.

14. For the text see *Law, Regulations & Decree and Single Article Concerning the Attraction and Protection of Foreign Investment in Iran*.

15. F. Daftary and M. Borghey, *Multinational Enterprises and Employment in Iran*, pp. 11-13.

16. *U.S. International Commerce Overseas Business Reports*, p. 10. This represented over half of the total foreign investment in Iran at the time.

17. *Ibid.*, p. 12.

18. Of course, during the Qajar rule the Iranian armed forces were largely made up of tribal troops, regular army, and gendarmerie/police; Iran had no air force or navy, which were initiated under Reza Shah and expanded during the rule of Mohammad Reza Shah. For background see R. K. Ramazani, "The Military in Iran," unpublished paper. For an account of Reza Shah's military policies, see M. S. Bahar, *Tarikh-e Ahzab-e Siyasi*, vol. 2.

19. *U.S. Office of Statistics and Reports*, p. 12. For a review of the purpose of the grants, see R. K. Ramazani, *Iran's Foreign Policy, 1941-1973*, pp. 158-59. Also, *U.S. State Department, Bulletin* no. 418 (July 6, 1947), p. 47; no. 467 (August 15, 1948), pp. 210-11.

20. *U.S. State Department, Bulletin* no. 22 (June 26, 1950), p. 1,048.

21. U.S. Congress, House, Committee on Foreign Affairs, Sub-Committee on the Near East and South Asia, Hearings, *New Perspectives on the Persian Gulf*, June 6, 1973, p. 105, testimony of Marvin Zonis.

22. *The Military Balance 1959/60, 1960/61.*

23. F. Halliday, *Arabia Without Sultans*, p. 474.

24. *Iran Almanac, 1966*, pp. 207-208.

25. For details of SAVAK's organization and operations, see U.S. Congress, House of Representatives, Committee on Foreign Affairs, Sub-Committee on International Organizations, Hearings, *Human Rights in Iran*, August 3 and September 6, 1976, esp. pp. 7-8, 14-16, 37-52, 70-83. Also see D. N. Wilber, *Contemporary Iran*, pp. 129-30; and M. Zonis, *The Political Elite of Iran*, p. 115.

26. *U.S. State Department, Bulletin* 28 (February 9, 1953), p. 212; (June 15, 1953), pp. 831-36.

27. For a discussion of this, see S. K. Asopa, *Military Alliance and Regional Cooperation in West Asia*, pp. 52-71.

28. In a statement on November 29, 1956, the United States supported the Baghdad Pact and the objectives of collective security on which it was based. Moreover, it stressed, "The United States reaffirms its support for the collective efforts of these nations [Iran, Pakistan and Turkey] to maintain their independence. A threat to the territorial integrity or political independence of the members would be viewed by the United States with the ultimate gravity." The United States, however, never became a full member of the pact. The text of the statement is in R. H. Magnus, ed., *Documents on the Middle East*, pp. 81-83.

29. Asopa, *Military Alliance and Regional Cooperation in West Asia*, p. 78.

30. Pahlavi, *Mission for My Country*, pp. 294-96.

31. L. P. Elwell-Sutton, "Nationalism and Neutralism in Iran," pp. 20-21; L. Binder, *Iran: Political Development in a Changing Society*, p. 324. Even General Hasan Arfa, a loyal supporter of the Shah, acknowledged the public opposition to Iran's entry into the Baghdad Pact. He wrote, "During that year [1955] responsible public opinion in Iran was divided between those who were for the Pact and those who were against it. The former followers of Mossadeq, the fellow-travellers, the crypto-communists and most of the intellectuals on the one hand and the Anglophiles on the other, were against it. Most of the military, an important section of the people of Azerbaijan, part of the middle class and of the business community were in favor of the Pact." *Under Five Shahs*, p. 414. For a review of the arguments in favor of and against Iran joining the pact, see H. Hekmat, "Iran's Response to Soviet-American Rivalry, 1951-1962," Ph.D. dissertation, pp. 170-73.

32. The Shah apparently used the Iraqi upheaval not only to justify

the continuation of Iran's membership in the Baghdad Pact (now CENTO), but also to seek the further strengthening of military ties with the United States. U.S. Congress, Senate, Committees on Foreign Relations, Hearings, *The Mutual Security Act, 1959*, pp. 637 and 690. For a detailed discussion of the military and economic aims of CENTO and its structure, as well as the Soviet condemnation of it, see Commonwealth of Australia, Senate, Standing Committee on Foreign Affairs and Defence, *Reference: Australia and the Indian Ocean Region, 1976*, Annexure A-51-65.

33. The text is in Magnus, *Documents on the Middle East*, pp. 83-85. This was to be in case of either direct or indirect aggression, for the preamble of the agreement affirmed the determination of the Baghdad Pact members to resist aggression, "direct or indirect."

34. The dramatic change after Mossadeq in the pattern of Iran's foreign policy behavior, with increasing pro-Western overtures and anti-Soviet overtones, was a manifestation of the Shah's growing dependence on the West. In surveying Iran's voting pattern in the United Nations in the 1950s, Hormoz Hekmat finds that during Mossadeq's period, Iran cast 40 percent of its total votes (44) on the Russian side, and only 30 percent with the United States. During the Shah's period, however, Iran cast nearly three times as many votes (126) on the American as on the Soviet side (47). For details of this, particularly in comparison with the voting patterns of Afghanistan and Egypt (two non-aligned states with friendly relations with the Soviet Union at the time) as well as Turkey (the pro-Western regional ally of Iran), see H. Hekmat, "Iran's Response to Soviet-American Rivalry," pp. 34-47.

35. *New York Times*, December 15, 1954.

36. For details see: Pahlavi, *Mission for My Country*, pp. 125, 130-60.

37. N. Jacobs, *The Sociology of Development: Iran as an Asian Case Study*, p. 113.

38. Amuzegar & Fekrat, *Iran: Economic Development under Dualistic Conditions*, p. 44.

39. For a detailed discussion of intervention in the Iranian economy and economic planning by the political authority for political gains, see Jacobs, *The Sociology of Development*, pp. 74-152.

40. P. Avery, *Modern Iran*, p. 451.

41. For a review of Ebtehaj's background and his criticism of the Iranian government and his imprisonment, see "Top Iran Economist, Aid–Waste Critic, Is Held Without Trial on Funds Charges," *Washington Post*, January 4, 1962; Zonis, *The Political Elite of Iran*, pp. 67-69.

42. Avery, *Modern Iran*, pp. 251, 416-49. R. W. Cottam, *Nationalism in Iran*, pp. 285-305. Zonis, *The Political Elite of Iran*, pp. 39-79, 116.

43. Wilber, *Contemporary Iran*, p. 242; U.S. Congress, House, Committee on Foreign Affairs, Hearings, *The Mutual Security Act, 1958*, p. 701.

44. Meanwhile, in an apparent attempt to subordinate the parliament permanently to the will of monarchy, the Shah instigated a constitutional amendment in 1957 that entrusted him with the power to veto any financial measure adopted by the Majlis. For the text of the amendment, see Qasemzade, *Hoquq-e Asasi*, p. 467.

45. Pahlavi, *Mission for My Country*, p. 162.

46. Citing Majlis records, Hormoz Hekmat discovers that "in fact, no Prime Minister and for that matter no cabinet member, appears to have failed a vote of no confidence in either 18th or 19th Majlis." Hekmat, "Iran's Response to Soviet-American Rivalry," p. 138.

47. J. A. Bill, *The Politics of Iran: Groups, Classes and Modernization*, p. 100. For a detailed discussion of this method, see Zonis, *The Political Elite of Iran*, pp. 39-79.

48. In April 1965, T. Cuyler Young wrote, "he [the Shah] since 1955, except for about 15 months during the premiership of Dr. Ali Amini (1961-62), steadily gathered to his own hands the reins of government, which is now one of his personal rule and dictatorship. By a combination of shrewd political ability and incomparable command of intelligence, together with some good luck and timely, though ruthless use of force, the Shah has managed to outwit, divide and break his opposition until today he dominates the government, dictating policies and procedures. His dictatorship is based on an increasingly modern military establishment, augmented by efficient and ubiquitous police forces—especially those of SAVAK, in all of which the officers, among whom none of remarkable ability or outstanding stature survives, are beholden to him for position and security. His rule is executed by a government similarly staffed, with no popular or independent personalities and generally of the category of young, modern bureaucrats. Even those few hardy souls who have some desire for independence and would like to disengage themselves by resigning find this impossible except at His Majesty's wish: so effective would be his avenging pursuit into the private sector where such men might otherwise make a living." "U.S. Policy in Iran since World War II," unpublished paper, pp. 24-25.

Bahman Nirumand cites Premier Manuchehr Eqbal admitting to the Majlis in 1958 that "I am His Majesty's Servant and am uninterested in the games played by the opposition and the government party. I stay as long as it pleases His Majesty: if he does not want me any longer, I go." B. Nirumand, *Iran: The New Imperialism in Action*, p. 97.

49. U.S. Congress, House, Committee on Foreign Affairs, Subcommittee on the Near East and South Asia, *New Perspectives on the Persian Gulf*, p. 114.

50. For details see P. Avery, "Trends in Iran in the Past Five Years," pp. 282-28. For the role of clergy, see R. K. Ramazani, "Church and State in Modernizing Society: The Case of Iran," pp. 26-28, 32-33.

51. For examples of the Iranian students' protests, see "Students Call Truce with Iran Envoy," *Washington Post*, July 12, 1961; "40 Iranians Picket White House," *Washington Post*, July 26, 1961.

52. Cited in Kazemzadeh, "Soviet-Iranian Relations: A Quarter Century of Freeze and Thaw," p. 69.

53. Shortly after the overthrow of Mossadeq, *Pravda* declared that "U.S. ruling circles are not satisfied merely with the establishment of 'friendly' relations between Iran and the West. They insist that the Iranian government show that if it is a truly non-communist government—a government which under the guise of struggle against the communists, is ready to establish a terrorist regime in the country, it is ready to prosecute any progressive leader who advocates his country's freedom and national independence." *Pravda*, September 5, 1953, quoted in *Current Digest of the Soviet Press* 5 (1953), 5.

54. Text in Royal Institute of International Affairs, *Documents on International Affairs, 1953*, p. 305.

55. Text, *ibid., 1954*, pp. 189-90.

56. Avery, *Modern Iran*, p. 459.

57. The Eisenhower Doctrine, which was supported by the Shah, essentially asserted U.S. readiness "to cooperate with and assist any nation or group of nations in the general area of the Middle East," both economically and militarily, including "the employment of the Armed forces of the United States," against "overt armed aggression from any nation controlled by International Communism." The doctrine was put into effect in Lebanon in July 1958, when President Eisenhower dispatched the Sixth Fleet and 114,357 troops to the country in support of the Lebanese pro-Western forces against what he regarded as the Soviet-backed Nasserite intervention there. For the text of the doctrine and American intervention in Lebanon, see H. Druks, *From Truman through Johnson: A Documentary History*, pp. 292-93; R. J. Barnet, *Intervention and Revolution*, ch. 7.

58. For the Shah's views on this, see his book, *Mission for My Country*, p. 122; Hekmat, "Iran's Response to Soviet-American Rivalry," pp. 229-32.

59. *Documents on International Affairs, 1959*, p. 335, n. 1.

60. For a review of Iranian-Israeli entente and cooperation, see M. G. Weinbaum, "Iran and Israel: The Discreet Entente," pp. 1,070-87.

61. In the wake of the breakdown of diplomatic relations between the two sides, President Nasser accused the Shah of selling himself to "imperialism" and "Zionism" at a cheap price. To Nasser, Zionism and imperialism were interlocked. "The battle with Zionism is also a battle with imperialism, imperialistic stooges, and the reactionary elements." See *Address by President Gamal 'Abd al-Nasser at the Arab Socialist Union in Celebration of the Anniversary of Unity Day, Cairo, February 22, 1966*, p. 27.

62. Following the Iraqi revolution, William M. Rontree, a senior official of the State Department, observed, "The Shah is concerned over the capability of his armed forces to maintain internal security against all kinds of subversion that he might reasonably anticipate would be fomented by the Communists, and to make it quite clear that he has the capacity to stand up against any local forces that might be turned against him." U.S. Congress, House, Committee on Foreign Affairs, Hearings, *The Mutual Security Act, 1959*, p. 691.

63. D. J. Dallin, *Soviet Foreign Policy after Stalin*, p. 211.

64. In December 1954, Moscow agreed to return to Iran nearly 11 million grams of gold taken to Moscow during World War II, and to deliver over $8 million worth of goods to satisfy Iran's financial claims. Similarly, in July 1955, it reportedly offered Iran the grant of technical assistance; and in late September 1955, it repatriated seventy-three Iranian nationals who had long been detained in the Soviet Union, thus bringing the total to three hundred and "removing another source of irritation for the Iranian government." Hekmat, "Iran's Response to Soviet-American Rivalry," pp. 206-207 and 212.

65. Pahlavi, *Mission for My Country*, p. 120.

III · THE WHITE REVOLUTION

1. In 1959/1960, when Iran's population was over 20 million (about 70 percent rural, of which one-fifth was nomadic, and about 30 percent urban), the country's gross national product was approximately Rls. 275.5 million ($3.7 billion), national income Rls. 24,416 ($3.3 billion), and per capita income Rls. 11,990 ($158). Iran was still a predominantly agricultural country, but only 11 percent of its land was cultivated, and only 13 to 15 million hectares of its land were planted in one year. *International Economic Survey*, April 1964, pp. 2-3.

2. For a detailed discussion of "groups" and "classes" in Iranian politics, see J. Bill, *The Politics of Iran: Groups, Classes and Modernization*.

3. M. R. Pahlavi, *Mission for My Country*, pp. 54-58. The Shah later wrote, "In whatever I have done, and in whatever I do in the future, I consider myself merely as an agent of the will of God, and I pray that He may guide me in the fulfilment of his will, and keep me from error." M. R. Pahlavi, *The White Revolution of Iran*, p. 16.

4. See Pahlavi, *Mission for My Country*, p. 328; *The White Revolution*, p. 2.

5. C. S. Prigmore, *Social Work in Iran since the White Revolution*, p. 8.

6. For relationship between landlords and peasants in Iran, see A.K.S. Lambton, *Landlord and Peasant*. For village conditions also see A. R. Arasteh and J. Arasteh, *Man and Society in Iran*, pp. 18-20;

H. H. Smith et al., *Area Handbook for Iran*, pp. 116-17; L. Binder, *Political Development in a Changing Society*, pp. 168-69.

7. M. H. Pesaran, "Income Distribution and Its Major Determinants in Iran," unpublished paper. Quoting Iranian sources, the *Washington Post*, August 26, 1962, reported that "three percent of the population owns 90 percent of the resources."

8. In early 1962, Jerrold L. Walden reported: "Despite large-scale American aid, Iran is now in more desperate financial straits than at the height of her misadventure in nationalization. When Mossadeq departed, despite a national debt of £210 million, the country nonetheless still possessed reserves exceeding $150 million in gold and foreign exchange. But by the end of 1960, Iran, for all its great oil income, . . . [had] nearly exhausted its foreign currency reserves. . . . Moreover, the nation had built up an enormous external debt, despite foreign aid." *Journal of Public Law*, Spring 1962, p. 120, cited in B. Nirumand, *Iran: The New Imperialism in Action*, p. 111.

Moreover, according to Farhad Kazemi, "the cost of living index began to rise sharply after 1958 especially between 1958 and 1961. The price of food index, for example, rose from 86 in 1958 to 112.4 in 1961. . . . The combination of economic recession in the early 1960s and the rise in the cost of living coincided with the violent events of the same period. These included a massive general strike and demonstration of teachers demanding higher salaries and better working conditions in 1961, which were preceded by election dispute, Cabinet changes, and finally the violent clashes of 1963." "Economic Indicators and Political Violence in Iran: 1946-1968," p. 81.

9. For an overall view of the system, see Bill, *The Politics of Iran*, pp. 39-51; N. Jacobs, *The Sociology of Development: Iran as an Asian Case Study*, pp. 24-42.

10. Interview with a top member of the "ruling elite" in September 1976.

11. For details of Bakhtiar's rise to power and his demise, see G. de Villiers et al., *The Imperial Shah: An Informal Biography*, pp. 198-200, 230-38; M. Zonis, *The Political Elite of Iran*, pp. 47-53.

12. For a discussion of the Iranian administrative system and its weaknesses, see Jacobs, *The Sociology of Development*, pp. 43-62, 64-69; F. M. Esfandiary, *Identity Card*.

13. By now one of the prominent domestic critics of the Shah's regime was Abol Hasan Ebtehaj, the former head of the Plan Organization. In September 1961, for the first time, he publicly signaled his distrust of the Iranian regime, and urged Washington to channel the future American aid to Iran through an "internationally administered agency" with strict control of compliance in order to discourage further Iranian "corruption, graft [and] suppression of freedom." Moreover, he asked Washington to modify its aid policy to Iran for America's

own sake, so that "the United States Government can refuse to be identified with policies and practices followed by recipient governments that are completely opposed to American traditions and principles." *Washington Post*, January 4, 1962. For more criticism of the U.S. support for the Shah's regime, see T. C. Young, "U.S. Policy in Iran since World War II," unpublished paper, pp. 24-29.

14. For some American criticisms, see "Iran's Financial Plight Laid to Irresponsibility," *Washington Post*, May 13, 1961; and "Prisoner in Iran," *ibid.*, January 8, 1962.

15. The report had concluded: "The conduct of the United States operations mission appears to have been based on the assumption that as long as United States aid funds were spent promptly it was not a matter of great consequence as to what they were spent for. Members of the mission who openly objected to the uncontrolled nature of the operation were either disciplined or labeled as incompetent. To those familiar with the involved and time-consuming processes for financing public works in the United States, in whole or in part with Federal funds, the cavalier, free-wheeling casual fashion in which huge sums of United States funds were committed in Iran must be shocking." Moreover, it stressed that the value of the enterprises funded by the United States in Iran, "in terms of economic development has been almost nil, and as demonstrations they appear chiefly to be monuments to a fumbling aid program." U.S. Congress, House, Committee on Government Operations, First Report. *United States Aid Operations in Iran*, January 28, 1957, pp. 3-4.

16. *New York Times*, December 15, 1959.

17. *Kayhan International*, November 5, 1977.

18. G. de Villiers et al., *The Imperial Shah*, pp. 235-36. For further documentation of American pressure, see U.S. Congress, House, Committee on Foreign Affairs, Hearings, *The International Development and Security Act, 1961*, p. 257; U.S. Congress, Senate, Committee on Foreign Relations, Hearings, *The International Development and Security Act, 1961*, p. 499.

19. *Kayhan International*, October 22, 1977; and *ibid.*, November 5, 1977.

20. *Washington Post*, May 31, 1961.

21. U.S. Congress, House, Committee on Foreign Affairs, Hearings, *The International Development and Security Act, 1961*, p. 255.

22. On Arsanjani's significant role in initiating the land reform, see Y. Armajani, *Iran*, p. 172. Also see Bill, *The Politics of Iran*, p. 142. About Amini's background, see "Notes of the Month," *The World Today* 17 (June 1961), 227-29.

23. *Washington Post*, April 13, 1962.

24. *Ibid.*, August 26, 1962.

25. This occurred during what was described as the Shah's private

and cultural visit to the United States in June 1964, when President Johnson saluted the Shah as a "reformist, 20th-century monarch." E. A. Bayne, *Persian Kingship in Transition*, pp. 215, 221.

26. *Washington Post*, July 19, 1962.

27. *Ibid.*, July 19 and 21, 1962.

28. Cited in Zonis, *The Political Elite of Iran*, p. 116.

29. Cited in D. Wright, "The Changed Balance of Power in the Persian Gulf," p. 259.

30. These points were confirmed to the author by two senior Iranian officials close to the Shah in private interviews in Tehran in September 1976.

31. Pahlavi, *The White Revolution of Iran*, p. 2.

32. Bill, *The Politics of Iran*, pp. 133-56; Zonis, *The Political Elite of Iran*, pp. 74-76; R. K. Ramazani, "Iran's 'White Revolution': A Study in Political Development," pp. 124-39; Prigmore, *Social Work in Iran since the White Revolution*, esp. chs. 3-8.

33. G. A. Almond, *Political Development: Essays in Heuristic Theory*, pp. 223-35.

34. *Decade of the Revolution 1963-1973*, pp. i-vii.

35. Pahlavi, *Mission for My Country*, pp. 162, 169-78.

36. *Ibid.*, pp. 178-94.

37. *Ibid.*, p. 193.

38. *Ibid.*, p. 160.

39. The Shah subsequently wrote, "[We] will base our future actions on far-reaching social reforms, economic development within the framework of free enterprise, cultural progress, and international co-operation; and at no times must the means of attaining our goal be in conflict with the individual's right of belief and freedom. I cannot conceive of any other procedure open to us that would be in keeping with the ancient traditions and spiritual mission of our nation. I can only give thanks to the Almighty for placing in my hands the reins of government of the nation I deeply love at a time when conditions at home and abroad are ripe for carrying out our plans." *The White Revolution of Iran*, pp. 1-2.

40. For details see Pahlavi, *Mission for My Country*, pp. 132-60.

41. *Outline of the Third Plan, 1341-1346*, pp. 40-41, 72; for the achievements of the Third Plan, see *Planning in Iran: A Brief Study*, pp. 11-14.

42. See issues of *The Military Balance*, 1964-65, 1965-66, 1966-67, 1967-68, and 1968-69.

43. *Ettela'at* (Tehran), January 31, 1963.

44. Pahlavi, *The White Revolution of Iran*, p. 4.

45. The Shah had already made some personal gestures in this respect. In 1950, he had announced that the 2,100 villages in the ownership of the crown (so-called crown lands) would be divided into small

holdings and sold on long-term credit to landless peasants. "One major reason for this move was to provide an example to other large land-owners." Prigmore, *Social Work in Iran since the White Revolution*, p. 17.

46. J. Amuzegar and M. A. Fekrat, *Iran: Economic Development under Dualistic Conditions*, pp. 116-21.

47. *Decade of the Revolution: 1963-1973*, pp. 41, 136. Also see *The Nationalisation of Water Resources in Iran*.

48. The Shah subsequently declared that one of the major objectives of the land reform was "to break up the big estates in the interests of farmers, to abolish for ever the landlord and peasant system, and to enable the latter to benefit both in terms of human dignity and by direct participation in the fruit of his labours." Pahlavi, *The White Revolution of Iran*, p. 35. For an overall view of the land reform, also see D. R. Denman, *The King's Vista*, pp. 124-53.

49. A. Sedehi and S. Tabriztchi, "A Theory of Economic Growth and Political Development: The Case of Iran," p. 429.

50. The factories excluded the "mother industries," such as oil, the railways, power generators, armaments, steel, and the mint, which were to remain the property of the state. *Decade of the Revolution*, p. 49.

51. Based on private interviews with senior Iranian officials in September 1976 in Tehran. For details and achievements of the reform, see *Sales of Factory Shares in Iran*.

52. See B. Mostofi, "The Petrochemical Resources and Potentials of the Persian Gulf."

53. Amuzegar and Fekrat, *Iran: Economic Development under Dualistic Conditions*, p. 48.

54. Markaz-e Amar-e Iran [Iran's Statistical Center], *Bayan-e Amar-e Tahavvolat-e Eqtesadi va Ejtema'i dar Dowran-e por Eftekhar-e Dudman-e Pahlavi*, p. 130.

55. These two industries continued to account for about 45 to 50 percent of manufacturing employment throughout the Third Plan. Ministry of Economy, *Iranian Industrial Statistics for 1964 and 1969*, reproduced in Daftary and Borghey, *Multinational Enterprises and Employment in Iran*, p. 36.

56. *Decade of the Revolution: 1963-1973*, p. 60. Also see: Pahlavi, *Mission for My Country*, ch. 4; *Workers' Profit-Sharing in Iran*; M. Shamlon, *Effects of the White Revolution on the Economic Development of Iran*, pp. 91-92.

57. *Decade of the Revolution: 1963-1973*, p. 79. In 1966, Iran's population was estimated at 25,789,000, of which 13,356,000 were men and 12,433,000 were women. In the same year the total number of educated people was estimated at 5,533,000, of which 3,907,000 were men and 1,626,000 were women. Of the last number, 1,390,000 were living in cities. Markaz-e Amar-e Iran, *op.cit.*, pp. 16, 37.

58. For details see Pahlavi, *Mission for My Country*, ch. 5.

59. *Decade of the Revolution, 1963-1973*, p. 66.

60. Amuzegar and Fekrat, *Iran: Economic Development under Dualistic Conditions*, p. 123.

61. *Decade of the Revolution*, pp. 100-101, 113. For the Shah's views on the Literacy and Health Corps, see *The White Revolution of Iran*, chs. 6 and 7. For the Development and Extension Corps also see *The Extension and Development Corps in Iran*; Pahlavi, *Mission for My Country*, ch. 8.

62. *The Houses of Equity in Iran*; Pahlavi, The White Revolution of Iran, ch. 9; *Decade of the Revolution*, pp. 122-26.

63. *Decade of the Revolution*, p. 154. For details also see *Reconstruction in Iran*.

64. *Decade of the Revolution*, p. 149.

65. See H. F. Farmayan, "Politics during the Sixties: A Historical Analysis" in E. Yar-Shater, ed., *Iran Faces the Seventies*, pp. 108-109, 113.

66. M. Weinbaum, "Iran Finds a Party System: The Institutionalization of Iran Novin"; Zonis, *The Political Elite of Iran*, pp. 39-79.

67. This was despite the fact that one of the Shah's subsequent advisors, Daryush Homayun, stated: "Not only the wellbeing of the country, but the interests of the leadership itself require a reform in the political direction, so as to maintain a balance with the rapidly changing social and economic structure. This is not only a matter of giving a sense of stability to the country. It is to ensure the very implementation of the modernization program." "Political Development of Iran," unpublished paper, pp. 26-27.

68. For details of these models, see S. P. Huntington and J. M. Nelson, *No Easy Choice: Political Participation in Developing Countries*, pp. 17-27.

69. Pahlavi, *The White Revolution of Iran*, pp. 173-74.

70. Pahlavi, *Mission for My Country*, pp. 306-307.

71. *The Week*, September 11, 1964, quoted in S. K. Asopa, *Military Alliance and Regional Cooperation in West Asia*, p. 136. For a detailed discussion of the formation of RCD, its aims, and its structure, see *ibid.*, pp. 130-58.

72. See S. Tahir-Kheli, "Iran and Pakistan: Cooperation in an Area of Conflict," pp. 476-77.

73. Announcing the end of the aid, President Johnson stated: "We are celebrating an achievement not an ending. . . . Now is the time when even stronger ties become possible . . . with one milestone behind us, we begin planting for a new harvest of friendship, trust and shared hopes." *Washington Post*, November 30, 1967.

74. In its edition of October 23, 1966, *Pravda* declared: "Although

Iran still maintains its ties with the West and the [Western oil] Consortium still controls the lion's share of the country's oil resources, and although the system of military and political agreements concluded in the post-war year still exists, the period of one-sided orientation has ended and the first results are apparent." *Current Digest of the Soviet Press*, 18, p. 43.

75. For details see B. Dasgupta, "Soviet Oil and the Third World," pp. 395-460.

76. Under the agreement the Soviets extended aid to Afghanistan in extracting the Afghan gas in the north and constructing a pipeline to the Soviet border. "In May 1967, just before the pipeline was opened, Afghanistan agreed to supply the U.S.S.R. with 58 billion cubic meters of natural gas through 1985 to repay the debts incurred in this venture and to finance additional imports from the Soviet Union." R. E. Kanet, ed., *The Soviet Union and the Developing Nations*, p. 222.

77. R. E. Hunter, "The Soviet Dilemma in the Middle East, Part II: Oil and the Persian Gulf," p. 7.

78. *Washington Post*, February 8, 1967. The paper wrongly reported that the deal involved only $90 million.

79. Despite the smallness of the deal, Washington was concerned because it saw "a new pattern in Soviet influence-seeking aimed at pro-Western nations and the Mideast." *Ibid.* In reacting to American criticism of his arms deal, the Shah for the first time felt secure enough to declare: "We cannot accept that you, the United States, should tell us what we want. . . . If we shop elsewhere, it is because of our limited resources. . . . Maybe we are not denouncing you enough to get more aid," although he stressed that he bore no grudge toward the United States, and Iran would stick by its alliance with CENTO. *Washington Post*, February 22, 1967.

IV · The Emergence of Iran as an Oil Power

1. M. R. Pahlavi, *Mission for My Country*, p. 289.

2. Markaz-e Amar-e Iran (Iran's Statistical Center), *Bayan-e Amar-e Tahavvolat-e Eqtesadi va Ejtema'i dar Dowran-e por Eftekhar-e Dudman-e Pahlavi*, pp. 162, 165-66.

3. A. Lufti, *OPEC Oil*, Appendix IV, pp. 112-13.

4. Address by Amir 'Abbas Hoveida, prime minister, on the occasion of the presentation to Majlis of the bill of the agreement for the sale and purchase of petroleum (Tehran, July 19, 1973), p. 2; he also cites the Shah's remark in 1960.

5. Pahlavi, *Mission for My Country*, p. 289.

6. For the text, see *Bank Melli Bulletin* (Tehran), Nos. 185-86 (August-September 1957), pp. 302-15.

7. *Oil in Iran*, pp. 41-47; Vezarat-e Omur-e Khareje (Ministry of Foreign Affairs), *Tahaqqoq-e Hakemiyat-e Melli bar Naft dar Panjah Sal-e Shahanshahi-ye Pahlavi*, pp. 58-59.

8. The Shah's speech in the Majlis, 1958, cited in *Iran Almanac, 1975*, p. 274.

9. Pahlavi, *Mission for My Country*, p. 282.

10. Between 1961 and 1964, while the consortium companies produced 2,035,600,000 barrels of crude, SIRIP and IPAC combined production reached 1,945,000 barrels. *Iran Almanac, 1966*, p. 394.

11. P. R. Odell, *Oil and World Power: A Geographical Interpretation*, pp. 16, 19-20.

12. B. Dasgupta, "Soviet Oil and the Third World," p. 351.

13. *OPEC Information Book*, p. 5.

14. A. Lutfi, *OPEC Oil*, pp. 112-13.

15. D. A. Rustow and J. F. Mugno, *OPEC: Success and Prospects*, p. 154.

16. *OPEC Information Book*, p. 6.

17. A. Sampson, *The Seven Sisters: The Great Oil Companies and the World They Shaped*, pp. 196-97.

18. See F. Rouhani, *A History of O.P.E.C.*, pp. 195f., 221, 245.

19. Rustow and Mugno, *OPEC: Success and Prospects*, p. 7.

20. A. Lutfi, *OPEC Oil*, p. 112.

21. J. Amuzegar and M. A. Fekrat, *Iran: Economic Development under Dualistic Conditions*, pp. 67, 138, 134; Markaz-e Amar-e Iran, *op.cit.*, pp. 162, 165-66. In the latter reference oil production and export are measured in "tons metric," and oil revenue in pounds sterling.

22. The agreement concerning the Madras refinery was concluded in November 1965. The NIOC's share amounted to 13 percent. Iran agreed to supply the refinery with 42 million tons of crude in the next twenty years. Moreover, the NIOC bought a 24.5 percent share in the Madras chemical fertilizer plant. Vezarat-e Omur-e Khareje, *op.cit.*, pp. 66-67.

23. See the production, export, and import tables in Rustow and Mugno, *OPEC: Success and Prospects*, pp. 128-29.

24. The Shah's speech at High Economic Council, 1965, cited in *Iran Almanac 1975*, p. 274.

25. For details see *Iran Almanac 1966*, p. 401.

26. Odell, *Oil and World Power*, pp. 157-58; L. Mosley, *Power Play: The Tumultuous World of Middle East Oil, 1890-1973*, pp. 272-85.

27. S. Chubin and S. Zabih, *The Foreign Relations of Iran: A Developing State in a Zone of Great Power Conflict*, p. 163.

28. Amuzegar and Fekrat, *Iran: Economic Development under Dualistic Conditions*, pp. 67, 138; Markaz-e Amar-e Iran, *op.cit.*, pp. 162, 165-66; *Iran Almanac 1975*, pp. 269, 275.

29. After the 1967 war, Saudi Arabia, Libya, and Kuwait undertook to pay a yearly subsidy to Egypt and Jordan of $378,000,000, so that they could repair their war machines and economies. L. Mosley, *Power Play*, p. 275.

30. For a discussion of this, see H. Hekmat, "OPEC and a New World Order; Some Preliminary Observations," unpublished paper; P. Windsor, *Oil: A Plain Man's Guide to the World Energy Crisis*, ch. 3; H. Madelin, *Oil and Politics*, ch. 2; F. Heard-Bey, "The Gulf States and Oman in Transition," pp. 14-22.

31. Rustow and Mugno, *OPEC: Success and Prospects*, pp. 129, 13.

32. The full text *ibid.*, Appendix C, pp. 166-72.

33. For details see Sampson, *The Seven Sisters*, pp. 251-62.

34. For the Shah's stance on this issue, see "Press Conference by His Imperial Majesty Shahanshah Aryamehr, London, 24 June 1972" (Tehran: Ministry of Information, n.d.).

35. In an interview with the American CBS network in October 1976, the Shah called Qaddafi an "absolutely irresponsible and crazy" man, and condemned him for giving aid to the Palestinian Liberation Organization (PLO); the Shah regarded the PLO as a group that bullied "the world . . . by terrorism and blackmailing," though he supported a "just" solution of the Palestinian problem. *New York Times*, October 22, 1976.

36. Rustow and Mugno, *OPEC: Success and Prospects*, p. 155.

37. The text in *BBC Summary of World Broadcast*, January 14, 1971, ME/3587. Cited hereafter as *BBCSWB*.

38. The Shah's speech to the Plan Organization, *BBCSWB*, December 29, 1971, ME/3575.

39. *Ibid.*

40. *Ettela'at*, January 18, 1971.

41. See the text of the committee's joint communique in *BBCSWB*, January 13, 1971, ME/3584.

42. Rustow and Mugno, *OPEC: Success and Prospects*, p. 21.

43. Text of the Shah's press conference in *BBCSWB*, February 5, 1971, ME/3502.

44. *Ibid.*

45. *Keesing's Contemporary Archives*, June 5-12, 1971, p. 24,648.

46. See *BBCSWB*, February 5, 1971, ME/3602.

47. *Ibid.*, February 9, 1971, ME/3605.

48. *Keesing's Contemporary Archives*, June 5-12, 1971, p. 24,649.

49. Rustow and Mugno, *OPEC: Success and Prospects*, p. 131.

50. For a discussion of this see P. R. Odell, "The World of Oil Power in 1975."

51. See *BBCSWB*, February 11, 1971, ME/3607.

52. Rustow and Mugno, *OPEC: Success and Prospects*, pp. 156-57.

53. The Shah subsequently declared, "They [Iraqis] have the right to nationalize; We support that, obviously." His press conference, London, June 24, 1972, p. 4.

54. *Ibid.*

55. *Ibid.*, p. 23.

56. "The Shah's Address to the National Congress Held to Mark the Tenth Anniversary of the Revolution of the Shah and the Nation, January 23, 1973" (Tehran: Ministry of Information, 1973), p. 8.

57. *Ibid.*, pp. 8-9.

58. *Keesing's Contemporary Archives*, May 21-27, 1973, p. 25,898.

59. Address by Amir 'Abbas Hoveida (Tehran, July 19, 1973), p. 9-11, 7.

60. *BBCSWB*, March 29, 1973, ME/4257.

61. *BBCSWB*, July 17, 1973, SU/4348.

62. *Keesing's Contemporary Archives*, November 12-18, 1973, p. 26,195.

63. *Ibid.*, November 26-December 2, 1973, p. 26,225.

64. *Newsweek*, April 9, 1973.

65. For a discussion of this, see H. J. Burchard, "Sovereignty over Petroleum Changes Hands," pp. 448-51; L. Turner, "The European Community: Factors of Disintegration," pp. 404-15.

66. King Faisal had issued his warning as early as August 31, 1973 in an interview with the U.S. National Broadcasting Corporation.

67. This was declared by the chairman and managing director of the National Iranian Oil Company (NIOC), Manuchehr Eqbal, during his official visit to Tokyo, *BBCSWB*, October 18, 1973, FE/4427.

68. *BBCSWB*, October 19, 1973, ME/4428.

69. *BBCSWB*, October 19, 1973, ME/4428. OAPEC was formed by the Arab oil states shortly after the Middle East War of June 1967.

70. *Keesing's Contemporary Archives*, November 26-December 2, 1973, p. 26,225.

71. *BBCSWB*, October 20, 1973, ME/4429.

72. *New York Times*, December 21, 1973.

73. *Ibid.*

74. *Keesing's Contemporary Archives*, February 18-24, 1974, p. 26,355.

75. The Shah's press conference at the Niavaran Palace, Tehran, December 23, 1973 (Tehran: Ministry of Information Press).

76. Rustow and Mugno, *OPEC: Success and Prospects*, p. 131.

77. *Newsweek*, January 21, 1974.

78. The Shah's interview with "Al-Hawadith," Tehran, November 24, 1973. *BBCSWB*, November 27, 1973, ME/4461.

79. For details see R. M. Burrell and A. J. Cottrell, "Iran, Afghanistan, Pakistan: Tensions and Dilemmas," pp. 28-37.

80. *Kayhan International*, January 26, 1974.

81. *Daily Telegraph*, February 7, 1974.

82. *The AGE*, January 13, 1975. Also see *Kayhan International*, January 25 and February 1, 1975.

83. For a discussion of this, see M. Timmler, "Africa Duped and Disappointed."

84. The Shah's press conference, Tehran, December 23, 1973. Also see *His Imperial Majesty Mohammad-Reza Pahlavi Aryamehr, Shahanshah of Iran on Oil and Other Topics, Press Conference and Interviews* (Tehran: Ministry of Foreign Affairs, January 19, 1974).

INTRODUCTION TO PART II

1. For details see the Shah's following speeches and interviews: address by the Shahanshah Aryamehr to the National Congress held to mark the Tenth Anniversary of the Revolution of the Shah and the Nation, January 23, 1973 (Tehran: Ministry of Information, 1973); the Shah's Navy Day speech, *BBCSWB*, ME/4140/D/1, November 9, 1972; the Shah's interview with *Der Spiegel*, *BBCSWB*, ME/4495/D/1, January 9, 1974; the Shah's interview for ITV, *BBCSWB*, ME/4514/D/1, January 31, 1974; the Shah's interview for Cairo *Al-Ahram*, *BBCSWB*, ME/4515/D/1, February 1, 1974; the Shah's interview with the *Daily Telegraph*, *BBCSWB*, ME/4523/D/1, February 1, 1974; the Shah's Now Ruz message, *BBCSWB*, ME/4558/D/1, March 23, 1974. The Shah's ideas concerning his goal of "Great Civilization" have been collected in *Basu-ye Tamaddon-e Bozorg*. Also see Amir 'Abbas Hoveida's speeches at Iran Novin party meetings in Bushire and Baluchistan, *BBCSWB*, ME/4112/D/1, October 7, 1972; ME/4111/D/1, October 6, 1972. The Shah's interview, *Kayhan* (Persian airmail edition), Ordibehesht 13, 2537 (May 3, 1978).

2. Discussing "middle powers," Carsten Holbraad perceptively writes, "they [middle powers] can be distinguished only on the grounds of the strength they possess and the power they wield. But to measure the strength and estimate it is extremely difficult. Since such measurements and estimates invariably involve a number of personal choices and since the divisions based on them in the last resort tend to be arbitrary, there is something to be said for openly relying heavily on impressionistic methods when classifying states lower than great powers." "The Role of Middle Powers," p. 82.

V · THE SHAH'S VISION

1. See M. R. Pahlavi, *Besu-ye Tamaddon-e Bozorg*, pp. 233-46 and 248-345; and *The White Revolution in Iran*, ch. 11.

2. The Shah's interviews for ITV, *BBCSWB*, January 31, 1974, ME/4514, and *Al-Ahram*, *BBCSWB*, February 1, 1974, ME/4515.

3. For the Shah's views on change of date see his interview for *Der Spiegel* in *His Imperial Majesty Mohammed-Reza Pahlavi Aryamehr, Shahanshah of Iran on Oil and Other Topics, Press Conference and Interviews* (Tehran: Ministry of Foreign Affairs, January 19, 1974), pp. 22-26.

4. The Shah considered the relationship between economic and military buildups as "compatible" and "essential." He stressed that "the one is worthless without the other. There is no economic power without military power." *Europa*, 111 (March 1976).

5. The Shah's Navy Day speech on Kharg Island, *BBCSWB*, November 9, 1972, ME/4140; the Shah's interviews for *Der Spiegel*, January 19, 1974; press conference by His Imperial Majesty Shahanshah Aryamehr, London, June 24, 1972 (Tehran: Information Department, Ministry of Information, n.d.).

6. In a press conference in June 1972, answering a question about Soviet activities against Iran in the region, particularly the Persian Gulf, the Shah stated: "What concerns me is the subversive activities of some of our neighbours there [in the Persian Gulf], and this is something to which we are very sensitive, and if necessary we shall take adequate measures." "Press Conference By His Imperial Majesty Shahanshah Aryamehr," London, June 24, 1972.

7. The Shah subsequently declared, "we are not prepared to face any [further] disturbances on our eastern flank. It would be a terrible blow to us if anything bad happened to Pakistan . . . and we cannot remain indifferent" to disintegration of Pakistan. *Ibid.*

8. *Oil and Gas Journal*, December 30, 1974. For a brief discussion of the significance of the Persian Gulf in the context of world politics, see H. Hekmat, "OPEC and New World Order, Some Primary Observations," unpublished paper. Also see A. Taheri, "Policies of Iran in the Persian Gulf Region," pp. 259-60; R. M. Burrell, "The Persian Gulf," *The Washington Papers: 1*.

9. The Shah's interview with the *Daily Telegraph*, February 8, 1974.

10. Even the Shah was very conscious of such differences when he made a clear distinction between the Arabs and the Persians as two distinct races: "The Arabs are Semites . . . the Jews are Semites and the Arabs are Semites too. We [Persians] are Arians and . . . Germans are Arians." He denied that religious ties were as strong between Arabs and Persians as the former claimed. The Shah's interview for *Der Spiegel*, January 4, 1974.

11. For background information, see H. Moghtader, "The Settlement of the Bahrain Question: A Study in Anglo-Iranian-United Nations Diplomacy"; R. K. Ramazani, *The Persian Gulf: Iran's Role*.

12. For details see R. K. Ramazani, *The Persian Gulf: Iran's Role*; C.J. Edmonds, "The Iraqi-Persian Frontier: 1639-1938"; S. Chubin and

S. Zabih, *The Foreign Relations of Iran: A Developing State in a Zone of Great-Power Conflict*, ch. 4.

13. For details see S. Chubin and S. Zabih, *The Foreign Relations of Iran*; Ramazani, *The Persian Gulf; Iran's Role*; R. M. Burrell and A. J. Cottrell, "Iran, Afghanistan, Pakistan: Tensions and Dilemmas," pp. 11, 57.

14. As recently as 1976 this issue prompted Iran to recall its ambassadors from several Arab states and warn them that it would review its relations with those states if they insisted on calling the Persian Gulf "the Arabian Gulf." *Canberra Times*, January 9, 1976. For background information see J. Marlowe, "Arab-Persian Rivalry in the Persian Gulf," pp. 22-31.

15. For the background to the Kurdish movement, see D. Kinnane, *The Kurds and Kurdistan*. See Burrell and Cottrell, "Iran, Afghanistan, Pakistan," pp. 11-14.

16. A. H. Raoof, "Confrontation and Detente in the Arabian-Persian Gulf: The Case of Iraq," unpublished paper.

17. For a detailed discussion, see J. O. Anthony, *Arab States of the Lower Gulf: People, Politics, Petroleum*; F. Heard-Bey, "The Gulf States and Oman in Transition"; F. Heard-Bey, "Social Changes in the Gulf States and Oman"; F. Halliday, *Arabia Without Sultans*; U.S. Congress, House, Committee on Foreign Affairs, Subcommittee on the Near East, Hearings, *The Middle East, 1971: The Need to Strengthen Peace: The Persian Gulf at the End of 1971*, July 15, 1971.

18. For details see Halliday, *Arabia Without Sultans*, chs. 10-11.

19. For a detailed discussion of the division and disputes, see Subcommittee on the Near East, Hearings, *The Middle East, 1971*, July 15, 1971; D. C. Watt, "The Persian Gulf—Cradle of Conflict?"

20. See U.S. Congress, House, Committee on Foreign Affairs, Subcommittee on the Near East, Hearings, *The Middle East, 1971*, July 15, 1971.

21. See D. Wright, "The Changing Balance of Power in the Persian Gulf," pp. 255-62. This was confirmed by a senior British diplomat in a personal interview in October 1976. The Trucial States were Abu Dhabi, Dubai, Sharjah, Ajman, Um al Qaiwain, Ras al-Khaimah, and Fujaira; they formed the United Arab Emirates (UAE) in 1971.

22. The Shah's interview for *Newsweek* as it appears in full in *Kayhan International*, January 22, 1976.

23. For details of the Helmand dispute, see A. Lamb, *Asian Frontiers: Studies in a Continuing Problem*.

24. During 1954-1976, the Soviet economic assistance alone to Afghanistan amounted to $1,253 million. *Strategic Survey 1977*, p. 66.

25. Joint Afghan-Soviet communique, February 1966, in N. M. Rahimi, ed., *The Kabul Times Annual*, pp. 26-28. For background to the

issue of Pushtunistan see A. R. Binava, *Pushtunistan*; O. Caroe, "The North-West Frontier, Old and New"; R. S. Newell, *The Politics of Afghanistan*, pp. 65-69.

26. The treaty provided for consultations between the two countries whenever their respective security was threatened by a third party. The text of the treaty is in Commonwealth of Australia, Senate, Hansard, Standing Committee on Foreign Affairs and Defence, *Australia and the Indian Ocean Region, 1976*, Annexure A-88-92. The Shah subsequently declared, "the integrity of Pakistan is vital for us. If it were threatened and some separatist movement started, this would create an absolutely intolerable situation for our eastern frontiers." The Shah's interview in Washington, reported in *Kayhan International*, October 20, 1973.

27. In his first policy statement as the leader of the coup, Daoud singled out Pakistan as the only country with which Afghanistan had a major political difference. He reiterated his firm support for the right of Pushtuns living in "Pushtunistan" to self-determination, and sought a political solution of the matter. For the full text of the statement see *Pamir* [in Dari], no. 33-34 (16 Asad, 1352 A.H.). For the Pushtunistan issue see D. Mukerjee, "Afghanistan under Daud [sic]: Relations with Neighbouring States."

28. This was emphasized by Tehran's belated recognition of the Daoud regime.

29. This eventually resulted in President Daoud's state visit to Iran in May 1975. Daoud said that Iran and Afghanistan were "duty-bound" to expand their cooperation, and expressed hope that his talks in Iran would lead to a "new phase in our friendly relations." *Kayhan International*, May 3, 1975. For the joint communique see *ibid.*

30. Personal interviews with senior Iranian officials and anti-Shah elements in Tehran in September 1976.

31. Mukerjee, "Afghanistan under Daud."

32. Personal interview with two senior foreign policy advisors of the Shah in Tehran in September 1976.

33. *Ibid.* R. K. Ramazani, "Emerging Patterns of Regional Relations in Iranian Foreign Policy," p. 1,052.

34. Personal interview with two senior foreign policy advisors of the Shah in Tehran in September 1976.

35. The Shah's Navy Day speech on Kharq Island, *BBCSWB*, November 9, 1972, ME/4140.

VI · RESOURCES CAPABILITY

1. For a detailed discussion of the difference between potential, power, and capability in political, socio-economic and military terms, see K. Knorr, *Military Power and Potential*; K. Knorr, *Power & Wealth: The Political Economy of International Power*.

2. See Chapter V, n. 1; also, A. Sampson, *The Arms Bazaar*, pp. 252-59.

3. See Chapter III; also *Outline of the Third Plan, 1341-1346; Report on the Performance of the Third Development Plan* (in Persian); *Fourth Development Plan 1968-1972.*

4. Charles Issawi claims that over the period 1957/58-1967/68 Iran's "compound rate of growth of 7 percent per annum and a per capita rate of about 4.5 percent . . . exceed[ed] those for all regions of the world. They . . . [were] equalled or surpassed by only a very small number of countries, such as Japan, Yugoslavia, Israel, Jordan, Greece, Mexico, Italy, West Germany and Taiwan." "The Economy: An Assessment of Performance," in E. Yar-Shater, ed., *Iran Faces the Seventies*, p. 47. For the rate of GNP and increases in oil revenues during 1959-1970, see J. W. Jacqz, ed., *Iran: Past, Present and Future*, p. 324.

5. Bank Markazi Iran, *Annual Report Balance Sheet, 1349* [as at March 20, 1971], pp. 17-18.

6. *Ibid.*, pp. 53-60, 61-65.

7. *Ibid.*, pp. 42-46.

8. *Ibid.*, pp. 46-47, 40.

9. Jacqz, *Iran: Past, Present and Future*, p. 63.

10. J. Amuzegar and M. A. Fekrat, *Iran: Economic Development under Dualistic Conditions*, p. 123.

11. Bank Markazi Iran, *Annual Report Balance Sheet, 1349*, pp. 77-78.

12. *Ibid.*, p. 79.

13. Personal interview with a senior Iranian economic advisor of the Ministry of Finance in September 1976.

14. Jacqz, *Iran: Past, Present and Future*, p. 98.

15. The Shah's speech, *BBCSWB*, August 13, 1974, ME/W788.

16. *Ibid.* See also *The Middle East*, no. 10 (July 1975), pp. 41-43.

17. Personal interviews with senior economic planners in Tehran in September 1976.

18. The Shah's speech, *BBCSWB*, August 13, 1974, ME/W788.

19. Knorr, *Military Power and Potential*, p. 3, and ch. 2; Knorr, *Power & Wealth*, p. 3.

20. *The Military Balance 1970/71 and 1971/72*; Stockholm International Peace Research Institute (SIPRI), *The Arms Trade with the Third World; SIPRI, Yearbook of World Armaments and Disarmaments* for 1969-1970 and 1970-1971.

21. For the comparative military strength of Iran with other regional countries, particularly Iraq, see *The Military Balance* for *1970/71* and *1971/72*. Iran's military capability was fulfilling the Shah's remark to the *Washington Post* in 1969: "We have to develop such a potential to keep this area secure after the British leave. Iran can do it because we have no territorial or colonial designs. Iran's role in the Persian Gulf is to present the image of strength, wisdom, and absolutely altruistic

purposes, and yet, without any thought of trying to play Big Daddy."
SIPRI, *The Arms Trade with the Third World, 1975*, pp. 222-23.

22. S. Chubin and S. Zabih, *The Foreign Relations of Iran*, pp. 178-85.

23. SIPRI, *The Arms Trade with the Third World, 1975*, p. 196.

24. F. Halliday, *Arabia Without Sultans*, pp. 139-40, 144; Chubin and Zabih, *The Foreign Relations of Iran*, pp. 96, 107.

25. For Iran's activities in the Gulf and Oman, see below, Chapter VII.

26. See Knorr, *Power & Wealth*, ch. 3.

27. *Ibid.*

28. D. A. Rustow and J. F. Mugno, *OPEC: Success and Prospects*, p. 131.

29. *U.S. Military Sales to Iran*, p. 13.

30. *SIPRI Yearbook 1977: World Armaments and Disarmaments*, pp. 319-20.

31. Jacqz, *Iran: Past, Present and Future*, p. 98. Rustow and Mugno, *OPEC: Success and Prospects*, p. 131.

32. *BBCSWB*, August 3, 1974, ME/4668.

33. *The Middle East*, no. 10 (July 1975), pp. 41-43; the Shah's speech, *BBCSWB*, August 13, 1974, ME/W788.

34. *U.S. Military Sales to Iran*, p. 13.

35. *Arab Record & Memo* 2 (February 13, 1978), 3-4.

36. *Kayhan International*, December 5, 1974; February 4, 1976.

37. *U.S. Military Sales to Iran*, pp. 16, 21, 27. *SIPRI Yearbook 1977*.

38. *Strategic Survey 1977* (London: IISS, 1978), p. 106.

39. *The Military Balance 1977/78*; *SIPRI Yearbook 1977*, pp. 318-20. For the Shah's comment on the Soviet purchase and his desire to shop around for arms, thus preferring the United States as the major but not exclusive source of arms supply, see *Kayhan International*, December 8, 1976.

40. This was caused by periodical drops in the rate of Iran's oil production and export due to fluctuations in the world market. See *Arab Report and Memo* 2 (February 20, 1978), 11.

41. *Kayhan International*, November 27, 1976.

42. Personal interview with a senior Pentagon official in October 1976. Also see *Sydney Morning Herald*, August 7, 1976.

43. *Sydney Morning Herald*, August 7, 1976.

44. *Canberra Times*, March 18, 1978.

45. *U.S. Arms Sale to Iran*, p. viii.

46. For the Shah's confirmation of his nonnuclear stance, see the Shah's interviews as published in *Kayhan International*, June 26, 1974, December 18, 1976.

47. *Canberra Times*, February 7, 1978.

48. "NPT: Paradoxes and Problems," in A. W. Marks, ed., *Arms Control Association*, p. 99.

49. See the Shah's interviews in *Kayhan International*, January 22, 1976; December 18, 1976; March 26, 1977; Amir 'Abbas Hoveida's speech, *Kayhan International*, March 18, 1976. In 1972, the Shah declared that given the danger of smaller countries, if not the superpowers, and the "impotency of the United Nations, . . . we have adopted what we call our independent foreign policy and first of all we are counting on ourselves and then on our friends, and it is very good for us to have friends. We are searching, in addition, to find good friends." *Press Conference by His Imperial Majesty Shahanshah Aryamehr*, London, June 24, 1972 (Tehran: Ministry of Information, 1972).

VII · PATTERN OF REGIONAL BEHAVIOR

1. Details of the Shah's regional policies may be found in S. Chubin and S. Zabih, *The Foreign Relations of Iran: A Developing State in a Zone of Great-Power Conflict*; S. Chubin and M. Fard-Saidi, "Recent Trends in Middle East Politics and Iran's Foreign Policy Options"; S. Chubin, "Iran: Between the Arab West and the Asian East"; R. K. Ramazani, *Iran's Foreign Policy, 1941-1973*; R. K. Ramazani, "Emerging Patterns of Regional Relations in Iranian Foreign Policy"; R. M. Burrell, "Iranian Foreign Policy: Strategic Location, Economic Ambition, and Dynastic Determination"; R. M. Burrell and A. J. Cottrell, "Iran, Afghanistan, Pakistan: Tensions and Dilemmas"; A. J. Cottrell, *Iran: Diplomacy in a Regional and Global Context*.

2. M. R. Pahlavi, *Mission for My Country*, p. 294.

3. *The Times* (London), June 13, 1969; *New York Times*, May 10, 1970; *Press Conference by His Imperial Majesty Shahanshah Aryamehr, London, 24 June 1972* (Tehran: Ministry of Information, 1972); *Kayhan International*, January 22, 1976 and June 12, 1976.

4. *Arab Report and Record*, 1969, p. 2.

5. For a concise discussion of the settlement, see H. Moghtader, "The Settlement of Bahrain Question."

6. Verbatim record of U.N. Security Council meeting no. 1536, May 11, 1970.

7. For a detailed discussion of this, see S. Chubin and S. Zabih, *The Foreign Relations of Iran*, pp. 214-21.

8. *Arab Report and Record*, 1968, pp. 14, 244, 329; and 1969, pp. 139, 383.

9. For the composition of UAE, see above, Chapter V, n. 21. For a full discussion of the creation of the federation and Iran's policy toward it, see Chubin and Zabih, *The Foreign Relations of Iran*, pp. 215-40.

10. Personal interviews with senior Iranian and British officials in September and October 1976.

238 · NOTES, CHAPTER VII

11. Burrell and Cottrell, "Iran, Afghanistan, Pakistan: Tensions and Dilemmas," p. 5.

12. Verbatim record of U.N. General Assembly meeting no. 1857, October 1, 1970, p. 7. Such a solution had been outlined earlier by Manuchehr Ganji, a close adviser to the Shah and Iran's minister of education during 1976-1978, in his book *Hoquq-e Bein al-Melali-ye 'Omumi*, pp. 220-27.

13. A. H. Raoof, "Confrontation and Detente in the Arabian-Persian Gulf: The Case of Iraq", unpublished paper; Burrell and Cottrell, "Iran, Afghanistan, Pakistan: Tensions and Dilemmas," pp. 1-8; R. M. Burrell, "Iranian Foreign Policy during the Last Decade," pp. 12-13. Another factor that complicated Iranian-Iraqi relations was Iraq's traditional claim over the islands of Warba and Bubiya, which have been under Kuwait possession since the latter's independence in 1963. Iraq regarded these islands as vital to its access to the Persian Gulf; *New York Times*, April 4, 1973. When talks between Kuwait and Iraq broke down in 1973, the latter opted for the use of force and on March 20, 1973, Iraqi troops occupied the Kuwaiti post of al-Simatah. Although the occupation was shortlived, it brought sharp reaction from Iran and Saudi Arabia. The Shah immediately declared that Iran would not tolerate Iraq's occupation of Kuwait (*Time*, April 1, 1974) and Saudi Arabia supported the Kuwait foreign minister in his assertion that "any attack on Kuwait is an attack on Saudi Arabia" (*Washington Post*, May 23, 1973). Subsequently, in September 1976, in a personal interview with the author, a senior advisor to the Shah claimed that it was largely because of Iranian pressure and the country's growing military strength that Iraq ended its occupation of al-Simatah within a few weeks and sought peaceful negotiations with Kuwait in August 1973.

14. Stressing the importance of close cooperation between Iran and Egypt, in August 1975, the Shah declared: "We believe Egypt must emerge as a very powerful country. . . . We have faith in the strength and importance of Egypt." Noting that Egypt had a population of 40 million, a large educated class, and an ancient history, the Shah described the cooperation between Iran and Egypt as "a base and foundation for the entire region, both the Arabian Peninsula and the Persian Gulf. We say this is a cooperation between the region of Asia and of Africa—if one can use these terms—and the countries of the Middle East. The cooperation between Iran and Egypt is thus of importance." He emphasized that for these reasons "we have extended help to her [Egypt] and we have large and joint projects for provisions of more extensive facilities to Egypt." The Shah's interview with the Kuwaiti newspaper, *al-Siyasah*, as reported in *Kayhan International*, August 13, 1975.

15. *Kayhan International*, December 1, 1973.

16. See Chubin, "Iran between the Arab West and the Asian East."

17. The Shah's interview with *Al-Ahram*, as published in *Kayhan International*, June 12, 1976.

18. *Kayhan International*, January 14, 1978.

19. *Kayhan International*, April 30, 1977 and December 31, 1977.

20. For details, see Burrell and Cottrell, "Iran, Afghanistan, Pakistan: Tensions and Dilemmas," pp. 24-28; *Kayhan International*, May 29, 1974 and November 27, 1974.

21. *Kayhan International*, September 23, 1975 and June 19, 1976.

22. *Ibid.*, June 12, 1976; *Ravabet-e Khareji-ye Iran dar Sal-e 2534 Shahanshahi*, p. 82. As early as June 1976, the Shah described Iranian-Egyptian relations as "excellent." He stated: "President Sadat's policies are courageous and wise. Ties of friendship between Iran and Egypt are further consolidated whenever the President and I meet. We two are always in contact. . . . Economic relations between Iran and Egypt are often based on the principle of mutuality. . . . At any rate, we spare no effort in helping Egypt eliminate economic difficulties imposed on it by war." The Shah's interview with *Al-Ahram*, as republished in *Kayhan International*, June 12, 1976.

23. *Kayhan International*, March 18, 1974; June 4, 1974; August 6, 1974.

24. See *Guardian Weekly*, February 29, 1976; Raoof, "Confrontation and Detente in the Arabian-Persian Gulf."

25. Personal interviews with senior Iranian officials in September 1976 in Tehran.

26. For the text of the communique, see *New York Times*, March 18, 1975.

27. *Qanun-e 'Ahdname Marbut be Marz-e Dowlati va Hosn-e Hamje-vari bein-e Iran va 'Eraq . . .*, p. 509.

28. *Kayhan International*, March 30, 1975.

29. In outlining his perception of Gulf "collective security," the Shah later declared he would accept anything, whether it was "a military, economic and political agreement or an understanding" agreed upon by a majority of the littoral states. "Our basic view is that the security of the region must rest with the regional states themselves, not with foreigners. For this reason, we will accept any proposal that wins the agreement of the majority, even if suggested by the small states" (of the Persian Gulf). He emphasized, however, that "All must realise that Iran will never be negligent on defence questions. It will obtain adequate military power to ensure the security of the region. If necessary we will do this alone. Naturally, we will be pleased if others cooperate with us in this area. . . . But if they do not do so, Iran will not endanger its own security. . . . Iran in practice has the capability of defending its just interests in this region of the world." The Shah's interview with *Al-Ahram*, as republished in *Kayhan International*, June 12, 1976.

30. Chubin, "Iran: Between the Arab West and the Asia East"; Burrell and Cottrell, "Iran, Afghanistan, Pakistan: Tensions and Dilemmas."

31. Burrell and Cottrell, "Iran, Afghanistan, Pakistan: Tensions and Dilemmas," p. 44; *Kayhan International*, June 11, 1977.

32. In early July 1973, the Shah reportedly said that "he was imploring it [Pakistan] to pursue a policy not only of peaceful co-existence but of active cooperation with India because it is evident to him that there could be no stability in Asia without it. Iran's own interests required peace in the sub-continent." *Times of India*, July 4, 1973.

33. D. Mukerjee, "Afghanistan under Daud: Relations with Neighbouring States," p. 307.

34. During President Ayyub's visit to Kabul between January 1 and 3, 1966, it was officially announced that "both sides [Afghanistan and Pakistan] discussed their points of view over the problems and agreed to explore all possibilities of further improvement of relationship in a spirit of cooperation and understanding." N. M. Rahimi, ed., *The Kabul Times Annual*, p. 25.

35. Daoud's speech: "Declaration of Republic," *Pamir*, no. 33-34 (Asad 16, 1352).

36. Mukerjee, "Afghanistan under Daud," pp. 308-309.

37. *Kayhan International*, February 21, 1973; January 31, 1974; May 14, 1974; May 2, 1975; May 13, 1975; Mukerjee, "Afghanistan under Daud," pp. 309-10; S. R. Ghauri, "Iran's Grand Design Runs into Trouble."

38. S. Tahir-Kheli, "Iran and Pakistan: Cooperation in an Area of Conflict," p. 484.

39. *Ibid.*, pp. 475-76.

40. *Times of India*, September 27, 1973.

41. For details see Tahir-Kheli, "Iran and Pakistan: Cooperation in an Area of Conflict," pp. 480-81.

42. J. W. Jacqz, *Iran: Past, Present and Future*, p. 324.

43. See *Kayhan International*, February 25, 1974; July 20, 29, 1974; August 6, 1974; September 2, 1974; October 24, 1974; February 18, 1975; March 11, 1975; May 6, 13, 1975; June 5, 1976; June 4, 1977; *Middle East Economic Digest*, 20 (July 2, 1976); R. Joseph, "Market Proposal Revived," *Canberra Times*, March 8, 1978.

44. R. Joseph, "Afghanistan Plans Railway to Link It to World," *Canberra Times*, February 1, 1978.

45. *Kayhan International*, October 5, 1974.

46. *Kayhan International*, April 21, 1974; May 1-6, 1974; April 29, 1975; May 2, 1975; February 4, 1978.

47. *Ibid.*, October 5, 1974.

48. For details see Joseph, "Market Proposal Revived."

49. *Kayhan International*, February 4, 1978.

50. The Shah's interview with the *Daily Telegraph*, *BBCSWB*, February 11, 1974, ME/4523.

51. See for the Shah's comments on "terrorism" *ibid.*; also *Press Conference by his Imperial Majesty Shaharnshah Aryamehr, London, 24 June 1972* (Tehran: Ministry of Information, 1972); *Kayhan International*, June 5, 1976.

52. The Shah's interview with the *Daily Telegraph*, *BBCSWB*, February 11, 1974.

53. For a detailed discussion of this, see B. M. Smolansky and D. M. Smolansky, "Soviet and Chinese Influence in the Persian Gulf," pp. 131-53.

54. The Shah's interview with *Der Spiegel*, in *His Imperial Majesty Mohammed Reza Shah Pahlavi Aryamehr, Shahanshah of Iran on Oil and Other Topics, Press Conferences and Interviews* (Tehran: Ministry of Foreign Affairs, 19 January 1974), p. 17.

55. See *Financial Times* (London), November 30, 1971; *New York Times*, December 1, 1971. For the statement by Sheikh Qasimi, the ruler of Sharjah, on the agreement, see *BBCSWB*, December 1, 1971, ME/3853.

56. *Keesing's Contemporary Archives*, December 25, 1971 to January 1, 1972, 25010.

57. For the reports of the Iranian military operation, see *BBCSWB*, December 2, 1971, ME/3854; December 4, 1971, ME/3856; December 7, 1971, ME/3858. For the statement by Premier Hoveida on the occupation of the islands, see *ibid.*, December 1, 1971, ME/3853.

58. For the details of increasing guerrilla activities, particularly by two major groups, the Mujaheddin Khalq (People's Strugglers), a "rightist-leftist" group, and Fedayien Khalq (People's Sacrificers), a leftist group—which both claimed responsibility for a number of explosions and killings, including slaying a number of American technical and military advisers to Iran between 1971-1978—and of the Shah's suppressive reaction to these groups, see *Keesing's Contemporary Archives*, July 29-August 24, 1974, p. 26,643; *New York Times*, February 29, 1976; *The Guardian Weekly*, February 15, 1976; *International Herald Tribune*, September 1, 1978; December 11, 1978.

59. The PFLOAG, however, claimed the number of the Iranian troops to be as high as 30,000. For details, see the *New York Times*, December 31, 1973.

60. *Canberra Times*, December 13, 1975.

61. *Kayhan International*, December 10, 1977.

62. *Keesing's Contemporary Archives*, March 17-23, 1971, pp. 27,016-27,018.

63. *The Australian*, February 18-19, 1978.

64. *Kayhan International,* December 31, 1977.
65. *Ibid.*
66. For details see *BBCSWB,* December 2-9, 1971, ME/3854-3860.

VIII · REPERCUSSIONS OF THE SHAH'S POLICIES

1. Personal interviews with senior Iranian planners in September 1976.

2. *Ibid.*

3. R. Graham, "When the Dreaming Had to Stop," *Australian Financial Review,* March 4, 1976.

4. For background to this and "the massive gulf in life-style between the bulk of north Tehrani residents and the bulk of those in the south," see J. Connell, "Tehran: Urbanisation and Development," unpublished paper; Hemmasi, *Migration in Iran;* A. Saikal, "Can the Shah Hold on?" *The AGE,* November 2, 1978.

5. *Economist,* August 28, 1976, p. 43.

6. For details of the agreement, see *Kayhan International,* December 4, 1976.

7. For a background discussion of this, see M. H. Pesaran, "Income Distribution in Iran."

8. R. Joseph, "Despite Oil Riches, Iran's Economy Faces a Slowdown," *Canberra Times,* February 8, 1978.

9. *Bank Markazi Iran: Annual Report,* 1853 [1976/77], p. 159.

10. F. Halliday, "The Major Obstacle on the Road to Democracy in Iran Is the Shah," *Canberra Times,* July 30, 1977.

11. F. Daftry and M. Borghey, *Multinational Enterprises and Employment in Iran,* pp. 35, 44, 45.

12. *U.S. Military Sales to Iran,* p. viii.

13. Personal interviews with senior Iranian officials in Tehran in September 1976.

14. *Kayhan International,* September 8, 1976.

15. *U.S. Military Sales to Iran,* p. viii.

16. By 1977, about half of Iran's population still lived in the country, and the gap between its income and that of the city people was widening: the ratio rose from 1.91 in 1965 to 3.21 in 1972; and this was expected to rise about 10.0 in the 1980s. F. Vakil, "Iran's Basic Macroeconomic Problems: a 20-year Horizon," p. 90. As for the widening gap between the minority rich and majority poor, during 1959/60 the top 20 percent of the population in urban areas accounted for 51.79 percent of the total consumption expenditure, and the bottom 40 percent for only 13.90 percent, but in 1973/74 the corresponding figures were 55.56 and 11.96 percent, respectively. In the absence of any comprehensive policy for redistribution of wealth, this trend in the income distribution was bound to continue in the coming years. M. H. Pesaran,

"Income Distribution and Its Major Determinants in Iran," p. 5. Also see Pesaran, "Income Distribution Trends in Rural and Urban Iran," unpublished paper; R. Joseph, "Corrupt Acts in Iran," *Canberra Times*, March 12, 1976; *Kayhan International*, February 28, 1976; E. Rouleau, "Iran: The Myth and the Reality," *The Guardian Weekly*, October 24, 1976.

17. See Rouleau, "Iran: The Myth and the Reality"; Connell, "Tehran: Urbanisation and Development"; personal observations.

18. *Canberra Times*, January 17, 1977. For background see E. Pace, "Iran, Despite Her Oil Wealth, Is Borrowing on a Grand Scale," *New York Times*, August 15, 1975.

19. Against the background of this situation, the Shah set up in 1977 "the Imperial Commission for Efficient Resources Application" to investigate the economic shortcomings and suggest measures for improvement. In January 1978, the Commission's findings considered the shortcomings to be a direct result of what may be called "uncoordinated leap forward" and "irreparable losses" in Iran's development. It reported that several hundred Fifth Plan projects remained incomplete because they had been unrealistically planned. The head of the Commission stressed that the new generation must be "faithful to the principles of . . . efficiency"; and "projects must be based on a logical assessment of financial and manpower and other resources"; and that the government, especially the planning authorities, should constantly supervise and follow up every project, for the implementation of which it is responsible. *Kayhan International*, January 21, 1978. For an overall discussion of the economic situation, see Joseph, "Despite Oil Riches, Iran's Economy Faces a Slowdown." For an official Iranian criticism of the economic shortcomings, see the comments by the Shah's special bureau director, Nosratollah Moinian, in *Kayhan International*, July 16, 1977.

20. *The Australian*, August 27-28, 1977.

21. Personal interviews. The Shah himself had already declared that in contrast with the Fifth Plan, the Sixth Plan should avoid temporary "showcase" projects. It "must stress infrastructure, wise use of resources, increased productivity and spiritual and cultural growth. The temptation to indulge in wasting resource through devotion to surface refinement—like extravagant exterior decoration—must be resisted." In view of a continuous drop in Iran's agricultural production, he stressed that the Plan must aim at further mechanization of agriculture without causing the destruction of rural and traditional agriculture. *Kayhan International*, August 21, 1976.

22. For a detailed discussion of this, see R. Baraheni, "Terror in Iran," *New York Review of Books*, October 28, 1976, pp. 21-25.

23. *Kayhan International*, March 8, 1975.

24. Personal interviews and observation.

25. In August 1976, however, William Butler, chairman of the International Commission of Jurists Executive Committee, claimed that SAVAK had up to 200,000 full-time employees "operating in every nook and cranny of the Iranian system, and also in many places, and especially in places where Iranian students are congregating both in the United States and in West Germany, and in other parts of the world." U.S. Congress, House, Committee on International Relations; Subcommittee on International Organizations, Hearings, *Human Rights in Iran*, August 3 and September 6, 1976, p. 7.

26. For details see *Kayhan International*, September 9, 1976; *Kayhan* (daily Persian edition), Sharpūr 15, 2535.

27. M. Zonis, *The Political Elite of Iran*, p. 13.

28. For a summary of guerrilla activities and the Shah's stern actions against them, see *Keesing's Contemporary Archives*, July 29-August 4, 1974, pp. 26,643-44. For the Shah's view of "Islamic-Marxism" as "an inane farce," see *Kayhan International*, May 7, 1977.

29. This was largely evident from the appearance of critical articles concerning the performance and functions of the public authorities. For examples of them, see the issues of *Kayhan International* and *Ettela'at* during 1977.

30. Personal interviews with senior officials, including a top adviser to Amir 'Abbas Hoveida on social and political affairs.

31. Personal interview with a top aid of the Shah and senior official of the Rastakhiz party.

32. Personal interviews. See also I. Murray, "Battle for Iran's Soul"; "A Frail Man Prays as Iran Erupts," *Sydney Morning Herald*, November 9, 1978.

33. For a discussion of the role played by the religious zealots at the early stages of the crisis see R. Joseph, "Iran's Mosques become Centres of Political Dissent," *Canberra Times*, May 29, 1978.

34. Conservative estimates of the death toll in the fifteen months leading to the collapse of the Shah's regime put the number at 10,000. *The Australian*, February 15, 1979.

35. For details, see the Shah's interview with West German journalists, as appeared in *Kayhan* [airmail edition in Persian], May 3, 1978. Also see *Kayhan International*, August 20, 1978; March 4, 1978.

36. *Canberra Times*, August 28, 1978.

37. *The AGE*, August 30, 1978; *Kayhan International*, September 3, 17, 1978.

38. R. Joseph, "Sombre City after the Massacre," *Canberra Times*, September 27, 1978.

39. *The Australian*, November 8, 1978.

40. A. Saikal, "Military Rule 'Not a Long-Term Option,'" *Canberra Times*, November 12, 1978.

41. *The Australian*, December 12, 1979.

42. *International Herald Tribune*, December 30-31, 1978.

43. It was reported that in late November 1978 alone, $2,400 million was transferred to foreign banks by the Iranian political and economic leaders, including members of the royal family. Australian Broadcasting Commission program, "Four Corners," December 2, 1978.

44. *The Australian*, December 10, 1978. B. Gwertzmen, "U.S. Now Feels Shah Will Leave Shortly," *International Herald Tribune*, January 10, 1979. For a full discussion of the failure of the United States to foresee the Iranian crisis and formulate its policy accordingly, see A. K. Mansur, "The Crisis in Iran: Why the U.S. Ignored a Quarter Century of Warning"; U.S. Congress, House, Staff Report, *Iran: Evaluation of U.S. Intelligence Performance Prior to November 1978*.

45. *International Herald Tribune*, December 30-31, 1978; January 2, 1979.

46. For details see the issues of *International Herald Tribune*, January 4, 8, 10, 1979.

47. For example, the Saudi purchase of sixty F15 fighters, approved by the U.S. Congress in May 1978; see "Middle East Plane Sales Backed by Senate Vote in Major Carter Victory," *Congressional Quarterly* 36 (May 20, 1978), 1,263-64.

48. For a discussion of the arms race, see E. M. Kennedy, "The Persian Gulf: Arms Race or Arms Control." On Afghanistan, personal interview with a senior Afghan diplomat. For Indian concern over the Shah's military build-up, see especially *New York Times*, July 3, August 27, 1973.

49. See "Saudi Arabia," A Report by Senator Mike Mansfield, Majority Leader, United States Senate to the Committee on Foreign Relations, United States Senate, October 1975 (Washington, D.C.: Government Printing Office, 1975.)

50. *Canberra Times*, January 15, 1977; *The Australian*, January 8, 1977.

51. *Canberra Times*, January 11, 1977.

52. *Canberra Times*, January 17, 1977.

53. *Kayhan International*, December 25, 1976. The Shah himself went as far as to say that any oil production increases by Saudi Arabia and UAE that seriously affected Iran's balance of payments would constitute "an aggression against us." For details, see *Kayhan International*, January 29, 1977.

54. The exact amount of Iranian aid to Afghanistan was never officially disclosed. Press reports put it between 1 and 3 billion dollars. The figure of $1.2 billion, reported in the *Christian Science Monitor*, May 8, 1978, seems about right.

55. *The Economist*, May 13, 1978.

CONCLUSION

1. See "United States' Foreign Policy for the 1970s: A New Strategy for Peace" in the weekly compilation of presidential documents, Monday, February 23, 1970; D. Landan, *Kissinger: The Uses of Power*, p. 120.

2. Interview, Washington, D.C., October 1976.

3. *U.S. Military Sales to Iran*, p. 5.

4. *The AGE*, August 9, 1976.

5. *Sydney Morning Herald*, November 17, 1977.

6. Statement made by Philip Habib, under-secretary of state, to U.S. Senate, Committee on Foreign Relations, September 16, 1976.

7. A. Sampson, *The Arms Bazaar*, p. 257.

8. *U.S. Military Sales to Iran*, p. 1.

9. Personal interviews and observations in Tehran in 1976.

* BIBLIOGRAPHY *

PERSIAN-LANGUAGE SOURCES

'Alanur, P. *Hezb-e Tude-ye Iran Sar-e do Rah* [The Tudeh Party of Iran on Two Ways]. Tehran, 1947.

'Alavi, B. *Panjah va se Nafar* [Fifty-three People]. Tehran, n.d.

Aprim, P. *Che Bayad Kard?* [What Must Be Done?]. Tehran, 1946 and September 20, 1950.

Asadi, A. et al. *Naqsh-e Rasaneha dar Poshtibani-ye Towse'e-ye Farangi* [Communication Networks in Support of Cultural Development]. Tehran: Iran Communications and Development Institute, 1976.

'Azima, J. *Jombesh-e Melli-ye Iran* [Iran's National Movement]. N.p., 1959.

Bahar, M. S. *Tarikh-e Ahzab-e Siyasi* [History of Political Parties]. Vols. 1 and 2. Tehran: Amir Kabir, 1944.

Davudi, W. et al. *Naqsh-e Rasaneha dar Poshtibani-ye Towse'e-ye Siyasi* [Communication Networks in Support of Political Development]. Tehran: Iran Communications and Development Institute, n.d.

Fateh, M. *Panjah Sal-e Naft-e Iran* [Fifty Years of Iranian Oil]. Tehran, 1956.

Ganji, M. *Hoquq-e Bein al-Melali-ye' Omumi* [General International Law]. Vol. 1. Tehran: Danishyari Danishgahi Tehran, 1348 [1969/70].

Hamzalu, B., and Homapur, N. *Naqsh-e Rasaneha dar Poshtibani-ye Towse'e-ye Eqtesadi* [Communication Networks in Support of Economic Development]. Tehran: Iran Communications and Development Institute, n.d.

Kayostovan, H. *Siyasat-e Movazane-ye Manfi dar Majles-e Chahardahom* [The Politics of Negative Equilibrium in the Fourteenth Majlis]. Tehran: Ibn Sina, 1329 [1950/51].

Kermani, H. K. *Az Shahryar-e 1320 ta Faje'e-ye Azerbaijan* [From Shahryar 1941 to the Crisis of Azerbaijan]. Vol. 2. Tehran: Mazahiri, 1329 [1950/51].

Kiyanuri. *Mobarazat-e Tabaqati* [Class Struggles]. Tehran, 1948.

M. H. *Farmanrava'i-ye Proletariya* [Dictatorship of the Proletariat]. Tehran, n.d.

————. *Jang-e Dakheli* [Civil War]. Tehran, 1945.

Mahmud, M. *Tarikh-e Ravabat-e Siyasi-ye Iran ba Englis dar Qarn-e Nuzdahom-e Miladi* [The History of Iran's Relations with England in the Nineteenth Century A.D.] 5 vols. Tehran, 1328-1329 [1949/ 50-1950/51].

Maleki, K. *Niru-ye Sevvom Chist?* [What Is the Third Force?]. Tehran, 1951.

———. *Niru-ye Sevvom Piruz Mishavad* [The Third Force Will Succeed]. Tehran, 1951.

———. *Takamol-e Tarikh-e Sosiyalism* [The Historical Evolution of Socialism]. Tehran, n.d.

Mobarez, P. *Aya Hezb-e Tude Shekast Khorde Ast?* [Is the Tudeh Party Defeated?]. Tehran, 1946.

———. *Dar Piramun-e Hezb-e Demokrat-e Iran* [About Iran's Democratic Party]. Tehran, 1946.

Mohid, M. A. *Naft-e ma va masa'el-e Hoquq-e An* [Our Oil and Its Legal Aspects]. Tehran: Shirkati Sahami Entesharati Khwarazmi, 1353 [1974/75].

Mo'meni, B. *Iran dar Astane-ye Enqelab-e Mashrutiyat* [Iran on the Threshold of the Constitutional Revolution]. Tehran: Shabgir, 1352 [1973/74].

Nazari. *"Niru-ye Sevvom" va Tude'iha dar baraye "Solh"* ["Third Force" and Tudeh-ites about "Peace"]. Tehran, n.d.

Pahlavi, M. R. *Besu-ye Tamaddon-e Bozorg* [Toward the Great Civilization]. Tehran: Sherkat-e Offset-e Sahami-ye 'Amm, 1978.

Qasemi, A. *Chand Mowzu' az Eqtesad* [Some Issues from Economics]. Tehran, 1948.

———. *Qanun Chist va Chegune be Vojud Amad?* [What Is Law and How Did It Come About?]. Tehran, 1947.

Qasemzade. *Hoquq-e Asasi* [Constitutional Law]. Tehran: Ibn Sina, 1340 [1961].

Radmanesh. *Dar Baray-e Qanun-Shekaniha-ye Dowlat: Matn-e Sokhanrani-ye Dr. Radmanesh dar Konferanse-e Matbu'ati* [About the Government's Lawlessness: The Text of Dr. Radmanesh's Speech at a Press Conference]. Tehran, n.d.

Rahimi, M. *Qanun-e Asasi-ye Iran va Osul-e Demokrasi* [Iran's Constitution and System of Democracy]. Tehran: Ibn Sina, 1354 [1975/76].

Ravandi, M. *Tafsir-e Qanun-e Asasi-e Iran* [The Details of Iran's Constitution]. Tehran, n.d.

Sa'id-Vaziri, A. *Nizam-e Kapitolasiyon va Nata'ije an dar Iran* [The System of Capitulation and Its Consequences in Iran]. Tehran: Vezarat-e Omur-e Khareje [Ministry of Foreign Affairs], 1976.

Shahed. *Hezb-e Tude che Migoft va che Mikard? Jebhe-ye Melli che Karde va che Bayad Bekonad?* [What Did the Tudeh Party Say and What Did It Practice? What Has the National Front Done and What Should It Do?]. Tehran, n.d.

Siddiq, J. *Melliyat va Enqelab dar Iran* [Nationality and Revolution in Iran]. New York: Entesharat-e Fanus, 1352 [1973/74].

Tabari, I. *Chand Mas'ale-ye Ejtema'i* [Some Social Issues]. Tehran, 1948.

Tamadduum, M. H. *Dar Baraye Jebhe-ye Matbu'ati Zedd-e Diktaturi* [About the Press Front against Dictatorship]. Tehran, 1948.

Tehranian, M. *Naqsh-e Rasaneha dar Poshtibani-ye Towse'e-ye Melli-ye Iran* [Communication Networks in Support of Iran's National Development]. Tehran: Iran Communications and Development Institute, n.d.

Zahra, S. *Namayandegan-e Majles-e Showra-ye Melli dar Bist va yek Dowre-ye Qanun-Gozari: Motala'ai az Nazar-e Jame'a-Shenasi-ye Siyasi* [The Majlis Deputies in the Twenty-First Legislative Session; A Study from a Political-Sociological Point of View]. Tehran: Daneshgah, 1965.

E'lamiyeha-ye moshtarak [Joint Communiques]. Vezarat-e Omur-e Khareje, 1349 [1970/71].

Enqelab-e Sefid va Siyasat-e Mostaqel-e Melli-ye Iran [The White Revolution and the National Independent Policy of Iran]. Tehran: Vezarat-e Omur-e Khareje, 1351 [1972/73].

Hezb-e Demokrat-e Iran [Iran's Democratic Party]. *Aya Shah Mitava-nad Mostaqiman dar Omur-e Mamlekat Modakhala Konad?* [Can the Shah Directly Intervene in the Country's Affairs?] Tehran, November 16, 1949.

Khelaf-e Jarayan [Against the Current]. No. 1, Autumn 1955.

Koliyat dar Bare-ye Ravabet-e Dowlat-e Shahanshahi-ye Iran ba Doval-e Howze-ye Mas'uliyat-e Edare-ye Avval-e Siyasi ('Eraq, Arabastan-e Sa'udi, Koveit, Jomhur-e 'Arab-e Yaman) Tei-ye Panjah Sal-e Shahanshahi-ye Pahlavi [A Book about the Relations of the Imperial Government of Iran with the Region, Charge of the First Political Department (Iraq, Saudi Arabia, Kuwait, the Arab Republic of Yemen) during the Fifty Years of Pahlavi Imperial Rule]. Tehran: Vezarat-e Omur-e Khareje, Edare-ye Entesharat va Madarek, 1976.

Koliyat dar Bare-ye Ravabet-e Dowlat-e Shahanshahi-ye Iran ba Doval-e Howze-ye Mas'uliyat-e Edare-ye Dovvom-e Siyasi (Ettahad-e Ja-mahir-e Showravi-ye Sosiyalisti, Jomhur-e Mardomi-ye Lehestan, Jomhur-e Sosiyalisti-ye Rumani, Jomhur-e Sosiyalisti-ye Chekoslo-vaki . . .) Tei-ye Panjah Sal-e Shahanshahi-ye Pahlavi [A Book about the Relations of the Imperial Government of Iran with the Region, Charge of the Second Political Department (USSR, the People's Republic of Poland, the Socialist Republic of Romania, and Socialist Republic of Czechoslovakia . . .) during the Fifty Years of Pahlavi Imperial Rule]. Tehran: Vezarat-e Omur-e Khareje, Edare-ye Entesharat va Madarek, 1976.

Komite-ye Masharakat dar Omur-e Refahi [The Committee for Participation in Affairs of Welfare]. Tehran: Plan and Budget Organization, 1976.

Komite-ye Siyasatye Refahi va Kaifeyate Zendage [The Committee for the Policies of Welfare and Quality of Life]. Tehran: Plan and Budget Organization, 1976. First and second seminar.

Markaz-e Amar-e Iran [Iran's Statistical Center]. *Bayan-e Amar-e Tahavvolat-e Eqtasad va Ejtema'i dar Dowran-e por Eftekhar-e Dudman-e Pahlavi* [Statistical Report of the Economic and Social Developments of Iran during the Triumphant Rule of the Pahlavi Dynasty]. Tehran, 2535 [1976/77].

Nashriya-e Akhbar va Asnad: Az Farvardin ta Shahrivar-mah-e 1349, 1350, 1352 [Publication of News and Documents from Farvardin to Shahrivar, 1970/71, 1971/72, 1973/74]. Tehran: Vezarat-e Omur-e Khareje, n.d.

Nashriya-e Akhbar va Asnad: Az Mehr ta Esfand va az Farvardin ta Shahrivar-mah-e 1351 [Publication of News and Documents from Mehr to Esfand and Farvardin to Shahrivar, 1972/73]. Tehran: Vezarat-e Omur-e Khareje, n.d.

Qanun-e 'Ahdname Marbut be Marz-e Dowlati va Hosn-e Hamjevari Bein-e Iran va 'Eraq. . . . [The Law of the Agreement of Official Border and Good Neighborliness between Iran and Iraq. . . .] Tehran: Vezarat-e Dadgostari [Ministry of Justice], 2535 [1976/77].

Ravabet-e Khareje-ye Iran dar Sal-e 1350, 1351, 1352, 2533 Shahanshahi, 2534 Shahanshahi, 2535 Shahanshahi [Iran's Foreign Relations in 1971/72, 1972/73, 1973/74, 1974/75, 1975/76, 1976/77]. Tehran: Vezarat-e Omur-e Khareje, 1350, 1351, 1352, 2533, 2534, 2535.

Sharayet-e Konuni-ye Mobareze-ye Ma [The Present Conditions of Our Struggle]. The Union of the Patriots of Kurdistan, January 1976.

Siyasat-e Bein al-Melali-ye Iran: Bargozide'i Az Neveshteha va Sokhanraniha-ye Shahanshah-ye Aryamehr [Iran's International Policy: Excerpts from Shahanshah Aryamehr's Writings and Speeches]. Tehran: Vezarat-e Omur-e Khareje, n.d.

Vezarat-e Omur-e Khareje [Ministry of Foreign Affairs]. *Tahaqqoq-e Hakemiyat-e Melli bar Naft dar Panjah Sal-e Shahanshahi-ye Pahlavi* [The Realization of National Sovereignty over Petroleum during the Fifty Years of Pahlavi Imperial Rule]. Tehran: Edare-ye Entesharat va Madarek [Office of Publications and Documents], 1976.

ENGLISH-LANGUAGE SOURCES

Books

Acheson, D. *Present at the Creation: My Years in the State Department.* New York: W. W. Norton, 1969.

Adamiyat, F. *Bahrein Island: A Legal and Diplomatic Study of the British-Iranian Controversy.* New York: Praeger, 1955.

Adelman, M. A. *The World Petroleum Market.* Baltimore: Johns Hopkins University Press, 1974. Published for Resources for the Future.

Alker, H. R., Jr.; Bloomfield, L. P.; Chouci, N. *Analyzing Global Interdependence.* Vols. 1, 2. Cambridge, Mass.: Center for International Studies, Massachusetts Institute of Technology, 1974.

Almond, G. A. *Political Development: Essays in Heuristic Theory.* Boston: Little, Brown and Co., 1970.

al-Otaiba, M. S. *OPEC and the Petroleum Industry.* London: Croom Helm, 1975.

Amirie, A., ed. *The Persian Gulf and Indian Ocean in International Politics.* Tehran: Institute for International Political and Economic Studies, 1975.

Amuzegar, J. *Technical Assistance in Theory and Practice: The Case of Iran.* New York: Praeger, 1966.

———, and Fekrat, M. A. *Iran: Economic Development under Dualistic Conditions.* Chicago: University of Chicago Press, 1971.

Anthony, J. D. *Arab States of the Lower Gulf; People, Politics, Petroleum.* Washington, D.C.: Middle East Institute, 1975.

Arberry, A. J. *The Legacy of Persia.* London: Oxford University Press, 1953.

Arasteh, A. R., and Arasteh, J. *Man and Society in Iran.* Leiden: Brill, 1964.

Arfa, H. *Under Five Shahs.* London: Murray, 1964.

Armajani, Y. *Iran.* Englewood Cliffs, N.J.: Prentice-Hall, 1972.

Asopa, S. K. *Military Alliance and Regional Cooperation in West Asia: A Study of the Politics of Northern Tier.* Meerut: Meenakshi, Prakashan, 1971.

Avery, P. *Modern Iran.* London: Benn, 1965.

Banani, A. *The Modernization of Iran, 1921-1941.* Stanford: Stanford University Press, 1961.

Barnet, R. J. *Intervention and Revolution: The United States in the Third World.* London: Paladin, 1972.

Bartold, V. V. *Four Studies on the History of Central Asia.* 3 vols. Leiden: Brill, 1956-1962.

Bartsch, W. H. *The Economy of Iran, 1940-1970: A Bibliography.* Durham: University of Durham, 1971.

Bausani, A. *The Persians, from the Earliest Days to the Twentieth Century*. London: Elek, 1971.

Bayne, E. A. *Persian Kingship in Transition: Conversations with a Monarch Whose Office is Traditional and Whose Goal is Modernization*. New York: American Universities Field Staff, 1968.

Beer, S. H. *The British Political System*. New York: Random House, 1974.

Berque, J. *The Arabs: Their History and Future*. New York: Praeger, 1964.

Bey, E. *Reza Shah: Feldherr, Kaiser, Reformer*. Leipzig: Passer, 1956.

Bharier, J. *Economic Development in Iran, 1900-1970*. London: Oxford University Press, 1971.

Bill, J. A. *The Politics of Iran: Groups, Classes and Modernization*. Columbus, Ohio: Merrill, 1972.

Binava, A. R. *Pushtunistan*. Kabul: Matba'e-ye 'Omumi, A.H. 1330 [1951].

Binder, L. *Iran: Political Development in a Changing Society*. Berkeley and Los Angeles: University of California Press, 1962.

Browne, E. G. *The Persian Revolution of 1905-1909*. Cambridge: The University Press, 1910.

Burrell, R. M. *The Persian Gulf*. The Washington Papers. Vol. 1. Beverly Hills: Sage Publications, 1972.

————, and Cottrell, A. J. *Iran, Afghanistan, Pakistan: Tensions and Dilemmas*. The Washington Papers. Vol. 2, no. 20. Beverly Hills: Sage Publications, 1974.

The Cambridge History of Iran. Cambridge: Cambridge University Press, 1968-.

Campbell, J. C. *Defense of the Middle East: Problems of American Policy*. 2nd ed. New York: Praeger, 1960.

————. *The United States in World Affairs, 1945-47*. New York: Council on Foreign Relations, 1947.

Chubin, S., and Zabih, S. *The Foreign Relations of Iran: A Developing State in a Zone of Great-Power Conflict*. Berkeley and Los Angeles: University of California Press, 1974.

Churchill, W. *Triumph and Tragedy*, Vol. 6 of *The Second World War*. London: Cassell, 1964.

Cottam, R. W. *Nationalism in Iran*. Pittsburgh: University of Pittsburgh Press, 1964.

Cottrell, A. J. *Iran: Diplomacy in a Regional and Global Context*. Washington, D.C., 1975.

Curzon, G. N. *Persia and the Persian Question*. Vol. 1. Reprint, London: Frank Cass & Co., 1966.

Daftary, F., and Borghey, M. *Multinational Enterprises and Employment in Iran*. Geneva: International Labour Office, 1977.

Dallin, D. J. *Soviet Foreign Policy after Stalin*. Philadelphia: Lippincott, 1961.

Denman, D. R. *The King's Vista: A Land Reform which Has Changed the Face of Persia*. Berkhamsted, Eng.: Geographical Publications, 1973.

Druks, H. *From Truman through Johnson: A Documentary History*. New York: Spellar and Sons, 1971.

Eden, A. *Full Circle*. London: Cassell, 1960.

Eisenhower, D. D. *Mandate for Change, 1953-1956*. London: Heinemann, 1963.

Elwell-Sutton, L. P. *Persian Oil: A Study in Power Politics*. London: Lawrence & Wishart, 1955.

Emmanuel, A. *Unequal Exchange*. New York: Monthly Review Press, 1972.

Engler, R. *The Politics of Oil; A Study of Private Powers and Democratic Direction*. Chicago: University of Chicago Press, 1967.

English, P. W. *City and Village in Iran: Settlement and Economy in Kirman Basin*. Madison: University of Wisconsin Press, 1966.

Esfandiary, F. M. *Identity Card: A Novel*. New York: Grove Press, 1966.

Fatemi, N. S. *Oil Diplomacy: Powderkeg in Iran*. New York: Whittier Books, 1954.

Feldman, H. *From Crisis to Crisis: Pakistan 1962-1969*. London: Oxford University Press, 1972.

Fischer, L. *The Soviets in World Affairs*. 2 vols. Princeton: Princeton University Press, 1951.

Frank, A. G. *Latin America: Underdevelopment or Revolution*. New York: Monthly Review Press, 1970.

Frye, R. N. *Persia*. London: Allen & Unwin, 1968. First published 1960 under the title *Iran*.

Gobineau, J. A. *The World of the Persians*. London: J. Gifford, 1971.

Grenville, J.A.S. *The Major International Treaties 1914-1973. A History and Guide with Texts*. London: Methuen, 1974.

Halliday, F. *Arabia Without Sultans*. Baltimore: Penguin, 1974.

Hansen, R. D. *The U.S. and World Development: Agenda for Action, 1976*. New York: Praeger, 1976.

Hekimatzadeh, F., ed. *Mass Communications Policy in Rapidly Developing Societies: Report of the Mashad Symposium*. Tehran: Iran Communications & Development Institute, 1975.

Hemmasi. *Migration in Iran*. Shiraz, 1974.

Heravi, M. *Iranian-American Diplomacy*. Brooklyn, N.Y.: T. Gaus' Sons, 1969.

Hunter, R. E. *The Soviet Dilemma in the Middle East Part II: Oil and the Persian Gulf.* Adelphi Papers, no. 60. London: The Institute for Strategic Studies, October, 1969.

Huntington, S. P., and Nelson, J. M. *No Easy Choice: Political Participation in Developing Countries.* Cambridge: Harvard University Press, 1976.

Hurewitz, J. C. *Diplomacy in the Near and Middle East—A Documentary Record, 1535-1914.* 2 vols. Princeton: Van Nostrand, 1956.

Inkeles, A., and Smith, D. H. *Becoming Modern: Individual Change in Six Developing Countries.* London: Heinemann Educational, 1975.

Issawi, C. *Oil, the Middle East, and the World.* The Washington Papers. Vol. 4. Beverly Hills: Sage Publications, 1974.

Jacobs, N. *The Sociology of Development: Iran as an Asian Case Study.* New York: Praeger, 1966.

Jacqz, J. W., ed. *Iran: Past, Present and Future.* New York: Aspen Institute for Humanities, 1976.

Jalil, T. *Workers of Iran: Repression and the Fight for Democratic Trade Unions.* London: C.R.T.U.I., July 1976.

Janjua, A. R. *Modern Iran in 20th Century.* Tehran, 1966.

Kanet, R. E., ed. *The Soviet Union and the Developing Nations.* Baltimore: Johns Hopkins University Press, 1974.

Kazemzadeh, F. *Russia and Britain in Persia, 1864-1914: A Study in Imperialism.* New Haven: Yale University Press, 1968.

Kennedy, G. *The Military in the Third World.* London: Duckworth, 1974.

Kent, M. *Oil and Empire: British Policy and Mesopotamian Oil, 1900-1920.* London: Macmillan, 1976.

Kinnane, D. *The Kurds and Kurdistan.* London: Oxford University Press, 1964.

Kinross, J.P.D.B. *Atatürk: The Rebirth of a Nation.* London: Weidenfeld, 1964.

Knorr, K. *Military Power and Potential.* Lexington, Mass.: Heath, 1970.
———. *Power & Wealth: The Political Economy of International Power.* London: Macmillan, 1973.

Lamb, A. *Asian Frontiers: Studies in a Continuing Problem.* London: Pall Mall, 1968.

Lambton, A.K.S. *Landlord and Peasant in Persia: A Study of Land Tenure and Land Revenue Administration.* London: Oxford University Press, 1953.

Landan, D. *Kissinger: The Uses of Power.* London: Robson Books, 1974.

Landis, L. *Politics and Oil: Moscow in the Middle East.* New York: Dunellen, 1973.

Lang, M. *The Shah.* London: Sidgwick & Jackson, 1977.

Lederer, I. J., ed. *Russian Foreign Policy: Essays in Historical Perspective.* New Haven: Yale University Press, 1962.

Leifer, M. *The Foreign Relations of the New States.* Camberwell, Australia: Longman, 1974.

Lenczowski, G. *Russia and the West in Iran, 1918-1948: A Study in Big-Power Rivalry.* Ithaca: Cornell University Press, 1949.

———, ed. *United States Interests in the Middle East.* Washington, D.C.: American Enterprise Institute for Public Policy Research, 1973.

Lewis, B. *The Middle East and the West.* London: Weidenfeld, 1964.

Lohbeck, D. *Patrick J. Hurley.* Chicago: H. Regnery, 1956.

Longhurst, H. *Adventures in Oil: The Story of British Petroleum.* London: Sidgwick & Jackson, 1959.

Longrigg, S. H. *Oil in the Middle East: Its Discovery and Development.* 3rd ed. London: Oxford University Press, 1968.

Lutfi, A. *OPEC Oil.* Beirut: Middle East Research and Publishing Center, 1968.

McCarthy, M. M. *Anglo-Russian Rivalry in Persia.* Buffalo, N.Y.: University of Buffalo Series 4, No. 2, June 1925.

Maddox, J. R. *Beyond the Energy Crisis.* London: Hutchinson, 1975.

Madelin, H. *Oil and Politics.* Lexington, Mass.: Lexington Books, 1975.

Magnus, R. H., comp. *Documents on the Middle East.* Washington, D.C.: American Enterprise Institute for Public Policy Research, 1969.

Manderson-Jones, R. B. *The Special Relationship: Anglo-American Relations and Western European Unity 1947-1956.* London: London School of Economics and Political Science, 1972.

Markham, C. R. *A General Sketch of the History of Persia.* London: Longman, Green, 1874.

Marks, A. W., ed. *Arms Control Association.* Washington, D.C.: Carnegie Endowment for International Peace, 1975.

Marlowe, J. *Iran: A Short Political Guide.* London: Pall Mall Press, 1963.

———. *The Persian Gulf in the Twentieth Century.* London: Cresset, 1962.

Miller, D. W., and Moore, C. D., eds. *The Middle East Yesterday and Today.* New York: Bantam Books, 1970.

Miller, L. H., and Pruessen, R. W., eds. *Reflection on the Cold War. A Quarter Century of American Foreign Policy.* Philadelphia: Temple University Press, 1974.

Millspaugh, A. C. *Americans in Persia.* Washington, D.C.: Brookings Institution, 1946.

Missen, D. *Iran: Oil at the Service of the Nation.* Transorient, 1969.

Mosley, L. *Power Play: The Tumultuous World of Middle East Oil, 1890-1973.* London: Weidenfeld and Nicolson, 1973.

Motter, T.H.V. *The Persian Corridor and Aid to Russia.* Washington,

D.C.: Office of the Chief of Military History, Department of the Army, 1952.

Myrdal, G. *Against the Stream: Critical Essays on Economics*. New York: Vintage Books, 1972.

Newell, R. S. *The Politics of Afghanistan*. Ithaca: Cornell University Press, 1972.

Nirumand, B. *Iran: The New Imperialism in Action*. New York: Monthly Review Press, 1969.

Nixon, R. *U.S. Foreign Policy for the 1970s*. Washington, D.C.: U.S. Government Printing Office, May 3, 1973.

Nollau, G., and Wiehe, H. J. *Russia's South Flank: Soviet Operations in Iran, Turkey, and Afghanistan*. New York: Praeger, 1963.

O'Connor, H. *World Crisis in Oil*. London: Elek, 1962.

Odell, P. R. *Oil and World Power: A Geographical Interpretation*. Harmondsworth: Penguin, 1970.

Pahlavi, M. R. *Mission for My Country*. London: Hutchinson & Co., 1961.

———. *The White Revolution of Iran*. Tehran: Imperial Pahlavi Library, 1967.

Poullada, L. B. *Reform and Rebellion in Afghanistan, 1919-1929*. Ithaca: Cornell University Press, 1973.

Prigmore, C. S. *Social Work in Iran since the White Revolution*. University: University of Alabama Press, 1976.

Reppa, R. B. *Israel and Iran: Bilateral Relationships and Effect on the Indian Ocean Basin*. New York: Praeger, 1974.

Rahimi, N. M., ed. *The Kabul Times Annual, 1967*. Kabul: Kabul Times Publishing Agency, 1967.

Ramazani, R. K. *The Foreign Policy of Iran: A Developing Nation in World Affairs, 1500-1941*. Charlottesville: University Press of Virginia, 1966.

———. *Iran's Foreign Policy, 1941-1973: A Study of Foreign Policy in Modernizing Nations*. Charlottesville: University Press of Virginia, 1975.

———. *The Northern Tier: Afghanistan, Iran and Turkey*. Princeton: Van Nostrand, 1966.

———. *The Persian Gulf: Iran's Role*. Charlottesville: University Press of Virginia, 1972.

Rothstein, R. L. *Alliances and Small Powers*. New York: Columbia University Press, 1968.

Rouhani, F. *A History of O.P.E.C.* New York: Praeger, 1971.

Rustow, D. A., and Mugno, J. F. *OPEC: Success and Prospects*. New York: New York University Press, 1976.

Sampson, A. *The Arms Bazaar, the Companies, the Dealers, the Bribes: From Victers to Lockheed*. London: Hodder and Stoughton, 1977.

————. *The Seven Sisters: The Great Oil Companies and the World They Shaped.* New York: Bantam Books, 1976.

Sanghvi, R. *Aryamehr: The Shah of Iran: A Political Biography.* New York: Stern & Day, 1968.

Seal, P. *The Struggle for Syria: A Study of Post-War Arab Politics, 1945-58.* London, 1965.

Shafa, S. *Facts about the Celebration of the 2500th Anniversary of the Founding of the Persian Empire by Cyrus the Great.* Tehran: Committee of International Affairs of the Festivities, 1971.

Shamlon, M. *Effects of the White Revolution on the Economic Development of Iran.* Scientific and Economic Publication no. 2. Tehran: Tehran Chamber of Commerce, 1969.

Sharpe, E. *A Visit to Iran.* London, 1972.

Sheehan, M. K. *Iran: The Impact of United States Interests and Policies, 1941-1954.* Brooklyn, N.Y.: T. Gaus' Sons, 1968.

Shuster, W. M. *The Strangling of Persia.* New York: Century, 1920.

Shwadran, B. *Middle East Oil and the Great Powers.* New York: Praeger, 1955.

Siddiqui, K. *Conflict, Crisis and War in Pakistan.* London: Macmillan, 1972.

Smith, H. H. et al. *Area Handbook for Iran.* Washington, D.C.: U.S. Government Printing Office, 1971.

Smith, W. B. *Moscow Mission, 1946-1949.* London: 1950.

Tanzer, M. *The Political Economy of International Oil and the Underdeveloped Countries.* Boston: Beacon Press, 1969.

Tehranian, M. *Iran.* Tehran, 1974-75.

Thomas, L. V., and Frye, R. N. *The United States and Turkey and Iran.* Cambridge: Harvard University Press, 1952.

Tiratsoo, E. N. *Oilfields of the World.* Beaconsfield, Eng.: Scientific Press, 1973.

Truman, H. S. *Memoirs.* Vol. 2. *Years of Trial and Hope, 1946-1952.* Garden City: Doubleday, 1956.

Tugendhat, C. *Oil: The Biggest Business.* London: Eyre & Spottiswoode, 1968.

Ulam, A. B. *The Rivals: America and Russia since World War II.* London: Allen Lane, 1973.

Upton, J. M. *The History of Modern Iran: An Interpretation.* Cambridge: Distributed for the Center for Middle Eastern Studies of Harvard University by Harvard University Press, 1961.

Uri, P. *Development Without Dependence.* New York: Praeger, 1976.

Vicker, R. *The Kingdom of Oil; The Middle East: Its People and Its Power.* London: Robert Hale, 1974.

de Villiers, G. et al. *The Imperial Shah, An Informal Biography.* Boston; Atlantic Monthly Press, 1976.

Vital, D. *The Inequality of States: A Study of the Small Power in International Relations.* Oxford: Clarendon Press, 1967.

———. *The Survival of Small States: Studies in Small Powers/Great Power Conflict.* New York: Oxford University Press, 1971.

Warne, W. E. *Mission for Peace: Point 4 in Iran.* Indianapolis, Bobbs-Merrill, 1956.

Wilber, D. N. *Contemporary Iran.* New York: Praeger, 1963.

———. *Iran: Past and Present.* 8th ed. Princeton: Princeton University Press, 1976.

Windsor, P. *Oil: A Plain Man's Guide to the World Energy Crisis.* London: Maurice Temple Smith, 1975.

Wise, D., and Ross, T. B. *The Invisible Government.* London: 1962.

Yar-Shater, E., ed. *Iran Faces the Seventies.* New York: Praeger, 1971.

Zabih, S. *The Communist Movement in Iran.* Berkeley and Los Angeles: University of California Press, 1966.

Zonis, M. *The Political Elite of Iran.* Princeton: Princeton University Press, 1971.

Articles

Abadi, A. "The Crisis of Arab Nationalism." In K. H. Karpat, ed. *Political and Sociological Thought in the Contemporary Middle East.* New York: Praeger, 1968.

Abrahamian, E. "Factionalism in Iran: Political Groups in the 14th Parliament (1944-46)." *Middle Eastern Studies* 14 (January 1978). 22-55.

Amuzegar, J. "Ideology and Economic Growth in the Middle East." *Middle East Journal* 28 (Winter 1974), 1-9.

Avery, P. "Iran 1964-8; the Mood of Growing Confidence." *World Today* 24 (November 1968), 453-66.

———. "The Many Faces of Iran's Foreign Policy." *New Middle East* no. 47 (August 1972), pp. 17-19.

———. "The Shah's Proclamation on Reform." *Middle East Journal* 16 (Winter 1962), 86-92.

———. "Trends in Iran in the Past Five Years." *World Today* 21 (July 1965), 279-90.

Ballis, W. S. "Soviet-Iranian Relations during the Decade 1953-64." *Bulletin of the Institute for the Study of the USSR* (November 1965).

Bartsch, W. H. "The Industrial Labor Force of Iran: Problems of Recruitment, Training and Productivity." *Middle East Journal* 25 (Winter 1971). 15-30.

Beckett, P.H.T., and Gordon, E. D. "Land Use and Settlement Round Kerman in Southern Iran." *Geography Journal* 132 (December 1966).

Bentwich, N. "Impressions of Iran." *Contemporary Review* 208 (January 1966), 21-24.

Bharier, J. "Economic Growth in Iran." *Contemporary Review* 214 (January 1969), 15-19.

Bill, J. A. "Modernization and Reform from above: the Case of Iran." *Journal of Politics* 32 (February 1970).

―――. "The Plasticity of Informal Politics: The Case of Iran." *Middle East Journal* 27 (Spring 1973), 131-51.

―――. "The Social and Economic Foundations of Power in Contemporary Iran." *Middle East Journal* 17 (Autumn 1963), 400-18.

Binder, L. "The Cabinet of Iran: a Case Study in Institutional Adaptation." *Middle East Journal* 16 (Winter 1962), 29-47.

―――. "Iran: Political Development in a Changing Society." *Review World Politics* 16 (October 1963).

―――. "Iran's Potential as a Regional Power." In P. Y. Hammond and S. S. Alexander, eds. *Political Dynamics in the Middle East*. New York: American Elsevier, 1972.

Blandy, R., and Nashat, M. "The Education Corps in Iran: a Survey of Its Social and Economic Aspects." *International Labour Review* 93 (May 1966), 521-29.

Boyle, J. A. "The Il-Khans of Persia and the Christian West." *History Today* 23 (August 1973), 554-63.

Budenheimer, S. "Dependency and Imperialism: the Roots of Latin American Underdevelopment." *Politics and Society* (May 1971), pp. 327-57.

Burchard, H-J. "Der Souveränitätswechsel beim Erdöl." *Aussen Politik* 25/4 (1974), 447-60.

Burrell, R. M. "Iranian Foreign Policy during the Last Decade." *Asian Affairs* 61 (February 1974), 7-15.

―――. "Iranian Foreign Policy: Strategic Location, Economic Ambition, and Dynastic Determination." *Journal of International Affairs* 29 (Fall 1975), 129-38.

Burt, R. "Power and the Peacock Throne: Iran's Growing Military Strength." *Round Table* no. 260 (October 1975), pp. 349-56.

Caporaso, J. A. "Dependence and Dependency in the Global System: A Structural and Behavioral Analysis." *International Organization* 32 (Winter 1978), pp. 13-43.

Carey, J.P.C., and Carey, A. G. "Industrial Growth and Development Planning in Iran." *Middle East Journal* 29 (Winter 1975), 1-15.

―――. "Oil and Economic Development in Iran." *Political Science Quarterly* 75 (March 1960), 66-86.

Caroe, O. "The North-West Frontier, Old and New." *Royal Central Asian Journal* 48 (1961), pp. 289-98.

Chubin, S. "Implications of the Military Build-up in Non-Industrial

States: The Case of Iran," Research Paper. Tehran: Institute for International Political and Economic Studies, 1976.

———. "Iran: Between the Arab West and the Asian East." *Survival* (July/August 1974). 172-83.

———, and Fard-saidi, M. "Recent Trends in Middle East Politics and Iran's Foreign Policy Options." *The Tehran Papers, No. 3.* Tehran: The Institute for International Politics and Economic Studies, n.d.

Cottrell, A. J. "Iran, the Arabs and the Persian Gulf." *Orbis* 17 (Fall 1973), 978-88.

"Crisis in Iran." *World Today* 17 (June 1961), 227-29.

Croizat, V. J. "Stability in the Persian Gulf." *U.S. Naval Institute Proceedings* (July 1973).

Cumming-Bruce, N. "Iran: Main Beneficiary of Increased Oil Revenues." *Middle East Economic Digest* 18 (April 26, 1974), 468-69, 488.

Dasgupta, B. "Soviet Oil and the Third World." *World Development* 3:5 (1975).

Dos Santos, T. "The Structure of Dependence." *American Economic Review: Papers and Proceedings* 60 (May 1970), 231-36.

Dupree, L. "A Suggested Pakistan-Afghanistan-Iran Federation." *Middle East Journal* 17 (Autumn 1963), 383-99.

Edmonds, C. J. "The Iraqi-Persian Frontier: 1639-1938." *Asian Affairs* 62 (June 1975), 147-54.

Elwell-Sutton, L. P. "Nationalism and Neutralism in Iran." *Middle East Journal* 12 (Winter 1958), 20-32.

Gable, R. W. "Culture and Administration in Iran." *Middle East Journal* 13 (Autumn 1959), 407-21.

Galtung, J. "A Structural Theory of Imperialism." *Journal of Peace Research* 8:2 (1971), 81-117.

Ganji, M. and Milani, A. "Iran: Development during the last 50 years." In Jacqz, J. W., ed. *Iran: Past, Present and Future.* New York: Aspen Institute for Humanistic Studies, 1976.

Ghauri, S. R. "Iran's Grand Design Runs into Trouble," *Far Eastern Economic Review*, 93 (July 16, 1976), 31-32.

Gibb, H.A.R. "Social Reform: Factor X" in Lacqueur, W. Z., ed. *Middle East in Transition.* London, 1958.

Grady, H. "Tensions in the Middle East with Particular Reference to Iran." *Proceedings of the Academy of Political Science* 24 (January 1952), 114-20.

Hameed, K. A., and Bennett, M. N. "Iran's Future Economy." *Middle East Journal* 29 (Autumn 1975), 418-32.

Harkness, R., and Harkness, G. "America's Secret Agents: the Mysterious Doings of CIA." *Saturday Evening Post* 227 (November 6, 1954), 34-35, 64-68.

Heard-Bey, F. "The Gulf States and Oman in Transition." *Asian Affairs* 59 (February 1972), 14-22.

———. "Social Changes in the Gulf States and Oman." *Asian Affairs* 59 (October 1972), 309-16.

Hess, P. "Trouble in Baluchestan." *Swiss Review of World Affairs* (November 1973).

Higgott, R. "Competing Theoretical Perspectives on Development and Underdevelopment: a Recent Intellectual History." *Politics* 13 (May 1978), 26-41.

Holbraad, C. "The Role of Middle Powers." *Cooperation and Conflict* 6:2 (1971), 77-90.

Housego, D. "Iran in the Ascendant: Economic Strengths, Political Weaknesses." *Round Table* no. 248 (October 1972), pp. 497-507.

Huntington, S. "The Change to Change: Modernization, Development, and Politics." *Comparative Politics* 3 (April 1971), 283-322.

Hurewitz, J. C. "Regional and International Politics in the Middle East." In Stevens, G., ed. *The United States and the Middle East.* Englewood Cliffs: Prentice-Hall, 1964, pp. 78-112.

Issawi, C. "Iran's Economic Upsurge." *Middle East Journal* 21 (Autumn 1967), 447-61.

Jack [now Kent], M. "The Purchase of the British Government's Shares in the British Petroleum Company 1912-1914." *Past and Present* 39 (April 1968), 139-68.

Jandaghi, A. "The Present Situation in Iran." *Monthly Review* 25 (November 1973), 34-47.

Johnson, P. "The Trouble with Persia." *New Statesman* 66 (September 20, 1963), 350-51.

Kazemzadeh, F. "Soviet-Iranian Relations: A Quarter-Century of Freeze and Thaw." In Lederer, I. J., and Vucinich, W. S., eds. *The Soviet Union and the Middle East: the Post-World War II Era.* Stanford: Hoover Institute Press, 1974, pp. 55-77.

Kazemi, F. "Economic Indicators and Political Violence in Iran: 1946-1968." *Iranian Studies* 8 (Winter-Spring 1975), 70-86.

Kennedy, E. M. "The Persian Gulf: Arms Race or Arms Control?" *Foreign Affairs* 54 (October 1975), 14-35.

Kingsley, R. "Premier Amini and Iran's Problems." *Middle Eastern Affairs* 13 (August-September 1962), 194-98.

Lambton, A.K.S. "Persia Today." *World Today* 17 (February 1961), 76-87.

Lenczowski, G. "United States' Support for Iran's Independence and Integrity, 1945-1959." *Annals of the American Academy of Political and Social Science* no. 401 (May 1972), pp. 45-55.

Lockhart, L. "The Constitutional Laws of Persia: an Outline of Their Origin and Development." *Middle East Journal* 13 (Autumn 1959), 372-88.

Lowe, F. "Iran: Emerging Power in the Middle East." *New Politics* 10 (Winter 1973), 41-46.

McLachlan, K. "Strength through Growth: Iran on the March. . . ." *New Middle East* (June 1973).

MacLeod, A. "Shah of the Indian Ocean?" *Pacific Community* (April 1976).

Mansur, A. K. "The Crisis in Iran: Why the U.S. Ignored a Quarter Century of Warning." *Armed Forces Journal International* (January 1979), pp. 26-33.

Marlowe, J. "Arab-Persian Rivalry in the Persian Gulf." *Journal of the Royal Central Asian Society* 51 (January 1964), 23-31.

Melamid, A. "The Shaṭṭ al-'Arab Boundary Dispute." *Middle East Journal* 22 (Summer 1968), 350-57.

Mestoli, B. "The Petrochemical Resources and Potentials of the Persian Gulf." *Iran Oil Journal* (December 1968).

Miller, W. G. "Political Organization in Iran: from Dowreh to Political Party." *Middle East Journal* 23 (Spring 1969), 159-67; (Summer 1969), 343-50.

Moghtader, H. "The Settlement of the Bahrain Question: A Study in Anglo-Iranian-United Nations Diplomacy." *Pakistan Horizon* 26:2 (1973), 16-29.

Mostofi, B. "The Petrochemical Resources and Potentials of the Persian Gulf." Iran Oil Journal (December 1968), pp. 10-22.

Mukerjee, D. "Afghanistan under Daud: Relations with Neighboring States." *Asian Survey* 15 (April 1975), 301-12.

Murray, I. "Battle for Iran's Soul." *The AGE* (January 19, 1979).

Odell, P. R. "The world of oil power in 1975." *The World Today* 31 (July 1975), 273-282.

Paterson, W. E. "Small States in International Politics." *Cooperation and Conflict* 4/2 (1969), 119-123.

Pesaran, M. H. "Income Distribution in Iran." In Jacqz, J. W., ed. *Iran: Past, Present and Future.* New York: Aspen Institute of Humanistic Studies, 1976, pp. 267-86.

Peiris, D. "India's new rival [Iran's relations with India and other Indian Ocean region countries; India's defences]" in *Far Eastern Economic Review*, Vol. 80. June 4, 1973.

Pfaff, R. H. "Disengagement from Traditionalism in Turkey and Iran." *Western Political Quarterly* 16 (March 1963), 79-98.

Pfau, R. "The Legal Status of American Forces in Iran." *Middle East Journal* 28 (Spring 1974), 141-53.

Pranger, R. J. "Currents in Iranian Nationalism." *Current History* 36 (February 1959), 102-106.

Ramazani, R. K. " 'Church' and State in Modernizing Society: the Case of Iran." *American Behavioral Scientist* 7 (January 1964), 26-28.

———. "Emerging Patterns of Regional Relations in Iranian Foreign Policy." *Orbis* 17 (Winter 1975), 1043-70.

———. "Iran's Changing Foreign Policy: A Preliminary Discussion." *Middle East Journal* 24 (Autumn 1970), 421-37.

———. "Iran's Search for Regional Cooperation." *Middle East Journal* 30 (Spring 1976), 173-86.

———. "Iran's 'White Revolution': a Study in Political Development." *International Journal of Middle East Studies* 5 (April 1974), 124-39.

Ridout, C. F. "Authority Patterns and the Afghan Coup of 1973." *Middle East Journal* 29 (Spring 1975), 165-78.

Roosevelt, A., Jr. "The Kurdish Republic of Mahabad." *Middle East Journal* 1 (July 1947), 247-69.

Rossow, R., Jr. "The Battle of Azerbaijan, 1946." *Middle East Journal* 10 (Winter 1956), 17-32.

Rothman, S. "Functionalism and Its Critics: an Analysis of the Writings of Gabriel Almond." *Political Science Reviewer* 1 (Fall, 1971), 236-76.

Saikal, A. "Afghanistan: Revolution of April 1978." In *Asia and Marxism*. Canberra: Australian National University Press, forthcoming.

———. "Can the Shah Hold On?" *The AGE* (November 2, 1978).

———. "Khomeiny: the Way of Salvation or the Way of Ruin for Iran?" *The AGE* (January 27, 1979).

———. "Military Rule not a Long-Term Option." *Canberra Times* (November 12, 1978).

Salzman, P. C. "National Integration of the Tribes in Modern Iran." *Middle East Journal* 25 (Summer 1971), 325-36.

Schulz, A. T. "A Leadership Role for Iran in the Persian Gulf?" *Current History* 62 (January 1972), 25-30.

Sedehi, A., and Tabriztchi, S. "A Theory of Economic Growth and Political Development: the Case of Iran." *International Studies* 13 (July-September 1974), 424-40.

Shamton, M. "Effects of the White Revolution on the Economic Development of Iran." In *Scientific and Economic Publication*, no. 2. Tehran: Tehran Chamber of Commerce, 1969.

Smolansky, B. M. and Smolansky, D. M. "Soviet and Chinese Influence in the Persian Gulf." In Rubinstein, A. Z., ed. *Soviet and Chinese Influence in the Third World*. New York: Praeger, 1976.

Stauffer, T. R. "The Economics of Nomadism in Iran." *Middle East Journal* 19 (Summer 1965), 284-302.

Taheri, A. "Policies of Iran in the Persian Gulf Region." In Amirie, A., ed. *The Persian Gulf and Indian Ocean in International Politics*. Tehran: Institute for International Political and Economic Studies, 1975, pp. 259-86.

Tahir-Kheli, S. "Iran and Pakistan: Cooperation in an Area of Conflict." *Asian Survey* 17 (May 1977), 474-90.

Tarokh, A. "Iran and the Arab States." *New Outlook* 9 (January 1966), 23-28.

Timmler, M. "Getäuschte oder enttäuschte Afrikaner." *Aussen Politik* 25:3 (1974), 329-40.

Torrey, G. H., and Devlin, J. F. "Arab Socialism." *Journal of International Affairs* 19:1 (1965), 47-62.

Toynbee, P. "Behind Iran's Seething Nationalism." *New York Times Magazine* (October 7, 1951), pp. 13, 54-56.

Turner, L. "Politics of the Energy Crisis." *International Affairs* 50 (July 1974), 404-15.

Vakil, I. "Iran's Basic Macroeconomic Problems: A 20-Year Horizon." In Jacqz, J. W., ed. *Iran: Past, Present and Future.* New York: Aspen Institute of Humanistic Studies, 1976.

Watt, D. C. "The Persian Gulf—Cradle of Conflict?" *Problems of Communism* 21 (May-June 1972), 32-40.

Weinbaum, M. "Iran Finds a Party System: The Institutionalization of *Iran Novin.*" *Middle East Journal* 27 (Autumn 1975), 439-55.

Weinbaum, M. G. "Iran and Israel: The Discreet Entente." *Orbis* 18 (Winter 1975).

Wright, D. "The Changed Balance of Power in the Persian Gulf." *Asian Affairs* 60 (October 1973), 255-62.

Zabih, S. "Change and Continuity in Iran's Foreign Policy in Modern Times." *World Politics* 23 (April 1971), 522-43.

———. "Communism in Iran." *Problems of Communism* 14 (September-October 1965), 46-55.

———. "Iran Today." *Current History* 66 (Fall 1974).

———. "Iran's International Posture: De Facto Nonalignment within a Pro-Western Alliance." *Middle East Journal* 24 (Summer 1970), 302-18.

Publications by Governments and Other Organizations

A Decade of American Foreign Policy. Washington, D.C.: Government Printing Office, 1950.

Address by President Gamel 'Abd al-Nasser at the Arab Socialist Union in Celebration of the Anniversary of Unity Day, Cairo, February 22, 1966. Cairo: National Publication House.

Bank Markazi Iran: Annual Report and Balance Sheet as at March 20, 1969, 1970, 1971, 1973, 1974, 1975. Tehran: Bank Melli Iran Press, 1969, 1970, 1971, 1973, 1974, 1975.

Bank Markazi Iran Bulletin. July-August 1963.

Bank Melli Bulletin. Nos. 185-186. August-September 1957.

Central Treaty Organization, *Economic Division. Economic Data and*

Development Plans for the CENTO Region Countries. . . . Ankara, 1965.

Commonwealth of Australia. Senate. Standing Committee on Foreign Affairs and Defence. *Reference: Australia and the Indian Ocean Region, 1976.* Canberra: Commonwealth Government Printer, 1976.

Correspondence between His Majesty's Government with United Kingdom and the Persian Government, and Related Documents Concerning the Oil Industry in Persia: February 1951 to September 1951. London: His Majesty's Stationery Department, 1951.

Decade of the Revolution 1963-1973. Tehran: Echo Print, n.d.

The Extension and Development Corps in Iran. Tehran: Ministry of Information, Publications Department, 1973.

Foreign Relations of the United States, 1943, Diplomatic Papers. Vols. 4, 5. Washington, D.C.: Government Printing Office.

Foreign Relations of the United States, 1945, Diplomatic Papers. Vol. 8. Washington, D.C.: Government Printing Office.

Foreign Relations of the United States, 1946, Diplomatic Papers. Vol. 7. Washington, D.C.: Government Printing Office.

Foreign Relations of the United States, Diplomatic Papers: The British Commonwealth, the Near East and Africa. Washington, D.C.: Government Printing Office, 1959.

Fourth Development Plan 1968-1972. Tehran: Plan Organisation, 1968.

History and Text of Iranian Oil Agreement. Tehran: NIOC, 1966.

The Houses of Equity in Iran. Tehran: Ministry of Information, Publications Department, 1973.

Iran Almanac, 1966-1976. Tehran: Echo of Iran, 1966-1976.

Iran Today. Tehran: General Department of Publications and Broadcasting, n.d.

Law, Regulations & Decree and Single Article Concerning the Attraction and Protection of Foreign Investment in Iran. Tehran: Ministry of Economy, Center for the Attraction and Protection of Foreign Investment, n.d.

National Income of Iran, 1338-50 (1959-72). Mordad: Bank Markazi Iran, 1353 (1974/75).

The Nationalisation of Water Resources in Iran. Tehran: Ministry of Information, Publications Department, 1973.

Oil in Iran. Tehran: INALO Ltd., 1971.

OPEC Information Book. Vienna: OPEC, 1975.

Outline of the Third Plan, 1341-1346. Tehran: Plan Organisation, 1342 (1963/64).

Planning in Iran: A Brief Study. Tehran: Plan Organisation, 1970.

Reconstruction in Iran. Tehran: Ministry of Information, Publications Department, 1973.

Report on the Performance of the Third Development Plan. Tehran: Plan Organisation, 1347 (1968/69) . (in Persian).

Royal Institute of International Affairs. *Documents on International Affairs, 1953, 1954, 1959.* London, 1957, 1958, 1962.

Sales of Factory Shares in Iran. Tehran: Ministry of Information, Publications Department, 1973.

Stockholm International Peace Research Institute (SIPRI). *The Arms Trade with the Third World.* New York: Humanities Press, 1971.

———. *The Arms Trade with the Third World, 1975.* Baltimore: Penguin, 1975.

———. *Yearbook of World Armaments and Disarmament, 1969-70; 1970-1971; 1971-1972; 1972-1973; 1973-1974; 1974-1975; 1975-1976; 1976-1977; 1977-1978.* New York: Humanities Press, 1970, 1971, 1972, 1973, 1974, 1975, 1976, 1977, 1978.

Strategic Survey 1977. London: The International Institute for Strategic Studies (IISS), 1978.

U.S. Congress. House. Committee on Foreign Affairs. Hearings. *The Mutual Security Act of 1954.* Washington, D.C.: Government Printing Office, 1954.

———. *Mutual Security Act, 1957.* Washington, D.C.: Government Printing Office, 1957.

———. *The International Development and Security Act, 1961.* Washington, D.C.: Government Printing Office, 1961.

———. *The Mutual Security Act, 1958.* Washington, Government Printing Office, 1958.

———. Subcommittee on International Organizations. Hearings. *Human Rights in Iran, August 3 and September 6, 1976.* Washington, D.C.: Government Printing Office, 1976.

———. Subcommittee on the Near East. Hearings. *The Middle East, 1971: the Need to Strengthen Peace: The Persian Gulf at the end of 1971, 15 July 1971.* Washington, D.C.: Government Printing Office, 1971.

———. Subcommittee on the Near East and South Asia. Hearings. *New Perspectives on The Persian Gulf, 6 June 1973.* Washington, D.C.: Government Printing Office, 1973.

U.S. Congress. House. Committee on Government Operations. First Report. *United States Aid Operations in Iran.* Washington, D.C.: Government Printing Office, 1957.

U.S. Congress. House. Permanent Select Committee on Intelligence. Sub-Committee on Evaluation. Staff Report. *Iran: Evaluation of U.S. Intelligence Performance Prior to November 1978.* Washington, D.C.: Government Printing Office, 1979.

U.S. Congress. Senate. Committee on Foreign Relations. Hearings. *The Mutual Security Act, 1959.* Washington, D.C.: Government Printing Office, 1959.

————. Subcommittee on Multinational Corporations. Hearings. *Multinational Corporations and United States Foreign Policy.* Parts 1-10. Washington, D.C.: Government Printing Office, 1975.

————. Sub-Committee on Foreign Assistance. Staff Report. *U.S. Military Sales to Iran, July 1976.* Washington, D.C.: Government Printing Office, 1976.

U.S. *International Commerce Overseas Business Reports.* Washington, D.C.: Department of Commerce, May 1966.

U.S. Office of Statistics and Reports. *Internal Administration, Foreign Assistance and Assistance from International Organizations, July 1, 1945 through June 30, 1966.* Washington, D.C.: Government Printing Office, 1967.

Workers' Profit-Sharing in Iran. Tehran: Ministry of Information, Publications Department, 1973.

Wūzārat-i Ittilā'āt. Celebration of the 2500th anniversary of the Founding of the Persian Empire by Cyrus the Great. Tehran, 1971.

Unpublished Sources

Connell, J. "Tehran: Urbanisation and Development," Institute of Development Studies Discussion Paper, no. 32. September 1973.

Hekmat, H. "Iran's Response to Soviet-American Rivalry, 1951-1962; A Comparative Study." Ph.D. dissertation, Columbia, 1974.

————. "OPEC and New World Order, Some Primary Observations." Paper delivered at the Edinburgh IPSA Congress of August 16-21, 1976.

Homayun, D. "Political Development of Iran." Paper prepared for Seminar on Iranian Studies on Problems of Contemporary Iran. Harvard University, April 17, 1965.

Pesaran, M. H. "Income Distribution and Its Major Determinants in Iran." August 1975.

————. "Income Distribution Trends in Rural and Urban Iran." Paper presented to the International Conference on the Social Sciences and Problems of Development, Perspectives, Iran. 1974.

Ramazani, R. K. "The Military in Iran." Paper prepared for Seminar on Iranian Studies on Problems of Contemporary Iran. Harvard University, April 17, 1965.

Raoof, A. H. "Confrontation and Detente in the Arabian-Persian Gulf: The Case of Iraq." Paper delivered at the Tenth Annual Meeting of the Middle East Studies Association. Los Angeles, California, November 11-13, 1976.

Richardson, J. L. "World Society: The 'Structural Dependence' Model." Department of International Relations, Australian National University, Canberra, August 4, 1975.

Tabari, K. "Iran's Policies toward the United States during the Anglo-

Russian Occupation, 1941-1946." Ph.D. dissertation, Columbia, 1967.

Young, T. C. "U.S. Policy in Iran Since World War II." Paper presented for Seminar on Problems of Contemporary Iran. Harvard University, April 17, 1965.

Newspapers and Periodicals

The AGE
Arab Record and Memo
Arab Record and Report
The Australian
BBC Summary of World Broadcasts
Canberra Times
Congressional Quarterly
Current Digest of the Soviet Press
Christian Science Monitor
Daily Telegraph
The Economist
Ettela'at
Europa
The Guardian Weekly
International Economic Survey

International Herald Tribune
Kabul Times
Kayhan (Persian edition)
Kayhan International
Keesings Contemporary Archives
The Military Balance
New York Times
Oil and Gas Journal
Oil Forum
Pamir
Sydney Morning Herald
The Times
Times of India
U.S. State Department Bulletin
Washington Post

* INDEX *

LIBRARY OF CONGRESS CATALOGING IN PUBLICATION DATA

Saikal, Amin, 1951-
  The rise and fall of the Shah.

  Bibliography: p.
  Includes index.
  1. Iran—Politics and government—1941-1979.
I. Title.
DS318.S244   955'.053   80-7462
ISBN 0-691-03118-5